GOING SOLO

The Best Resources
for
ENTREPRENEURS & FREELANCERS

Stanley I. Mason, Jr.
Editor

A RESOURCE PATHWAYS GUIDEBOOK

Seattle, Washington

651795

Published by Resource Pathways, Inc.
22525 S.E. 64th Place, Suite 253
Issaquah, WA 98027

Editor: Stanley I. Mason, Jr.,
        Founder and President, Simco, Inc., Weston, Connecticut

Managing Editor:
        Jacquelline Cobb Fuller, MPP

Associate Editor:
        Dana Lynch

Researchers:
        Dana Lynch and Julie Glassmoyer

Book Design and Production:
        Sandra Harner and Kelly Rush
        Laing Communications Inc., Redmond, WA

Printing: DeHart's Printing Services Corporation,
        Santa Clara, CA

Publisher's Cataloging-in-Publication

Going solo : the best resources for entrepreneurs &
    freelancers / Stanley I. Mason, editor. -- 1st ed.
        p. cm.
        Includes bibliographical references and index.
        ISBN: 1-892148-12-9

    1. Entrepreneurship--Bibliography. 2. Small
business--Management--Bibliography.
3. Self-employed--Bibliography.   I. Mason, Stanley
I. II. Resource Pathways (Firm)

Z7164.C81G65 1999   016.65802'2
                QBI99-1153

CONTENTS

INTRODUCTION

Going Solo In 2000 & Beyond

So you want to start your own business? Strike out on your own as a consultant? You've been thinking about this big step for a long while and have decided that now is the time. You're not alone.

When I was a pilot during World War II, I used to fly over the innumerable towns in the countryside and think about how hardly any of those towns had large businesses. They were populated with small businesses, all started and run by individuals. Even the large companies of today started out as small ones.

My own father always had a business of his own. He was an electrician by trade, but he could do anything. His father had the only large truck in town and so had a moving company. His grandfather was a farmer. Each owned their own businesses and hired help when they needed it.

I grew up thinking my uncle, who worked for a large steel company, was rather strange for having joined a giant company and giving up his freedom, much like a slave who came home at night.

Perhaps you've come upon the idea of working for yourself after years of feeling like you did not fit well in a corporate cubicle. Or perhaps you have entered a season of life where you need a flexible career, one that allows you to schedule work around children or dependent adults in your care. Men and women who choose to go solo have a variety of reasons for wanting to step out on their own, but they share common characteristics.

The entrepreneur (and I use this term to describe any person who directs his own work) may take direction from another, but not easily. She doesn't accept anything blindly, but filters information and decides for herself. The entrepreneur is comfortable making decisions quickly because he knows the world is filled with many opportunities. She is willing to take a calculated risk when necessary, and she doesn't waste time beating herself up for mistakes or failures. But most of all, the entrepreneur thrives on bringing a business to life through their own series of brilliance and flubs. Entrepreneurs revel in being the boss: casting the vision for the enterprise, setting its goals and giving it structure.

Am I describing you? Before you dive into starting a business, first ask yourself some tough questions:

- Do you truly want to run your own business, or are you mainly interested in the obvious, though not easily attainable benefits, such as an unlimited salary potential or reduced work week?

- Are you willing and disciplined enough to get up early every day and work long hours into the night to establish your business?

- Is your family supportive of your goals? Are you prepared financially to live on the lean side while your business is growing? Is your family prepared to do so?

Some folks are more or less forced into their businesses because they were either fired or downsized, and that's fine. We tend to see things differently, and we are not always appreciated by large corporations. Being able to land on your feet shows that you have some entrepreneurial skill. But though you can fall into a business, you can't fall into success.

After observing my success with various invention-based businesses, my neighbor decided to go into business for himself. We talked and I suggested some ideas to him which he promptly ignored.

First he leased an expensive sports car and turned his living room into a beautiful home office. He bought expensive mahogany furniture, filing cabinets and a beautiful carpet. Then he got to work hunting for consulting business! Because it was slow to develop he lost his house and almost went broke before he got clients.

My neighbor could have avoided financial ruin by observing some time-tested advice:

- Be creative, and realistic, in raising the capital you will need to operate your business. Remember that if you take out a home equity loan to finance your business that your house is on the line as collateral! I started out with only $3500 and have been behind since the beginning.

- The telephone is not your enemy; it is your link to new business. If you are unable to answer the phone yourself, get an answering machine or voice mail service and return calls as soon as possible.

- Keep yourself very presentable and well groomed at all times. You never know where you will meet a potential client or a person who will tell someone about you and your business.

- If you don't have a computer, buy one. In the last year prices have dropped tremendously. Choose a model a little faster than you think you need. You'll soon grow into its extra computing power. Then learn to use it professionally.

- Get a letterhead. It should be designed carefully and well. I suggest going to a local college and establish friends with the design department. Give them the assignment and they will create a very fine letterhead for you to carry forward.

- Begin to outline a "how to" book about your business. In creating this copy you will learn much more about what you will need to run your business. This book will become your business plan establishing your goals for the future.

- Try to stick to what you know well, but always be open to new opportunities as they arise. Experiment with your ideas before you go "whole hog" into it.

- Research carefully. Don't be afraid to ask questions. Become an expert in the field. Ground yourself in the mechanics of running a business. Though entrepreneurs are risk-takers, they don't "wing it."

This last tip is the most important. I have seen more entrepreneurs fail for lack of planning and research than for any other reason. Fortunately, publishers have responded to the explosion in the number of entrepreneurs, consultants, freelancers, and home-businesses with a flood of resources. By using our guide you won't have to waste hours and dollars chasing the right books and websites for your particular needs. We have gathered 150 of the best resources available in print and on the Internet, reviewing each thoroughly and objectively.

Good luck to you in your entrepreneurial adventure!

How This Book Is Organized

This guidebook is designed to help you take control of the issues you will face when you go solo. We have:

- Identified the key issues faced by entrepreneurs and consultants.

- Created detailed reviews which describe and evaluate some 150 resources, so you can identify those best suited to your interests and needs.

- Provided multiple indices which serve as clear "pathways" to the most useful resources for each key issue, or for a particular type of entrepreneur, such as women or minorities.

We have divided the guidebook into seven sections. Following this introductory section, you will find:

Section II—Exploring Self-Employment

Am I cut out to be an entrepreneur? This section addresses the question at the heart of the matter. *Reflective Guides To Creating The Work And Life You Want*, contains resources that pull back and look at the big picture. Some offer self-assessment tools, others an inspirational look at the value of creating not just a business but a way of life. *Stories From Successful And Not-So-Successful Soloists* allow us to glimpse the successes and the failures of some of the world's best known entrepreneurs.

Section III—Creating & Managing Your Own Business

The heart of the book, filled with resources addressing *How To Start And Manage Your Own Business*. These resources can help you with the fundamentals of building a business, from creating a business plan to paying self-employment taxes. In *Ideas For Entrepreneurial Businesses*, we review a series of directories designed to help you choose the right entrepreneurial business for you. A final chapter covers resources specifically designed for *High-Tech And Internet-Based Businesses*.

Section IV—Working As A Freelancer Or Consultant

Several national trends: corporate downsizing, increased outsourcing, and market specialization, have led to an explosion in the number of professionals going into business for themselves. We let you know which consulting resources will save you time, money and headaches, and which to avoid.

Section V—Working From Home: The Home-Based Revolution

Setting Up And Running A Home-Based Business can be a challenge. Educate yourself and take charge with one of the resources we recommend. *Home Business Guides For Mothers, Women And Couples* are tailored to the unique strengths and particular needs of these kinds of home business soloists. A final chapter, *Ideas For Home-Based Businesses* evaluates the guides on the market designed to help you find the right home-based business for you.

Section VI—Insider Advice

Some people learn best by studying a how-to manual, others enjoy sitting at the feet of the "gurus" and absorbing their *Success Strategies*.

Always remember, going solo doesn't mean you have to go it alone. The Internet has created many new ways for entrepreneurs to share ideas, compare notes and be encouraged by the virtual community of like-minded soloists. We evaluate websites and other *Resources For Networking, Support And Advice* in this final section of reviews.

Section VII—Resources Of Interest To Specific Groups

My assistant looked all around her neighboring vicinity to try and find a support group for women like herself: professionals raising young children and running a home-based business. Though she couldn't find a group in her area, she was able to connect with such a community online. These "mompreneurs," who met through one of the websites we review, share information, advice and encouragement via the Internet. Perhaps you are looking for a book or a website that is tailored to your particular life situation. In this section we present abbreviated descriptions of all the resources of special interest to women, parents, minorities and young entrepreneurs. If after reading the short description you want to learn more, we indicate the page number of the full-page description.

Section VIII—Indices

Five resource indices arranged alphabetically by title, author, publisher, and media type, and by overall star rating in the subject index, to help you get to the information you need quickly.

THE REVIEW PROCESS

Our editors and researchers have identified virtually all available sources of consumer-oriented information focused on going solo, including books, software and websites. We have arranged these reviews into chapters based on the subject matter primarily addressed. Some resources comprehensively cover more than one aspect of going solo, and in these cases we note in the side-bar a secondary subject.

Each chapter provides background information and time-saving advice. Reviews of resources covering each topic form the heart of each chapter. These full-page, fact-filled, candid reviews offer an appraisal that's rich in specifics. And each follows the same format.

We separate evaluations from descriptions, so you can focus either on what a resource contains or what we think of it, and why. Facts of publication appear in a sidebar. A phrase sums up ease of use and our overall rating, and we give each 1–4 stars. We always list the highest-rated resources first. If there is more than one resource with the same Star Rating, we list them alphabetically by title. Abbreviated "non-rated" reviews are used for resources that warrant your attention but not a full review.

FOUR STAR RATING SYSTEM

★★★★　Highly recommended! Top quality at a fair price.
★★★　Well done; a good resource but not outstanding.
★★　Worth considering; check the description for strong chapters.
★　Your time and money could be better spent elsewhere.

Because our mission is to help you find your way through this "forest" of information and take control of the issue at hand, we also make carefully considered recommendations on which resources will best serve your needs. Only 25 percent of the resources we review are recommended. We base our recommendations on the resource's value relative to its peers in the same subject category.

- **Printed Books**: We read the book from cover to cover, identify the particular focus taken by each author, and make a judgment about how the book's contents could be best applied. Our judgment about the relative quality of each source is based upon readability, organization, depth, and style. We make every effort to ensure that the latest editions of books are reviewed, and that no out-of-print resources are included.

- **Internet Websites & Online Services**: We review all websites and online services that have any significant amount of original material related to the subject of going solo. Our reviews include judgments about the site's graphic and navigation design, as well as the usefulness of material provided relative to that available in other media. We revisit sites frequently to stay abreast of changes and improvements.

- **CD-ROM & Software**: We carefully review each facet of the CD, including all branches and multimedia options, and thoroughly test software applications. Our reviews include judgments about the "cost/benefit" of multimedia additions, as well as the usefulness of the content provided relevant to the similar offering in other media. We note technical problems in loading or using programs provided.

A NOTE ON WEBSITES

We include the current "address" (URL) of the home page or a specific page within a website to facilitate direct access on the Internet. Of course, the World Wide Web is a dynamic place, and many URLs will change over time. If you find that an address is outdated, we recommend that you simply delete the last expression in the address and hit the "Enter" or "Return" key again.

This procedure will point your browser to a file "further up" in the website's file directory. In most cases, you will return to the website's home page (indicated by the phrase ending in ".com," ".edu," ".gov," etc.). From there, you can navigate your way to the specific information or page you were looking for.

EXPLORING
SELF-EMPLOYMENT

II

REFLECTIVE GUIDES TO CREATING THE WORK & LIFE YOU WANT

Many people either lived through the depression or were raised by parents who were "depression kids." They were told by their parents to get jobs and hunt for security. "Be a teacher, or work for the city, or find a large and stable company." I did what I was advised. I went to college, got a teaching degree and worked to support my family at large corporations. Those occupations were stable, but as an entrepreneur at heart, those jobs were a poor fit for me.

Entrepreneurs are the risk-takers; those who are not afraid of the future; those who seek opportunity. Many successful business executives have the technical expertise to advise clients, but not all are cut out to be management consultants. A teacher may be excellent in one-on-one math instruction, but may not have the desire to strike out on her own as a freelance tutor. How can you know if going solo is right for you?

Do I Have What It Takes To Go Solo?

A burning desire to be your own boss, the possibility of unlimited income and the assurance of possessing the next "great idea" draw many people to consider self-employment. According to a recent Gallup poll, at any given time 30% of the population is mulling over the idea of going into business for themselves.

Before plowing ahead, it pays to do some soul searching to determine if you have what it takes to go solo. Though their interests, level of education, business plans and personalities differ greatly, successful entrepreneurs (and consultants) share a set of common characteristics. Scan the list below to see how you compare to the ideal entrepreneur profile. Successful soloists are:

Optimistic

Bottom line, the glass is always half-full. People are attracted to business people who are enthusiastic about their product and confident in their services. Case studies of successful start-ups are filled with ups and downs, sometimes lots of downs. You must be able to weather the storms and be your own cheerleader.

Self-Starting

Coming up with a great idea for a product is only half the battle. You must also be able to create your own goals, schedule and structure. If networking is not second nature for you, consider whether you have the initiative to make the cold calls or sales presentations required to build your client base.

Willing To Risk

In the financial markets, reward is typically correlated with risk. The same concept applies in business. The entrepreneurial path is strewn with weighty decisions: Should I invest in an expensive four-color brochure? Is it time to move out of my home office and add an employee? It is not enough to be decisive, you must be willing to take calculated risks.

Organized

Being excellent at your craft will bring in the clients, but if you're not on top of the paperwork, your own success will drown you. Through the years I have been amazed at the number of self-employed people I have worked with whose business floundered because they "overlooked" an essential aspect of the process, such as paying estimated taxes or obtaining a business license. I once had a plumber who "forgot" to collect payment for a thousand dollars worth of work he did on my bathroom remodel. I had to remind him twice to send a bill!

Comfortable Working Alone

Good riddance to office politics and glass ceilings, but will you miss the support and interaction with colleagues you enjoyed in your old job? If you start your own company, you will probably begin alone, and often remain alone. Will this independence be liberating or become stifling? Even introverts may need to break up the isolation of being in a solitary business. A friend who works as a freelance writer enjoys setting up shop at her "virtual office" by bringing her laptop and notes to a local coffee shop, where she enjoys the hum of background activity and occasional banter with other regulars.

The resources in this chapter can help you continue to explore whether going solo is right for you. Many include self-assessment tools such as interest inventories, awareness exercises and guided reflection. Others focus on the "spiritual dimension of entrepreneuring" as one author puts it, offering guidance in creating not just a business, but a balanced and creative way of life.

★★★★

Overall Rating
★★★★
A balanced look at achieving a balanced life; philosophy for work and life

Design, Ease Of Use
★★★★
Written with passion and energy

1–4 Stars

Author:
Jay Conrad Levinson
Levinson is the president of Guerrilla Marketing Information. He is a best selling author and entrepreneur.

Publisher:
Houghton Mifflin

Edition:
1997

Price:
$19.95

Pages/Run Time:
242

ISBN:
0395770181

Media:
Book

Principal Subject:
Reflective Guides To Creating The Work & Life You Want

THE WAY OF THE GUERRILLA
Achieving Success And Balance As An Entrepreneur In The 21st Century

Recommended For:
Reflective Guides To Creating The Work & Life You Want

Description:

The "Old American Dream," which measures success in dollars and seems to demand workaholism, personal sacrifice, and greed, is a 20th century model that, author Levinson says, is being supplanted by a "New American Dream" for the 21st century. The new dream is based on a balance between work success and a satisfying personal life; it is achieved through the "way of the guerrilla." That is the philosophy at the heart of this 4-part guide, which combines business strategies with personal life strategies in a holistic approach to entrepreneurism.
Part 1 begins by examining "The Goals" of the guerrilla entrepreneur, addressing such issues as changes in business practices, integrating your business with your life, maintaining balance, and sharing your profits. Part 2 applies guerrilla tactics to customer relations, supplier relations, business structuring, and time management. In Part 3, Levinson details the tools guerrillas need: i.e. focus, hiring and management skills, the ability to delegate, technological awareness, and modular profit alliances. "The Secrets" are revealed in Part 4, which includes chapters on using psychology, adaptability, marketing, getting interactive, and sustaining passion for your work.

Evaluation:

Levinson's juxtaposition of the "Old American Dream" against the "New" one is a classic for our times. Not only does it speak to the changes in American's collective consciousness—where personal needs are gaining emphasis over material wealth—it's also an apt description of the different schools of thought found in today's entrepreneurial guides. There are traditional guides (Dan Kennedy's are good examples) which primarily focus on financial success, and then there are guides like this one, in which financial success is a means—not an end—and the goal is to "have it all." If you relate to this second school, where entrepreneurism is more about achieving balance and freedom than it is about making a million dollars, the "Way of the Guerrilla" is the book for you. Though it shares thematic similarities with such spiritual/psychological entrepreneur guides as "To Build the Life You Want, Create the Work You Love" (see review), Levinson's work distinguishes itself from that genre by explaining how its philosophy impacts business practices and how to apply guerrilla tactics to specific business situations, i.e. managing employees. This guide is as much about succeeding in business as it is about succeeding in life as whole, an uncommon, welcome combination. This is a truly balanced look at achieving a balanced life.

Where To Find/Buy:

Bookstores and libraries.

Reflective Guides To Creating The Work & Life You Want

TO BUILD THE LIFE YOU WANT, CREATE THE WORK YOU LOVE
The Spiritual Dimension Of Entrepreneuring

 Recommended For:
Reflective Guides To Creating The Work & Life You Want

Description:

That you are always in business for yourself (even if your working for someone else) has become the mantra for 21st century employment, where entrepreneurism will provide the greatest job security. But going solo isn't just about job security for author Sinetar (or for most people); it's about taking control of your life and your work, of building a "meaningful vocation" that is tied to your spiritual (creative) needs and helps you become a "unique, whole person." That is the main premise of this guide, which combines Sinetar's advice and guidance with personal stories from successful, fulfilled individuals. The book begins with an examination of work discontent, work and life meaning, and the "vocational awareness" pyramid. Sinetar also describes the 7 "inclinations" shared by entrepreneurs: an inventive inclination, authentic focus, meaningful purposes, "figuring-out" skills, risk-taking effectiveness, a strategic outlook, and high spiritual intelligence. Each of the 7 chapters focuses on one of these "inclinations;" for example, Chapter 5 discusses risk-taking and provides tools for self-assessment while Chapter 6 looks at strategic planning. A "Q & A" session with Sinetar comprises the Afterword.

Evaluation:

There are wide variety of reasons for going solo; no two entrepreneurs are alike. Some are in it for the money, some for the joy of running their own business, some for the independence, some for the flexibility. Sinetar's approach to entrepreneurism as spiritually beneficial—the general theme of her guide—won't appeal to every self-employed (or potentially self-employed) person. When Sinetar talks about entrepreneurism, she sees it as a path to "authenticity," to a holistic life that combines work with personal development and self-actualization. Hers isn't a new idea; it's a mix of eastern and western religious thought, psychology, and "pop" existentialism. The difference in this book and others with similar, "find your true vocation" themes is that Sinetar believes that, odds are, your true vocation will have to be created by you, not found in someone else's business or company. That's where the self-employment angle comes into play. This isn't a guide to becoming an entrepreneur, per se. Rather, it's a self-exploratory guide designed both to inspire readers to reach for a more fulfilling life and to discover what their "right" work is. The interactive exercises are predictably "touchy-feely," but there are plenty of genuine insights to make this an encouraging read for the existentially dissatisfied. A good choice in its genre.

Where To Find/Buy:

Bookstores and libraries.

Overall Rating
★★★★
An inspiring view of self-employment as a route for self-fulfillment

Design, Ease Of Use
★★★
A combination of success stories, philosophy, and interactive exercises

1–4 Stars

Author:
Marsha Sinetar

Ms. Sinetar is an author whose books include *Do What You Love, the Money Will Follow* and *Developing a 21st Century Mind*.

Publisher:
St. Martin's Griffin

Edition:
1995

Price:
$10.95

Pages/Run Time:
209

ISBN:
0312141416

Media:
Book

Principal Subject:
Reflective Guides To Creating The Work & Life You Want

★★★

Overall Rating
★★★
A new approach to career planning; inspiring, insightful, creative

Design, Ease Of Use
★★★★
Engaging; involves time commitment (approximately 12 weeks)

1–4 Stars

Author:
Carol Lloyd

Ms. Lloyd is a writer, performer, and entrepreneur. She is the founder of The Writing Parlor, a San Francisco literary arts center, and has led Life Worth Living workshops for over seven years.

Publisher:
HarperPerennial

Edition:
1997

Price:
$14.00

Pages/Run Time:
309

ISBN:
0060952431

Media:
Book

Principal Subject:
Reflective Guides To Creating The Work & Life You Want

CREATING A LIFE WORTH LIVING

Description:

In Lloyd's experience, many artistic and innovative people feel frustrated by the traditional approaches to career planning. In response to that frustration, she created workshops which apply the creative process to career building. Since this book grew out of those workshops, it is designed to be read and practiced in weekly segments. (The program should take twelve weeks.) Part 1, "The Dive," begins by "strengthening your relationship to your dreams" via a series of daily tasks, i.e. "ecstatic tasks" like dancing or meditation, and "idea-generating" exercises. In Part 2, "The Dig," the reader uses memories to resurrect "forgotten career paths," clarifies their non-artistic needs, and explores their "creative type." The reader's ideas are given concrete form in Part 3, "The Design," wherein exercises combat indecisiveness, confront competing interests, and "map out" goals. Part 4, "The Doing," takes the reader from conceptualization to action through specific techniques for reinventing "your workday," forming support networks, and "balancing your life." Interviews with "artists and innovators" are interspersed throughout the chapters and "spot profiles" are also included.

Evaluation:

An artist and innovator herself, Ms. Lloyd speaks to her audience as an equal who's "been there, done that." She is not a traditional career counselor, which is perfect for anyone disdainful of "the system." Rather than encouraging readers to find their niche, as so many career guides do, she urges them to create their place in the world based on their own agendas, and no one else's. Her approach relies heavily on self-analysis and self-discovery, but she also employs daily exercises, planning methods, and motivational techniques. This is not "all talk, no action." There are also lots of interviews with successful people who have self-styled careers. These interviews provide both examples and valuable insight; each person offers advice, discusses the creative process, and shares personal struggles. For readers who are committed to realizing their dreams, this is a smart, inspiring alternative to run-of-the-mill guides. That said, this book can only take you half way to success; it doesn't deal with the practicalities of starting your own business, marketing your talent, etc. That's not its mission. Its mission is to help you "invent the means to support your long-term dreams," not implement those "means." For square pegs longing to escape their round holes, this is the resource; it's the first step in the right direction!

Where To Find/Buy:
Bookstores and libraries.

GOING INDIE
Self-Employment, Freelance & Temping Opportunities

★★★

Description:

A new work age is dawning, an "Indie Revolution" in which new self-employment options are popping up every day. To welcome readers to the "Revolution," the first section in Kaplan's guide begins by exploring the various possibilities of self-employment. Section 2 continues with a section on how to choose the right business by discovering your talents, skills, and passions. Exercises, checklists, and focus questions are given. Individual chapters follow to tell you how to find out about business trends and opportunities, how to "put it all together" and test out your ideas. Anecdotes from successful "indies" are included along the way. Section 3, "Essential Skills," includes chapters on self-management, decision-making, and risk-taking, along with practical matters such as marketing, sales, and financial planning. The final chapter gives advice, interview-style, from "real indies"—a graphic designer, a hat designer, and an owner of a computer information systems business. A list of resources for self-employment entrepreneurs rounds out the book.

Evaluation:

"Going indie" is believed to be one of the smartest ways to tackle the modern job market, in which corporate downsizing and outsourcing have led to a decrease in traditional 9–5 jobs and a corresponding increase in self-employment opportunities. Here, Kaplan throws its hat into the ring with a book dedicated to exploring the ins and outs of succeeding "on your own." Kaplan's guide distinguishes itself from other books on this subject through its equal emphasis on the "intangibles" of self-employment, such as figuring out your marketable talents, and the "tangibles," such as marketing and sales. In self-employment, as in any business, one needs a dose of both vision and practicality. However, the coverage of the practicalities, such as financial planning, isn't detailed enough to provide full assistance in starting up or starting out; you'll need additional information before you can truly "go indie." Also, the book wanders into vagueness at times, as in the exercises focused on pinpointing your talents and skills, but this seems to be a danger related to the field itself, which is highly variable. Overall, readers will find this to be a generally useful guide to both the potentials and practicalities of the indie lifestyle. It's a good choice for beginning your investigation.

Where To Find/Buy:

Bookstores and libraries.

Overall Rating
★★★
Sensible and inspirational guide to self-employment; coverage is broad, not deep

Design, Ease Of Use
★★★
Easy to read and work through; chapters arranged from exploration to practice

1–4 Stars

Author:
Kathi Elster and Katherine Crowley

Kathi Elsteris an adjunct professor at Baruch College and the New School in New York City, where she runs The Business Strategy Seminar, a business support program. Katherine Crowley is a partner in The Business Strategy Seminar.

Publisher:
Kaplan (Simon & Schuster)

Edition:
1997

Price:
$15.00

Pages/Run Time:
240

ISBN:
0684837560

Media:
Book

Principal Subject:
Reflective Guides To Creating The Work & Life You Want

Secondary Subject:
Working As A Freelancer, Consultant or Contract Worker

II. Exploring

★★★

Overall Rating
★★★

Addresses the individual as the foundation of "self-bossing"

Design, Ease Of Use
★

No index, Table of Contents is not particularly revealing either

1–4 Stars

Author:
Barbara J. Winter

Barbara J. Winter is the founder of Winning Ways, a Minneapolis-based training and publishing firm that creates resources for self-bossers. Her writing has appeared in dozens of magazines as well as in her own bimonthly newsletter.

Publisher:
Bantam Book

Edition:
1993

Price:
$12.95

Pages/Run Time:
260

ISBN:
0553371657

Media:
Book

Principal Subject:
Reflective Guides To Creating The Work & Life You Want

Reflective Guides To Creating The Work & Life You Want

MAKING A LIVING WITHOUT A JOB
Winning Ways For Creating Work That You Love

Description:
Winter focuses on the psychological and spiritual aspects of "self-bossing." While acknowledging that some individuals will be happy as an employee, Winter addresses readers who seek to use self-employment as an avenue for "making a life, not just a living." By writing about her own experiences in a series of self-employment situations and those of clients whom she consults, Winter conveys her philosophy that "self-employment is the child of self-discovery and self-esteem." Her book is divided into five sections: "Getting to Know Your New Boss," "Doing Your Homework," "Exploring Your Options," "Turning Passions Into Profits," and "Creating World Headquarters." Many of these sections include mini-worksheets to guide readers through suggested exercises. Also, advice and ideas are shared such as "$100 Idea Starters." Mirroring the text within this book, "A Winner's Bookshelf and Resource Guide" offers further reading on the topics of personal growth, thinking prosperously, entrepreneurial inspiration, the nuts and bolts, marketing, developing creativity, and specific profit centers.

Evaluation:
Although this book was written several years ago (1993), it offers timeless advice. In every section, Winter discusses common topics from the unique perspective of personal and spiritual growth. Winter's guide is motivational, with spiritual overtones, and serves to help the reader discover personal clarity. Because this psychological focus is so persistent, nearly any section could be highlighted to convey the book's tone. For example, the "asset inventory" list is comprised of things such as "My curiosity and desire to learn new things," "My weekly twelve-step group meetings, which give me support," and "A generally optimistic attitude." Other examples included in this list pertain to the more common suggestions such as "My personal computer and telephone," "Experience gained in three diverse jobs," and "Good personal management." While Winter's influence appeals most strongly to the reader's psychological/spiritual nature, the discussion provides worthwhile application to the real world of making money. This book will appeal to readers who share a belief in Winter's message that self-esteem and self-employment are interconnected.

Where To Find/Buy:
Bookstores and libraries.

THE NAFE GUIDE TO STARTING YOUR OWN BUSINESS
A Handbook For Entrepreneurial Women

★★

Description:

Evaluative tools and strategies help readers discover What It Takes to Own and Run a Business. The authors define characteristics of successful women entrepreneurs and common obstacles that are encountered. Also, the pros/cons of having your own business are listed. Readers are given a list of questions to determine their personal strengths/weaknesses, and are requested to Commit Now by declaring a date when their vision will become a reality. Chapter two focuses on strategies to develop the skills of a visionary, communicator, networker, and leader skills characteristic of successful women entrepreneurs. Assuming that some readers will choose to start a businesses which will hire employees, the Relationship Manager and Supportive Team Builder characteristics are considered. Strategies for Overcoming the Seven Major Obstacles Confronting Women Entrepreneurs includes issues such as Building Self-Esteem, Establishing Credibility, Becoming a Risk Taker, Developing Leadership Skills, Maintaining Balance, and more. The emotional and action-oriented endeavor of Making the Transition From Employee to Entrepreneur, and Growing Your Business are concluding chapters.

Evaluation:

This guide operates as a textbook and a workbook. Readers are asked 98 questions in an Entrepreneurial Skills Assessment. The responses to this lesson are referred to repeatedly as readers are coached to develop themselves as individuals so that they can create a successful business. For example, collaboration skills are addressed by questions 14, 20, 22, 44, 48, 52, and 93; a score of 25–35 points indicates that "You're well on your way to becoming a skillful collaborator. You just need to refine a few skills." Readers are advised to think of one way to improve performance ratings of "occasionally or rarely" until questions elicit a "frequently" response. In addition to personal development, the authors seem to encourage an aggressive approach to business. Readers are advised to network intensely, and to contact local Human Rights Commission or SBA office to get more information regarding requirements for M/WBE (minority- and women-owned business enterprises) certification which can be a valuable asset in some business relationships. Necessary Skills for Entrepreneurs With Employees and Setting Measurements and Controls seems to assume that readers are wanting to grow a company that requires hiring a staff. Concluding, the authors discuss the interconnection between business interests and community service which is attributed to the new business paradigm being designed by women.

Where To Find/Buy:

Bookstores and libraries.

Overall Rating
★★
Very formulated considering its self-development emphasis

Design, Ease Of Use
★★★★
Interactive, logically-organized path of action

1–4 Stars

Author:
Marilyn Manning & Patricia Haddock

Manning is a professional speaker, a book author, and a co-founding partner with an organizational development and management consulting firm. Patricia Haddock is a consultant specializing in communications and creativity; she has also authored other books.

Publisher:
Irwin Professional Publishing

Edition:
1996

Price:
$16.95

Pages/Run Time:
180

ISBN:
0786304081

Media:
Book

Principal Subject:
Reflective Guides To Creating The Work & Life You Want

Secondary Subject:
How To Start and Manage Your Own Business

Of Interest To:
Women

Reflective Guides To Creating The Work & Life You Want

★★

Overall Rating
★★
Upbeat and inspiring; better for brainstorming than specific ideas

Design, Ease Of Use
★★★
Well-formatted; includes checklists, graphics, cartoons

1–4 Stars

Author:
Carol Eikleberry, Ph.D.

Dr. Eikleberry is a career counselor at the University of Pittsburgh Counseling Center.

Publisher:
Ten Speed Press

Edition:
1995

Price:
$11.95

Pages/Run Time:
198

ISBN:
0898157579

Media:
Book

Principal Subject:
Reflective Guides To Creating The Work & Life You Want

THE CAREER GUIDE FOR CREATIVE AND UNCONVENTIONAL PEOPLE

Description:

If you've ever been told that your dream job can only ever be a dream, that you can't make a living doing "that," Eikleberry's guide was written for you. Eikleberry defines Part 1 of her book as the "what's going on part." In it, she examines personality types, provides self-evaluative checklists, and takes an "inside look at the creative personality." Topics discussed include aesthetic sensitivity, "divergent thinking," and nonconforming behavior. Part 2 investigates career possibilities. Skills and ideas for jobs are discussed, as are options for "composing your own career," i.e. freelance work, small businesses, grants. Part 3 explores ways to "take action." There are strategies for motivation, thinking constructively, time management, and forming a support network. For an "intuitive approach" to setting goals, there is a "guided imagery/focusing exercise." To help readers find inspiration from within, Dr. Eikleberry leads readers on a metaphorical "journey" through their creative development, past, present, and future. "Real-life success stories" and quotes are scattered throughout; the appendix contains descriptions of 216 "creative" careers.

Evaluation:

For many "creative and unconventional people," support and encouragement may be just what they need to jump start a new career. In that case, this book is a fine choice: it's a warm bear hug and a touchy-feely "you're OK" comforter. Eikleberry provides insights into the psychology of the "creative personality," such as how "your unique sensitivity" can be translated into useful skills. She also acts as the reader's greatest advocate and most sympathetic counselor; for example, segments include "Our World Needs Your Work" and "It Takes Courage To Be Yourself." However, this is not a book for turning your talents and skills into a profitable business. While there are "ideas" for various career "trails," i.e. the "idea trail" (writers, performers) or the "ideas and people trail" (instructors, negotiators), these suggestions offer little more than categories for further thought. While you may come away from this guide with a commitment to pursing a career as a writer, interior decorator, or consultant, you'll have to look elsewhere for the nitty-gritty, beginning-a-business basics. The career descriptions are too brief to be helpful, either. This is a resource for boosting morale and brainstorming, not for career investigation or practical guidance.

Where To Find/Buy:

Bookstores and libraries.

Reflective Guides To Creating The Work & Life You Want

SECRETS OF SELF-EMPLOYMENT

Description:

Going solo means just that: going "out there" alone. For the Edwards, the psychology of being self-employed is just as important as the "how to." In their guide, which is divided into 8 chapters, they focus primarily on the personal side of being your own boss, though they do address such practicalities as organizing your office, cutting costs, and marketing. Stories, examples, and interactive exercises are used throughout the book to explore topics. Chapter 1 introduces the "new breed" of entrepreneur and the ways in which being self-employed requires a different psychological approach. Chapter 2 discusses "making the mental shift to independence." Time management and "getting the business to run itself" (i.e. using technology effectively, etc.) are examined in Chapters 3 and 4. Self-motivation is the subject of Chapter 5, which includes such questionnaires as "What Motivates You?" and "Are You Ready For Success?" "Riding the Emotional Roller Coaster," i.e. handling depression, is treated in Chapter 6, while Chapters 7 and 8 focus on "Staying Up" and "Overcoming Obstacles." A final segment on "Enjoying Your Success" concludes the book, along with an appendix of additional resources.

Evaluation:

With the exception of Chapter 4, which offers tips for using technology to help run your business and some general marketing theory, this guide isn't concerned with the practicalities of being self-employed. (This isn't the resource for writing a business plan, financing, or learning about taxes.) Whenever "how to" guidelines pop up, they seem out of place with the rest of the content, which is far more concerned with the mental health of the entrepreneur than the viability of his/her business. The vast majority of this book is made up of self-esteem boosters, i.e. when you make a mistake, the authors say "Compliment yourself for your courage and ingenuity in trying what you did. . . . Don't berate yourself." Other advice samples: "Get plenty of exercise," "Become an optimist," "Remind yourself of your own capabilities." Some of this type of advice is warranted; being self-employed can take a mental toll. After all, when everything's up to you—the success of your business, the decision-making, the planning—the pressure and stress can be quite high. (This is not, however, a guide for tackling serious, "unbearable" stress and anxiety.) If you're starting a business and it's moral and mental support you desire, this is the place to go. It's certainly upbeat! Look elsewhere for practical tips and how-to advice.

Where To Find/Buy:

Bookstores and libraries.

Overall Rating
★★
An interactive mental health workbook for the self employed; not "how to"

Design, Ease Of Use
★★★
Engaging, easy to read; conversational style with lots of stories and exercises

1–4 Stars

Author:
Sarah and Paul Edwards
Sarah and Paul Edwards are authors of the best-selling "Working From Home" book series. They are columnists for *Home Office Computing* magazine and speak frequently on radio, television, and online.

Publisher:
G.P. Putnam's Sons

Edition:
2nd (1996)

Price:
$13.95

Pages/Run Time:
381

ISBN:
0874778379

Media:
Book

Principal Subject:
Reflective Guides To Creating The Work & Life You Want

★★

Overall Rating
★★
An interesting guide for discovering a self-employment match for your personality

Design, Ease Of Use
★★
Too many pages devoted to "exploration"; not enough practical suggestions

1–4 Stars

Author:
Paul and Sarah Edwards

Paul and Sarah Edwards are the creators of books, radio and television shows, and columns devoted to information and advice about self-employment.

Publisher:
Jeremy P. Tarcher (Putnam)

Edition:
1996

Price:
$16.95

Pages/Run Time:
456

ISBN:
087477795X

Media:
Book

Principal Subject:
Reflective Guides To Creating The Work & Life You Want

Reflective Guides To Creating The Work & Life You Want

FINDING YOUR PERFECT WORK
The New Career Guide To Making A Living, Creating A Life

Description:
Paul and Sarah Edwards are the authors of another book on self-employment, as well as the creators of radio and TV shows, online resources, and a magazine column, all focused on the same subject. Here, they compile a number of anecdotes and exercises designed to help the reader find his or her "perfect work" within the realm of self-employment. Part I discusses the possibilities for going solo, and how the changing nature of "the job" is creating more independent workers through outsourcing, small business services, and growing niche markets. Part II includes exercises for self-reflection to help you discover talents you can "harvest," along with inspiring narratives of others who have successfully parlayed their talents and vision into thriving businesses or organizations. How to connect your abilities to the needs of consumers is the focus of Part III, including six ways to spot opportunities. An epilogue includes a "personal style survey" designed to help you determine what type of work comes naturally to you, and a directory of self-employment careers which is also broken down by personal styles.

Evaluation:
Some entrepreneurs transition to self-employment through the irresistible pull of a fabulous idea. Others find themselves drawn to a vision they've developed for a way of using a particular skill or talent to build a more independent life. However others are enamored by the self-employment lifestyle but have neither an idea for a company nor a readily identifiable skill to harness. This book is written for the latter category of folks who desire to go solo but need guidance in finding the path that will lead them there. The authors build an argument for the benefits of breaking away from traditional work and "finding your own way." Once your hunger for independence is stoked, the authors spend a great deal of time on self-assessment. The exercises, questionnaires, and guided reflection sections designed to tease out personality strengths/weaknesses and interests are not among the best we've seen for this purpose. The chapters tend to be long-winded and short on application. However, the bountiful anecdotes of others who have successfully paved their way to self-employment are interesting, and a helpful index lists hundreds of possible self-employment careers. These are almost—but not quite—worth the price of the book.

Where To Find/Buy:
Bookstores and libraries.

Reflective Guides To Creating The Work & Life You Want

THE PERFECT BUSINESS
How To Make A Million From Home With No Payroll, No Employee Headaches, No Debts, And No Sleepless Nights!

Description:

LeBoeuf experienced the transition from employee to self-employed when he retired in 1989 from the University of New Orleans where he had spent twenty years teaching courses in management, organizational behavior, and communication. The "perfect business" is based on the "Greatest Moneymaker in the World" which is the mind. LeBoeuf provides a distinction between the jobholder and the self-employed. For those who choose the self-employment avenue, questions and pointers are offered to help resolve that most important dilemma: what business to create. Avid learning and communicating are presented as the best way to increase your earning power; and trust is considered an essential aspect to the marketing strategy. Further, creating is favored over competing and corporate examples of successful creating are cited. As for time management, there is encouragement to substitute new habits for old ones keeping in mind the difference between efficiency vs. effectiveness, and urgency vs. importance. Technology and the partnership of other professionals are considered as possible aspects of an independent business. LeBoeuf shares his experiences and insights in relation to all of these topics.

Evaluation:

Although "How to Make a Million" is a part of the title, the views found here are not limited to the mechanics of making money. Instead, LeBoeuf shares his philosophy that the information age is prompting a major cultural transition just as the industrial revolution did in its day; the "old employee" is becoming the "new self-employed." This "new" mindset offers a unique perspective to many aspects of self-employment. Rather than expecting a ready-made business idea, LeBoeuf asks readers to consider that "you can create the life you want by choosing what to think about." The transition to self-employment needn't occur in one grand leap, but is aided if the focus is on opportunity instead of security, what sells instead of what you know, getting results instead of following routines, earning a profit instead of earning a paycheck, trying new ideas instead of avoiding mistakes, the vision instead of the short-term payoff. Still, some truths hold in both the "old" and the "new" culture. Networking, closing sales and keeping customers are still enhanced when a business can establish a foundation of trust, in addition to under promising and over delivering. LeBoeuf emphasizes the benefits of partnering with other professionals, especially a financial planner who can help you develop the "millionaire mindset" to work, save, and invest.

Where To Find/Buy:

Bookstores and libraries.

Overall Rating
★★
Focuses on establishing the mindset for successful self-employment

Design, Ease Of Use
★★
Although indexed, cover-to-cover reading is required to understand the message

1–4 Stars

Author:
Michael LeBoeuf

Michael LeBoeuf, PhD, is the author is six previous books, including *Working Smart* and *How To Win Customers And Keep Them For Life*. A popular business lecturer and consultant, LeBoeuf is also a professor emeritus at the University of New Orleans, where he taught for 20 years.

Publisher:
Fireside (Simon & Schuster)

Edition:
1997

Price:
$11.00

Pages/Run Time:
222

ISBN:
068483345X

Media:
Book

Principal Subject:
Reflective Guides To Creating The Work & Life You Want

Secondary Subject:
How To Start and Manage Your Own Business

STORIES FROM SUCCESSFUL & NOT-SO-SUCCESSFUL SOLOISTS

Finding factual information is one thing, finding inspiration is quite another. Most of us are looking for a little of both. The resources in this chapter primarily tell stories. Recognizing that we can learn a great deal from an enlightened account of how would-be millionaires failed, the authors include narratives of their flops as well as their victories.

Every entrepreneur plans for success, but it's important to be prepared for failure as well. I've experienced my share of fizzled projects as an inventor, but I've tried to learn from them. A friend of mine started a weight-loss business which he grew from a start-up with annual sales of $500,000 to a $10 million enterprise in just a few years. Then out of the blue, disaster struck. The local newspaper ran an extremely negative story on the front page. The story turned out to be untrue, but the damage was already done. The newspaper buried its retraction in the back pages.

He could have tossed in the proverbial towel, but my friend chalked up the loss as a valuable learning experience. We spoke together soon after and I told him about a product I had developed for incontinent people that I had sold to a large company. He became intrigued by the size of the market for incontinence products and services and looked for a business opportunity. He began a study on treating incontinent people and today, using nurses and doctors in his clinics, offers a valuable service, helping people with incontinence problems cure themselves.

He attributes his success in his second business to the lessons he learned from his first. He acted more conservatively with his finances, and he also learned to allow for the unexpected. My friend didn't waste time blaming himself for a failure that was out of his control—and neither should you!

LOSING MY VIRGINITY
How I've Survived, Had Fun, And Made A Fortune Doing Business My Way

 Recommended For:
Stories From Successful & Not-So-Successful Soloists

Description:
Branson's autobiography doesn't just recount the creation, growth, and staggering success of the Virgin Group; it details his personal life, his death-defying adventures, and his on-going love affair with hot air balloons. The disparate elements of his life have one thing in common: challenge. Personal challenge has been the leading force in this entrepreneur's life, from his early years as an intelligent, learning-disabled student in a school system that saw dyslexia as laziness (and beat him for it) to his entrance into business arenas where the competition was heavily entrenched (airlines, cola). The book describes Branson's life from his birth in 1950 to 1993. At 16, he left school to start "Student," a magazine that eventually led to a mail-order record business named Virgin. The evolution of Virgin Records to the Virgin Group involves money made from such famous names as the Sex Pistols and Phil Collins, several near bankruptcies, a night in jail for Branson (for evading customs), his surprise entry into the airline business, and the rescue of hostages from Baghdad before the Gulf War. His story also reveals his personal failures and triumphs and the events leading up to Virgin's victorious, notorious lawsuit against British Airways.

Evaluation:
When Branson chose the name Virgin, it was because he and his friends thought of themselves as "complete virgins at business." Branson wasn't quite as inexperienced as that name implies; he was selling advertising in "Student" at 15 and making deals with the Beatles' representative by 19. His is the story of a man for whom business isn't about making money but about having fun, for whom business acumen wasn't learned but developed instinctively, a by-product of his love of a good challenge. He eschewed "smart" business tactics. He lost one business partner when the company was losing money but he wanted to expand; he lost another when he began Virgin Airlines for the challenge. His consistent risk-it-all tactics sometimes took a toll on personal relationships, but, more often than not, his daring was the single most important factor in his phenomenal success. Though candid about his (few) failures and personal tragedies, Branson is never melodramatic. His matter-of-fact narrative is an ironic contrast to the excitement of his life: surviving balloon and ship wrecks, dodging bullets, gambling his fortune time and again. What can future entrepreneurs learn from this larger-than-life man? To trust your instincts, to break the rules, to invest time and love in your family, and, perhaps, as Branson says, to just "screw it and do it."

Where To Find/Buy:
Bookstores and libraries.

Overall Rating
★★★★
Thoroughly entertaining account of a larger-than-life entrepreneur

Design, Ease Of Use
★★★★
Full of humor, glamour, danger, and business intrigue

1–4 Stars

Author:
Richard Branson

Richard Branson is the founder and chairman of the Virgin Group of Companies, which includes Virgin Atlantic Airways and Virgin Records. Virgin began in 1970 as a mail-order record company and has since expanded into hundreds of diverse areas.

Publisher:
Time Books

Edition:
1998

Price:
$27.50

Pages/Run Time:
370

ISBN:
0812931017

Media:
Book

Principal Subject:
Stories From Successful & Not-So-Successful Soloists

★★★★

Overall Rating
★★★★
Intelligent guidance; clearly and interestingly conveyed

Design, Ease Of Use
★★★
Logically organized, good layout, chapter tabs and index for quick reference

1–4 Stars

Author:
David E. Gumpert

David E. Gumpert is an expert on small-business planning, management, and communications. He has served as editor for *Harvard Business Review* and *Inc.* magazines, has written books on business topics, and serves president of Online Services, Inc.

Publisher:
Goldhirsh Group

Edition:
3rd (1996)

Price:
$19.95

Pages/Run Time:
278

ISBN:
1880394243

Media:
Book

Principal Subject:
Stories From Successful & Not-So-Successful Soloists

Secondary Subject:
How To Start and Manage Your Own Business

Stories From Successful & Not-So-Successful Soloists

HOW TO REALLY START YOUR OWN BUSINESS
A Step-by-Step Guide Featuring Insights And Advice From The Founders Of Crate & Barrel, David's Cookies, Celestial Seasonings, Pizza Hut, Silicon Technology, Esprit Miami

Description:

Gumpert was involved in the production of a video entitled "How to Really Start Your Own Business." This video was originally intended to be a one hour production. Due to the volume of information, run time was extended to ninety minutes and then to two hours, but still there was more information to convey. Here, Gumpert hopes to provide "the depth and detail that only a book format is capable of." Topics of discussion include: The New World of Start-Up Businesses, The Idea, Testing the Idea, Protecting the Idea, The Right People, Structuring the Business, Your Cash Flow, Finding the Money, The Best Business Plan for You, Starting Out on the Right Foot, and Looking Ahead. Gumpert also includes exercises such as Individual Assessment, Idea Crunching, Data Sources, Using Your Research, Pricing, Intellectual Property Self-Assessment, Salaries, Outside Advisers, Assessing Competitors, Organizing Your Business, Cash-Flow Projection, Assessing Your Resources, Setting Up Your Business Plan, Testing Your Knowledge, and more. Pages 233 to 268 reproduce the complete collection of exercises, and are followed by an Index.

Evaluation:

Gumpert offers an appraisal of the start-up process that is practical, insightful and motivational. His writing style is a delight. He often inserts anecdotes, life-lessons and memorable quotations to illustrate his points. One example, from George Gendron, of Inc. magazine: "Go to an amusement park with a roller coaster. Buy a ticket. Board the ride. Fasten your seat belt and, just before the car starts on that first steep ascent, apply a blindfold. That is what building your business is going to be like emotionally." The emphasis throughout the book is on the reality of running your own business—both the thrill of success and the exhausting, sometimes tedious work required to build a business. Gumpert's realism is a welcome respite from the overly optimistic guides on the market that gloss over some of the hard realities of flying solo. We especially appreciate his guidance on testing your idea before proceeding. The exercises he includes are well worth the effort. Use them as tools for reinforcement, evaluation and application.

Where To Find/Buy:
Bookstores and libraries.

THE ENTREPRENEUR'S MIND

Description:

Unlike resources that focus on the business plan, financing, or other nuts and bolts aspects of entrepreneurship, EM (the Entrepreneur's Mind) answers the question "how does one start a business" by presenting the personal stories and first-hand accounts of successful entrepreneurs. In addition to the selected "Keynote Entrepreneur" and the "Launch Pad" business that are featured on the home page, visitors can browse archives of previously featured people/businesses. Each entrepreneur/business profile has its own "table of contents," for moving within the document, and examines such issues as "industry direction," "concept development," "marketing," and "product launch." Background on the company and its founders is also provided. (Archive profiles include HandsOnToys, Inc., Nantucket Nectars, and ID Software.) Besides the "real-life" profiles, there are articles on international business concerns (in "Global Perspective"), as well as advice from "industry experts" and the site's sponsor, Arthur Anderson.

Evaluation:

OK, so this isn't a "how to start a business" site, though there are some valuable articles in the "Expert's Corner" on creating an effective business plan, marketing strategies, etc. It is an entertaining, enlightening, insightful look into the real-life experiences of some of today's great (and often unlikely) success stories. Here, for budding entrepreneurs of any sort, is proof-positive that the American Dream can, and does, happen. The profiles cover a variety of businesses, and (for those technophobes) there are plenty that are not computer-based. There's the story of Nantucket Nectars, a multi-million dollar "new age" beverage company which began in a "dockside shanty," and the tale of HandsOnToys, Inc., a toy maker. Of course, there's also ID Software, Secure Technologies, and MecklerMedia. The stories aren't all "smiles and sunshine," they discuss the problems and difficulties, too. For example, the story of MecklerMedia describes a thirty-year battle to grow a company! (The perseverance paid off.) It's rare to find resources that are truly educational as well as engaging; these stories are just such a rarity. Best of all, this "advice" is from the "real" experts: the entrepreneurs themselves.

Where To Find/Buy:

On the Internet at http://www.benlore.com/index2.html

★★★

Overall Rating
★★★
Entertaining and insightful stories and advice from successful entrepreneurs; inspiring

Design, Ease Of Use
★★★★
Simple format, engaging design, easy to navigate

1–4 Stars

Author:
The Benlore Company offers technology and business planning strategies to both emerging and established businesses. Its product, "The Entrepreneur's Mind," is sponsored by Arthur Anderson Consulting.

Publisher:
Benlore Company

Media:
Internet

Principal Subject:
Stories From Successful & Not-So-Successful Soloists

★★★

Overall Rating
★★★
An entertaining look at 12 diverse entrepreneurs

Design, Ease Of Use
★★★
A good mix of narrative, anecdotes, and quotes; simple format

1–4 Stars

Author:
Gregory K. Ericksen
Ernst & Young's Entrepreneurial Services practice is dedicated to owner-managed and middle-market businesses. Mr. Ericksen is the firm's National Director of Entrepreneurial Services and is chairman of the Entrepreneur of the Year Institute.

Publisher:
John Wiley & Sons

Edition:
1997

Price:
$24.95

Pages/Run Time:
231

ISBN:
0471179981

Media:
Book

Principal Subject:
Stories From Successful & Not-So-Successful Soloists

Stories From Successful & Not-So-Successful Soloists

WHAT'S LUCK GOT TO DO WITH IT?
12 Entrepreneurs Reveal The Secrets Behind Their Success

Description:

Author Ericksen calls the 12 successful men and women he profiles representatives of the "entrepreneurs of the post industrial information age." Their stories demonstrate that the "new economy" demands innovation, and though their paths to success vary, they share one common trait: they have a vision which they "pursue wholeheartedly." Profiles include Jim McCann of 1-800-FLOWERS, who began with a flower shop "on the side," Ted Waitt, who started Gateway 2000 on his family's Iowa farm, and Pleasant T. Rowland, who couldn't find a satisfactory gift for her nieces and wound up with the $250 million Pleasant Company, which makes "The American Girls Collection" of dolls and books. There are also stories about Joanna Lau, who transformed a money-losing business into LAU Technologies, a company with $56 million in annual revenues, and Richard Schulze, who switched marketing strategies and transformed an audio supply business into Best Buy Co., Inc. Each chapter is dedicated to one profile and combines narrative from Ericksen with personal quotes and anecdotes from the featured entrepreneur.

Evaluation:

In addition to McCann, Waitt, Rowland, Lau, and Schulze, Ericksen also profiles Ely Callaway (Callaway Golf Company), Steven Hamerslag (MTI Technology Corporation), Gary Hirshberg (Stonyfield Farm), Jim Koch (The Boston Beer Company), Fran Sussner Rodgers (Work/Family Directions), Jack Stack (Springfield ReManufacturing Corporation), and William Ungar (National Envelope Corporation.) The book reads like a business person's "People Magazine:" the stories are glossy, engaging, and tend to focus on the victories, rather than the "down times." Though certainly a great deal of hard work and perseverance factors into all of these entrepreneurs' successes, you'll have to keep reminding yourself of that; the profiles do have a tendency to make it "look easy." There's also an odd dichotomy to the stories and Ericksen's approach. On the one hand, vision and tenacity are portrayed as the chief attributes for success; on the other hand, almost all of the entrepreneurs refer to "luck" or lucky timing at least once, which sends a mixed message to the reader. Still, there are a wide variety of businesses and individuals showcased here—a sort of "something for everyone" potpourri— which should increase your chances of finding inspiration or a hero to spur you on. As far as "success stories" go, this is a fine choice.

Where To Find/Buy:
Bookstores and libraries.

CREATING & MANAGING YOUR OWN BUSINESS

How To Start & Manage Your Own Business

When I began my product development consulting business nearly 30 years ago, there weren't many resources available for me to turn to with my questions. I began from scratch with not much of a plan and learned along the way. Looking back, I marvel at the time and money I could have saved—and the frustration I could have avoided—by having access to the resources we review in this chapter.

Starting a business is a serious endeavor, one that requires considerable preparation. While there is certainly no blueprint for success, entrepreneurs must have a thorough understanding of the key elements of the start-up phase (creating a business plan, analyzing your market, etc.). Consulting one of these guides early on can help position your business for success down the road.

As you read through our reviews, you'll note that while some guides are written for a general audience, many are tailored for a particular group, such as: novices, seasoned professionals, young people and those on a "shoe-string" budget. Resources for high-tech or Internet-based businesses are grouped together in the last chapter of this section. And for information on home-based businesses, see Section V "Working From Home: The Home-Based Revolution."

I'll supplement the practical advice you will find in these resources with some home-spun advice of my own.

Lessons From A Lifelong Entrepreneur

Many things have changed since I created my first invention at age seven. One dynamic that hasn't changed is that when starting your own business, your income begins slowly but your start-up costs arrive early and living expenses remain fairly constant. Thus, you must cut your expenses to the bone. It is important that your family understand that they must endure this period of low income until the business becomes profitable. If you have the opportunity to save in anticipation of going solo, this will increase your buffer.

A new business owner must pay attention to the calendar, because most likely no set amount of money is going to come in on a schedule of the first and the fifteenth of the month. Stay on top of your cash flow to avoid the embarrassment of running out of funds before the next check arrives.

One of the first things I learned after leaving a large corporate employer was that I was totally alone. I had to learn how to make my travel plans, get my lunch, clean the office, make appointments and phone calls. When I needed copies I had to go have them made. Fax machines were just starting to be used and we needed to go downtown, 10 miles, to send or receive faxes. All those services seamlessly supplied by my former employer now fell upon my own shoulders. And if I wasn't careful, I could spend most of my time just taking care of the tasks formerly performed by others.

Remember that your time is the most valuable capital you have. You need to consider how and why you are investing it. I realized when I found myself lining up the pencils in my desk drawer one day that I was doing wasteful things, not constructively building a business. It takes discipline to stay on track. At the beginning of a new business you can add up to 25% of time to your usual 8-hour workday, using the time formerly employed commuting to and from your job. This time should be spent getting new business.

I have a sign hanging on the wall above my desk which reads "We need to do creative procrastination, putting off a chore in order to have few minutes to think." (Author unknown) In the harried initial stages of building your business, make time to reflect! Even if you have to schedule such time.

With a little research you can find opportunities, so creativity counts. At the beginning of my business I learned to plan my travel so I can take advantage of intermediate stops along the route. For example, when I was starting a business in California, across the country from my home in Connecticut, I found out that for only $5.00 extra, the airline would allow me to stop in Dallas, and continue the flight several hours later. Thus, when I flew to California each month, I stopped in Dallas once on the way out and once on the way back, which helped me cultivate new business.

For the last four years, one of my neighbors has been checking my "in box" for his faxes. We receive 10 or 12 such communications a month for him. In beginning your new business, you may find that sharing resources expands your asset base—and provides some social interaction as well!

How To Start & Manage Your Own Business

★★★★

Overall Rating
★★★★

Interactive, informative, in-depth resource for budding entrepreneurs!

Design, Ease Of Use
★★★★

Simple, elegant design; easy to navigate and use

1–4 Stars

Author:
Jill Bond, an entrepreneur, founded "Entrepreneurial Edge" in 1990 to help small business owners. In 1995, "Edge" was acquired by the Edward Lowe Foundation, a nonprofit organization founded by the creator of Kitty Litter and Tidy Cat.

Publisher:
Edward Lowe Foundation

Media:
Internet

Principal Subject:
How To Start & Manage Your Own Business

ENTREPRENEURIAL EDGE ONLINE

 Recommended For:
How To Start & Manage Your Own Business

Description:
The online version of "Edge" magazine offers new entrepreneurs more than its archives; there's a "Business Toolbox," "Business Resources," and a "Virtual Network." In the "Toolbox," users will find a two types of free tools for starting and growing a small business: "business builders" and "interactive toolbox." The "Business builders" are a series of "training modules." These "modules" are interactive, educational worksheets that walk users step-by-step through such procedures as marketing, financing, managing, and promoting a business. The "interactive toolbox" includes financial management and financial assessment tools, i.e. a profit and loss statement, a cash budget, and capital search assistance. The section for "Business Resources" includes links to related sites, news and trends, and access to "smallbizNet," "Edge's" sister site, a database of 5,000 documents on small business issues. For networking, the "Virtual Network" has two features: a "brainstorming boardroom" and an "interactive forum." The site's archives contain hundreds of articles on entrepreneurism; topics range from business planning and using technology to legal issues and growth strategies.

Evaluation:
When you arrive at this site, don't be deceived by the blank space that takes up a large amount of the screen. Move the cursor to one of the section headings, i.e. "Business Resources," and the blank space is filled by a description of that section. And that's only the first pleasant surprise awaiting visitors. There are tons of delicious gems at this quiet, unassuming site, and they aren't hard to find. Everywhere you go has something valuable to offer, from the networking possibilities of the "Virtual Network" to the one-click-away "smallbizNet," with its enormous database of informational documents. The best surprise, however, is how easy it is to use the "Toolbox." To use one of the financial tools, such as the balance sheet, just plug in your numbers and hit "calculate." The "training modules" are fantastic, too: interactive, self-paced, educational, and readily available—you don't have to download anything! Plus, the modules cover a huge amount of information; they're miniature business courses. For example, in "Identify a Market," there are clear instructions for preparing a market analysis, identifying your customer and your segment of the market, and creating a customer profile. "Edge" is owned by a nonprofit organization, and the true love of helping shines through in every screen. Don't miss this one!

Where To Find/Buy:
On the Internet at http://www.edgeonline.com

How To Start & Manage Your Own Business

ENTREPRENEURMAG.COM
The Online Small Business Authority

 Recommended For:
How To Start & Manage Your Own Business

Description:
EntrepreneurMag isn't just the online version of "Entrepreneur;" it houses online versions of "Business Start-Ups" and "Entrepreneur International," as well as the home-based business e-zine, "HomeOfficeMag.com." Features and columns from all 4 magazines are accessible, as are archived articles from past issues. Plus, EntrepreneurMag.com has its own "front page features," such as Find Money Online and a series of Start-Up Kits. The site also contains a searchable library of archived articles, trade show information, classifieds and a resume bank (for hiring), links to additional resources (i.e. SmallBizBooks.com), and online forums and chat rooms for networking. There's a Small Business Resource Center, which offers segments on financing, starting out, home businesses, franchising, marketing, management, and technology; features include top business picks for 1999 and a week-by-week guide to launching a business. Users can download free business forms (with Adobe Acrobat) to assist with analysis, marketing, collection, inventory, etc., or browse the Entrepreneur's Database for ideas. The Database contains lists of home-based businesses, business opportunities, and 100 fastest-growing franchises. A detailed site map is provided.

Evaluation:
This site is overflowing with substantial tools and advice for entrepreneurs of any ilk. Not only does it harbor 4 online magazines, full of articles on everything from taxes to technology, there are hundreds of business ideas to browse: hot home business ideas, franchises, general business ideas, top international opportunities. In fact, for business ideas, this is one of the number one sites to visit! The free business forms are easy to download (all forms are in Portable Document Format and you can download Adobe Acrobat here) and they're more in-depth than similar freebies. For example, the marketing forms include questionnaires for determining basic demographic characteristics, customer motivation (for buying a product), and customer brand loyalty. You won't find those forms at other sites! Plus, as a high-traffic site, the community forums and start-up chat rooms are reasonable places to network; they're definitely worth a look. With so much material, navigating can be time-consuming, so be sure to familiarize yourself with the site map and take advantage of the excellent search engines. Combine this multi-faceted site with the clear directions of Entrepreneur Media's print resource, "Start Your Own Business" (see review), and you are, as the saying goes, in business.

Where To Find/Buy:
On the Internet using the URL: http://www.entrepreneurmag.com

Overall Rating
★★★★
Hundreds of business ideas, 4 online magazines, a wealth of information; great for all!

Design, Ease Of Use
★★★★
Too much information for the site map to cover everything; use the search engines

1–4 Stars

Author:
EntrepreneurMag.com is produced by Entrepreneur Media, the same company that produces the print publication, *Entrepreneur Magazine*.

Publisher:
Entrepreneur Media

Media:
Internet

Principal Subject:
How To Start & Manage Your Own Business

Secondary Subject:
Setting Up And Running A Home-Based Business

★★★★

Overall Rating
★★★★
A must for female entrepreneurs!

Design, Ease Of Use
★★★★
Includes an explicit table of contents and effective search engines

1–4 Stars

Author:
The Online Women's Business Center is a collaboration between SBA's Office of Women's Business Ownership, the North Texas Women's Business Development Center, and SBA Women's Business Centers across America.

Publisher:
The Online Women's Business Center

Media:
Internet

Principal Subject:
How To Start & Manage Your Own Business

Secondary Subject:
Websites For Networking, Support And Advice

Of Interest To:
Women

How To Start & Manage Your Own Business

THE ONLINE WOMEN'S BUSINESS CENTER

 Recommended For:
How To Start & Manage Your Own Business

Description:
Developed in conjunction with the SBA and SBA Women's Business Centers, "OWBC" styles itself as a business skills training site with one primary goal: to help women entrepreneurs. For navigating the enormous site, there's an explicit table of contents which outlines each of the site's main sections: Learning About Business, Running Your Business, Information Exchange, and Resources. Learning About Business comprises segments on Starting (i.e. business plans, self-assessment), Growing, and Expanding. Running Your Business includes the Finance Center (i.e. accounting, cash flow), the Management Institute (i.e. employee handbook samples), and the Marketing Mall (i.e. market plans, promotions). There's also a Procurement Place, with details on doing business with federal, state and local governments, and a Technology Tower directory, which covers computer basics and doing business on the Web. The Information Exchange section offers discussion forums and expert help (from SCORE), while Resources encompasses a resource database, FAQs, and Internet listings. A nationwide directory of WBCs and Success Stories from all types of businesses are provided, as is a Spanish version of the text.

Evaluation:
There's is simply too much information at this site to describe it all; needless to say, this is a fantastic, all-inclusive site for women entrepreneurs! In Starting Your Business, you'll find business plan tools, "your own personal business glossary," statistics, self-assessment tips, and encouragement, and Starting is only one of 12 sub-sections! There's also the educational Finance Center, with instruction on accounting, bookkeeping, budgeting, and more, and the expansive Marketing Mall, with step-by-step guidance for creating marketing plans, promotions, and advertisements. The Management Institute provides almost a complete Employee Handbook with details on everything from attendance and dress code to retirement plans. In Success Stories, you can read inspirational accounts of a variety of women-owned enterprises: Internet Success, Home-Based Business, Small Business, etc. Best of all, you can interact with other soloists, too, in the discussion rooms, or get expert assistance from SCORE. (See SCORE review.) Plus all these materials are free, free, free. This is a completely non-profit site, affiliated with the SBA, so you don't have to spend one wasted moment worrying about concealed advertisements or for-fee products/services. For women-centered entrepreneurial help, this is the place to go!

Where To Find/Buy:
On the Internet using the URL: http://www.onlinewbc.org

How To Start & Manage Your Own Business

SBA ONLINE

  Recommended For:
How To Start & Manage Your Own Business

Description:

The SBA's site offers a wide range of informational resources for small business owners, including sections on regulations, financing, expanding, and Starting Your Business. The Starting section has its own "main page" and its own menu, whereby visitors can access such pages as FAQs (Frequently Asked Questions), Do Your Research, Training, Counseling Help, Special Assistance, Patents & Trademarks, and Outside Resources. There's also a "Success" page, with links to articles and tips from "winning" small business owners, and a "Startup Kit." The "Startup Kit" examines all aspects of starting: i.e. types of business organizations, marketing, finding the money you need, government regulations, etc. For creating a business plan, users can download the SBA's "tutorial" or view the business plan outline, which explicitly defines each element of the plan, such as "description of the business." For learning about SBA assistance and financing, the Financing section details loan programs, provides loan forms, and contains information on lending studies, lender programs, electronic tax payments, and ACE-Net. Business and financial shareware, such as "files for starting your business," is also available.

Evaluation:

The government is notorious for creating "no frills" sites and the SBA site is no different. Still, what it lacks in glamour it more than makes up for in content. In fact, there's more information here than you can imagine. There are resources for starting, financing, and expanding your business, plus all the necessary information on government regulations and SBA financial assistance, and that's just the tip of the iceberg. (SBA is the nation's largest single financial backer of small businesses; their portfolio of business loans, loan guarantees, and disaster loans is worth more than $45 billion.) Begin with the Starting Your Business section, it's just what you need: straight, explicit talk about the nuts and bolts of becoming an entrepreneur. The Business Plan tutorial is easy to follow and understand, and the "Startup Kit" is a reference library of essays defining and discussing such particulars as business structure, borrowing money, how your loan request will be reviewed, etc. Though you can spend hours in the Starting section alone, be sure to give the Site Map at least a once over; it provides a detailed outline of the entire SBA site and will direct you to other pertinent segments. Keep in mind too, that there are special sections for both women and minorities, as well as for SBA-related programs and services.

Where To Find/Buy:

On the Internet at http://www.sbaonline.sba.gov

Overall Rating
★★★★
One of the best sites for starting a business; everything you need

Design, Ease Of Use
★★★★
Simple, no frills layout; easy to use and quick download (for tutorials)

1–4 Stars

Author:
The U.S. Small Business Administration, established in 1953, provides financial, technical and management assistance to help Americans start, run, and grow their businesses. SBA is the nation's largest single financial backer of small businesses.

Publisher:
U.S. Small Business Administration

Media:
Internet

Principal Subject:
How To Start & Manage Your Own Business

Secondary Subject:
Websites For Networking, Support And Advice

Of Interest To:
Women

III. Creating & Managing Your Own Business

★★★★

Overall Rating
★★★★
A fantastic resource for the nuts-and-bolts and ins-and-outs of starting up!

Design, Ease Of Use
★★★★
Well rounded, explicit contents, lots of examples, thorough

1–4 Stars

Author:
Rieva Lesonsky and the Staff of Entrepreneur Magazine

Rieva Lesonsky is the Editorial Director of *Entrepreneur Magazine*.

Publisher:
Entrepreneur Media

Edition:
1998

Price:
$24.95

Pages/Run Time:
675

ISBN:
1891984004

Media:
Book

Principal Subject:
How To Start & Manage Your Own Business

START YOUR OWN BUSINESS

 Recommended For:
How To Start & Manage Your Own Business

Description:
There are seven sections in this self-styled "one stop" guide to entrepreneurism. In Part 1, chapters offer advice on choosing a business, brainstorming for ideas, whether or not your business should be "all you" or "ready made," i.e. a franchise. Part 2 examines the "Building Blocks:" defining your market, conducting market research, naming your business, and creating a business plan. Selecting a business structure, business licenses and permits, and hiring a lawyer and accountant are also discussed. In Part 3, the focus is on financial matters: "do it yourself" financing, finding and attracting investors, debt financing, and government loans. Guidelines for "Setting the Stage" comprise Part 4, which contains chapters on choosing a business location and negotiating a lease, as well as chapters on creating a professional image, daily operations, employee benefit packages, and business insurance. Business equipment is the subject of Part 5, which covers phone systems, fax machines, copiers, and computers; a chapter on "going online" is included. Part 6 deals with advertising, marketing, "Net working," and promotion. Finally, Part 7 tackles "the books:" bookkeeping, financial statements, money management, taxes.

Evaluation:
It's difficult to recommend this all inclusive guide to entrepreneurs, but not because it isn't thorough (it is) or because it isn't useful (it's that too). The problem is, this book is so rich, so packed with detail, and so well organized that readers may be tempted to actually use it as their only resource. It literally does cover everything: self-assessment, market analysis, business plans, legal issues, financial issues, hiring employees, selecting an insurance agent. Plus, there are tips for going online, buying office equipment, keeping the books, and filing your taxes. There are also quizzes, interactive worksheets, sample ledgers, sample financial statements, sample marketing letters, sample loan applications, checklists, and glossary words. But, as suggested earlier, readers should be cautious of relying too heavily on any one resource. As incredible as this book is for the nuts-and-bolts of starting a business, entrepreneurs can always profit from diverse input, information, and ideas. Besides, though exceedingly educational, the text here can be a bit dry. This isn't a passionate, inspirational, get-rich-and-happy guide. Use this as your practical, primary resource, but supplement it with some of the more colorful, creative or inspiring resources available.

Where To Find/Buy:
Bookstores and libraries.

How To Start & Manage Your Own Business

HERS
The Wise Woman's Guide To Starting A Business On $2,000 Or Less

 Recommended For:
How To Start & Manage Your Own Business

Description:

Milano addresses readers who are contemplating creating a business, whether it be a million-dollar company or a part-time endeavor for supplemental income. She begins by presenting categories of businesses (Businesses for Everyone, Creative Professions, Fields for Persuasive Women, and A Little More Training . . . But Worth It) and offers examples of businesses that would fall within each topical heading. Milano also tells the stories of ten women who started a home business; here, she highlights problems that were encountered and solutions that worked. After being introduced to these business ideas, Milano makes suggestions for evaluating entrepreneurial capacity, choosing a business, and adapting to the different lifestyle that business ownership entails. She considers preliminary steps to starting a business such as researching the chosen field, finding a niche, and choosing a name. Then, in Getting Down to Business, there is advice on topics such as office setup, registration, and letterhead. Fifteen Women Who Love Being Their Own Bosses contains reports of women's actual business experiences. In Secrets of Low Cost Marketing, Milano states her Rules of Marketing and lists her twenty-seven favorite low-cost marketing techniques.

Evaluation:

Through her own marketing business and workshops she has taught, Milano has gained exposure to a diverse range of small businesses. The business ideas that she offers are categorized according to the training/ preparation required. For example, Businesses for Everyone lists ideas such as errand service or event planning that require no specific training/ credentials and can be researched via volunteer opportunities. Milano provides a short description of the business ideas, but not a detailed course of action. She acknowledges that small business ownership is not the best choice for everyone, and includes some examples of this among the True Stories. By looking at the pros and the cons of business ownership, Milano focuses on assisting readers in their decision to be either an employee or a business owner. Is Entrepreneurship for You? includes the stories of several individuals and some tools for self-discovery such as Your Self profile. Having spent several chapters addressing the decision to go solo, Milano turns her attention to starting a business on $2000 or less. She describes various strategies for keeping costs low; these suggestions pertain to business idea considerations, office setup, and marketing. For each, she offers rationale and/or a real story to illustrate her point. Due to the recent revision, there is also a chapter devoted to the Internet as a low-cost marketing tool.

Where To Find/Buy:

Bookstores and libraries.

Overall Rating
★★★★
Provides good reference for decision-making; introduces low cost options

Design, Ease Of Use
★★★
Alternates examples/advice throughout; good reference links

1–4 Stars

Author:
Carol Milano

Carol Milano is President of Milano Marketing, a marketing communications and consulting firm serving only small businesses. She is a regular columnist for *Home Office Computing* and the co-author of *Profitable Careers in Nonprofit*.

Publisher:
Allworth Press

Edition:
2nd (1997)

Price:
$16.95

Pages/Run Time:
185

ISBN:
1880559676

Media:
Book

Principal Subject:
How To Start & Manage Your Own Business

Secondary Subject:
Stories From Successful And Not-So-Successful Soloists

Of Interest To:
Women

Overall Rating
★★★★
Thoroughly addresses the needs of sole-proprietor without being overly complicated

Design, Ease Of Use
★★★
A possibly challenging topic simplified and clearly conveyed

1–4 Stars

Author:
Jan Zobel, EA

Jan Zobel has her own tax preparation/consultation business, specializing in self-employed people. She has prepared over 6,000 tax returns and has represented numerous taxpayers in audits. She is recipient of the SBA's Accountant Advocate of the Year Award.

Publisher:
EastHill Press

Edition:
2nd (1998)

Price:
$16.95

Pages/Run Time:
196

ISBN:
0965477894

Media:
Book

Principal Subject:
How To Start & Manage Your Own Business

Of Interest To:
Women

MINDING HER OWN BUSINESS
The Self-Employed Woman's Guide To Taxes And Record keeping

Description:
Similar to the tax and records-keeping class that she created, Zobel writes to provide answers to "all those questions" related to tax and money topics that she has encountered in her nearly twenty years of preparing tax returns for self-employed women. She begins by discussing the ramifications of designating a business entity, obtaining permits, banking, and balancing your checkbook. Keeping Records is outlined for both ledger book and computer systems. In regards to bookkeeping, Zobel recommends that readers find/devise a framework that is most suited to their particular business needs. In Deductible Expenses she describes the general conditions of What Makes Expenses Deductible, and specifies the tax implications related to start-up expenses, depreciation, deductions for home office, telephone, meals, travel, insurance, education and more. Tax Forms are explained and some illustrations are displayed. The employer and employee positions are both considered in relation to tax calculations. Appendices include How to Reconcile a Bank Statement, How to Calculate Estimated Tax Payments: A Step-By-Step Example, Resources for Small Business Owners, and Books and Other Publications for women.

Evaluation:
Zobel has found that many business owners are "number-phobic," and that this tendency is especially true for women. While advising readers as to the designation of a business entity and the maintenance of financial/inventory records as applied to the operation of a business, Zobel focuses on the tax ramifications of these choices. She primarily addresses sole proprietor, but much of the information could be applied to corporations. She discusses some unique activities of business ownership such as the "draw." This is a rare example of an operation that is of no special interest to the IRS. Deductions, on the other hand, are activities that must be thoroughly recorded/substantiated for acknowledgment by the IRS. Zobel clearly stipulates the types of deductions that will find acceptance by the IRS, what records are required, and the length of time such records must be kept on file. Similarly, Zobel thoroughly defines IRS guidelines for employees vs. independent contractors, allowable business write offs, and calculation/ payment of taxes. She talks readers through the rationale and provides examples for each of these important topics. Getting Help suggests options to consider when there is not enough money available to pay taxes that are due. Although this is a thorough resource for tax concerns, additional resources are noted.

Where To Find/Buy:
Bookstores and libraries.

How To Start & Manage Your Own Business

CCH BUSINESS OWNER'S TOOLKIT

Description:

From the CCH home page, small business owners (and potential entrepreneurs) can access the main sections of the site: the "SOHO Guidebook," "Power Tools," "Business Tools," and "News and Advice." Each of these main sections has its own table of contents for navigating. Within the "Guidebook," users will find tips and articles on such "essentials" as "starting and planning your business," "getting financing," "marketing your product," and "controlling your taxes." In the article on "starting," choosing a business, evaluating your chances of success, and examining start-up costs are among the issues discussed. "Power Tools" include business/credit reports, trademark and patent searches, and industry information. "Business Tools," for such categories as "Business Finance," "Marketing," and "Starting Your Business," comprise the basic "toolkit." There are step-by-step checklists (i.e. a Start-Up Checklist), model business documents (i.e. Loan Application Bank Review Form), and fill-in-the-blank financial spreadsheet templates. The site also features access to "SCORE's" free e-mail counseling and an archive of news items and "Ask Alice" advice columns.

Evaluation:

There are (primarily) two types of websites for budding entrepreneurs: the glamorous, inspirational, networking ones (like Idea Cafe or Fast Company, see reviews) and the practical, "nuts and bolts" sites, like this one. Used in tandem with the SBA's site (see review), CCH's "Toolkit" will help you get started on the practical side of starting your business: the money, the documents, the basics. In "Business Tools," the number one reason to check out this site, there are all sorts of quick and effective tools (checklists, model documents, financial spreadsheet templates) for getting organized. For example, the tools for "Starting Your Business" include a "Family Monthly Budget Form" as well as checklists for "Start-up," "Business Selection," and "Cost Assessment." While some of the tools are a little simplistic, they admirably fulfill their chief function: to get you ready for action. They will also help you appraise your business goals realistically and practically. (Keep in mind, too, that the more written documents and formal preparation you have, the better your chances for securing financial backers.) Plus, CCH is partnered with "SCORE" (see review), so there's access to free e-mail counseling. This truly is a "Business Owner's Toolkit!"

Where To Find/Buy:

On the Internet at http://www.toolkit.cch.com

Overall Rating
★★★
Lots of free tools and model documents for starting your own business

Design, Ease Of Use
★★★★
Easy to use, well formatted and well designed

1–4 Stars

Author:
CCH Incorporated is a provider of business, legal, and tax information and software to the business community.

Publisher:
CCH Inc.

Media:
Internet

Principal Subject:
How To Start & Manage Your Own Business

Secondary Subject:
Ideas For Entrepreneurial Businesses

III. Creating & Managing Your Own Business

How To Start & Manage Your Own Business

★★★

Overall Rating
★★★
Good balance between advice/information and motivational prompts

Design, Ease Of Use
★★★★
Efficient, a relatively self-contained reference with additional Resources

1–4 Stars

Author:
David H. Bangs, Jr.

David H. "Andy" Bangs, Jr., is the founder of Upstart Publishing and author of several books on small business. In addition to starting and managing his own small business, he has worked with growing businesses as a commercial lending officer at the Bank of America.

Publisher:
Upstart Publishing (Dearborn Publishing Group, Inc.)

Edition:
3rd (1998)

Price:
$22.95

Pages/Run Time:
179

ISBN:
1574101153

Media:
Book

Principal Subject:
How To Start & Manage Your Own Business

THE START-UP GUIDE
A One-Year Plan For Entrepreneurs

Description:
Bangs introduces the Basics of Business Ownership by contradicting The Six Myths of Business Ownership, and defining How to Lower the Risks of a Start-Up from the perspective of his business experiences. Information is conveyed along a timeline, and each segment of time concludes with an Action Plan chart. One year before start-up, the Action Plan calls for choosing the right business, testing assumptions, and improving business management skills. Six Months Before Start-Up, the objective is to know your industry thoroughly and find the best location for your business. Four Months Before Start-Up, choices of business name and form must be decided upon and contacts and education expanded. Three Months Before Start-Up, the focus turns to accounting and financial planning; forms are supplied to support text. Two Months Before Start-Up, financing should be obtained, a marketing plan established and preparations made for opening the business. One Month Before Start-Up, these tasks are nearing completion and are implemented during Start-Up and After. A Sample Business Plan is presented in Appendix 1; and Appendix 2 contains Forms and Worksheets. A fourteen page Resources list, a glossary and an index are also provided.

Evaluation:
Bangs strongly recommends taking the full year he has allocated for planning to start a business. He reasons that the "big picture" mentality of entrepreneurship is unparalleled by the corporate experience. Consequently, time and effort are required to accomplish both the learning and the unlearning that must take place. The One-Year Plan presented is a step-by-step guide for transitioning to small business ownership and management. Discussions and formats tend to be both informative and thought provoking. Topics are often addressed from various perspectives; for example, the business idea discussion includes the Personal Sense, Business Sense, Market Sense and Financial Sense. Bangs consistently clarifies the reality/expectations of creating a small business, and suggests strategy/resources for accomplishing tasks. The Action Plan sections explicitly provide prompts/monitors for progress towards The Start-Up. Bangs conveys the business plan as a working document that will continue to be worked throughout the life of the business. The example business plan located in Appendix 1 is thoroughly detailed and serves as an excellent representation of the teachings conveyed in the preceding chapters. So whether or not the time frame is a perfect match, this One-Year Plan for Entrepreneurs offers valuable guidance.

Where To Find/Buy:
Bookstores and libraries.

How To Start & Manage Your Own Business

BUSINESS START-UP GUIDE
How To Create, Grow, And Manage Your Own Successful Enterprise

Description:

In his (apparent) determination to cover the entire spectrum of "starting up," from conception to development and growth, Severance packs a wide range of information into 20 chapters. The first 3 chapters begin with self assessment ("Are you an entrepreneur?"), tips for finding/evaluating business ideas, and start-up options: starting a new business, buying a business, buying a franchise. Chapters 4–6 address such topics as developing a business plan, conducting market research, and forecasting sales. The next 3 chapters look at product decisions (i.e. features, benefits, names, logos), selling channels, and pricing. Facets of promoting your business, such as public relations, advertising, and personal selling, are dealt with next. Chapters 13–14 provide advice on financial assessment and resources, as well as choosing a business structure (sole proprietorship, partnership, corporation, etc.). Selecting a business location, handling leases, and such legal issues as licenses, taxes, and intellectual property rights, are discussed in Chapters 15–16. Subsequent chapters offer guidelines for personnel management, hiring employees, accounting and bookkeeping; the final chapter contains "12 Tips for Business Success."

Evaluation:

Most of the "all inclusive" guides for starting a business suffer the same complaint: they cannot provide in-depth coverage of every topic they address. Severance makes an effort to include as much pertinent information as possible, but he simply cannot—within the confines of the space available—provide all the information small business owners need. As a result, his book occasionally seems like an outline for a more thorough resource. For example, the chapter on business locations has lots of bold-print section headings, yet there are only a couple of paragraphs or lists of "things to consider" under each heading. Under the heading "Market Trends," Severance tells you to "evaluate the potential location from a broader, futuristic perspective" and "analyze why former occupants are no longer there" without any explanation of how to do either task. Despite these flaws, however, Severance does shine in certain areas. The chapters on business plans, market research techniques, and promotion possibilities are solid, detailed, and well-written. The break-down of business plan components is clear, concise, and useful; the tips for advertising are particularly insightful and educational. As far as "all inclusive" guides go, this is a "mixed bag:" some good, some bad. "Start Your Own Business" is a better choice. (See review.)

Where To Find/Buy:
Bookstores and libraries.

Overall Rating
★★★
A mixed bag; informative in some areas, too broad in others

Design, Ease Of Use
★★★
Includes an explicit table of contents and chapter summaries

1–4 Stars

Author:
Tom Severance

Mr. Severance is a Business and Tax Attorney and a Certified Public Accountant in private practice; he is also a Business Professor and Director of the Entrepreneur Center at MiraCosta College in California.

Publisher:
Tycoon

Edition:
1998

Price:
$19.95

Pages/Run Time:
294

ISBN:
0965321207

Media:
Book

Principal Subject:
How To Start & Manage Your Own Business

★★★

Overall Rating
★★★
A good choice for small business money matters: taxes, accounting, bookkeeping, etc.

Design, Ease Of Use
★★★
Well crafted and well written; includes a series of fill-in-the-blank ledgers

1–4 Stars

Author:
Bernard B. Kamoroff, CPA

Mr. Kamoroff is a business consultant, Certified Public Accountant, university instructor, author, columnist, and small business operator; he started and operated two of his own small businesses.

Publisher:
Bell Springs

Edition:
23rd (1998)

Price:
$16.95

Pages/Run Time:
180

ISBN:
0197510143

Media:
Book

Principal Subject:
How To Start & Manage Your Own Business

SMALL TIME OPERATOR

Description:
Operating your own business is a lot of work; so is starting one. To help readers through the entire process, from choosing a location to understanding taxation, Mr. Kamoroff has created a combination explanatory guide and workbook. There are six sections: "Getting Started," "Bookkeeping," "Growing Up," "Taxes," "Appendix," and "Ledgers." "Getting Started" explores such issues as financing, business location, legal structure, licenses and permits, and insurance. Business bank accountants, credit sales, recording expenditures, and profit and loss analysis are among the subjects examined in "Bookkeeping." Hiring help and such business structures as partnerships, incorporation and L.L.C. are primary topics in "Growing Up." "Taxes" provides an in-depth look at various tax issues, i.e. self employment tax, retirement deductions, state and local tax, etc., as well as business expenses, "the IRS and you," and federal information returns. The "Appendix" covers a potpourri of subjects, such as husband and wife businesses, home-based businesses, computers, freelancing, and consulting. Eight fill-in-the-blank ledgers, i.e. "year-end expenditure summary," comprise the final section.

Evaluation:
Many budding entrepreneurs blanche at the thought of daily ledgers and retirement deductions encroaching on their happy dreams of freedom and riches. Not surprisingly, most guides aimed at entrepreneurs deal at length with topics such as business ideas and marketing strategies. However, the author's background as a CPA is evident in this book's focus on taxes and other financial aspects of operating your own business. Though perhaps less inspiring than a series of vignettes about successful entrepreneurs, chapters on bookkeeping, taxes, licenses and other financial issues are quite necessary. For tackling these "drudge" elements of owning a business, this is the book to choose. It's not a fun read, but it is helpful, informative, and realistic. Mr. Kamoroff is excellent at defining terms and explaining important topics such as excise taxes, deductions, IRS regulations, etc. Plus, the included ledgers are truly useful. Although most of this material is aimed at small business owners and home-based businesses, the tax sections, in particular, are applicable to all types of solo ventures. Freelancers and consultants, for example, need to know about self-employment tax, incorporating themselves, and retirement deductions, too. This isn't a resource for choosing a business or writing a business plan, but for $17, it's a great paperback CPA.

Where To Find/Buy:
Bookstores and libraries.

How To Start & Manage Your Own Business

UPSTART START-UPS

★★★

Description:

The success stories of 34 young entrepreneurs are intermingled with how-to advice in Lieber's "start up" guide for people 30 and younger. In Chapter 1, "What It Takes (And What It Doesn't)," Lieber begins by examining the diverse routes entrepreneurs take to independence, how they accumulate experience, college vs. no college, graduate work, etc., and which traits "upstarts" share. Chapter 2 explores "where ideas come from" and assists with brainstorming and self-assessment. Chapter 3 offers a "quick primer on market research" (the entrepreneurs explain their own research techniques), while Chapter 4 discusses "the ups and downs of having a business partner." Finding financial backing, business plans, and marketing are addressed in Chapters 5 and 6. Chapter 7 provides insight into daily operations, including licensing, hiring, salesmanship, and pricing. "Management 101," which encompasses "playing shrink" as well as leadership, is found in Chapter 8. Finally, Chapter 9 tells you when and how to get help. The remaining pages contain a list of the "upstarts" (the entrepreneurs who participated in this book) and their businesses, and a resource guide to books and websites.

Evaluation:

One of the things that makes this book work is the seamless joining of "how to" advice and personal examples from successful, young entrepreneurs. While other, similarly formatted books are often chunky and disconnected, suffering from a case of "here's the advice . . . OK, now here's the example," Lieber's writing is so fluid there is almost no distinction between the two. This fluidity allows the reader to assimilate information almost effortlessly, so engaging are the entrepreneurs and their stories. (The 34 entrepreneurs who share their experiences include the owners of Jellyvision, Magnetic Poetry, and Geek Squad.) Most of the major issues are treated here, i.e. market analysis, business structures, and daily operations, though business plans are addressed only briefly. What is treated is treated well, though there are unfortunate omissions. Taxes, bookkeeping, and networking (the way many of the entrepreneurs started out) are among the topics you'll have to research elsewhere. There are also a few annoyances: because he's writing for "twentysomethings," Lieber incessantly uses words like "cool" and "killer" and more profanity than is typical for a career resource. Still, despite its effort at trendiness (or maybe because of it), this is an inspiring, useful, and often insightful guide for "up starts."

Where To Find/Buy:

Bookstores and libraries.

Overall Rating
★★★
Engaging, insightful mix of success stories and how-to advice

Design, Ease Of Use
★★★
If you can, like, stomach the teen-speak, it's way cool

1–4 Stars

Author:
Ron Lieber

Twenty-six year old Lieber writes for *Fortune* magazine and is co-author of *Taking Time Off*.

Publisher:
Broadway Books

Edition:
1998

Price:
$15.00

Pages/Run Time:
232

ISBN:
076790088X

Media:
Book

Principal Subject:
How To Start & Manage Your Own Business

Of Interest To:
Young Entrepreneurs

III. Creating & Managing
Your Own Business

How To Start & Manage Your Own Business

WORKING FOR YOURSELF
Full Time, Part Time, Any Time

★★★

Overall Rating
★★★
A fine all-inclusive introduction for traditional business ventures; no web information

Design, Ease Of Use
★★★
Includes pertinent resources' addresses and information, plus interactive exercises

1–4 Stars

Author:
Joseph A. Anthony
Mr. Anthony writes on small business and consumer issues for many national magazines and newspapers.

Publisher:
Kiplinger

Edition:
2nd (1995)

Price:
$15.00

Pages/Run Time:
343

ISBN:
0812926455

Media:
Book

Principal Subject:
How To Start & Manage Your Own Business

Description:
To cover the wide scope of issues involved in entrepreneurism, there are 26 chapters in this all-inclusive starting/managing a business guide. Chapters 1–5 begin with self-assessment, examining such subjects as Who Are The Self-Employed? and Why You Want To Work For Yourself, as well as cost assessment and Choosing A Business. Chapters 6–10 look at the early stages of business development: organization, business plans, copyrights and trademarks, market research, advertising. The form of your business (i.e. sole proprietorship, partners), naming your business, getting help (i.e. accountants, lawyers), and staffing are discussed in Chapters 11–15. In Chapters 16–17, costs of starting up and setting up shop are analyzed, as are early financing needs and strategies. The pros and cons of franchising, buying a business, and MLMs are debated in Chapters 18–20, while Chapter 21 helps you with licenses, permits, leases, insurance. Daily operation, bookkeeping, accounting, taxes and inventory control are among the subjects addressed in Chapters 22–25. The final chapter explores Managing Yourself, Managing Others. Cartoons, interactive exercises, and resource lists are scattered throughout.

Evaluation:
There are some very fine chapters in this all-inclusive guide. Of particular note is the attention given to self-assessment. Anthony provides tools for self-evaluation, calculating your net worth (to help you determine if you can afford to go solo), and start-up cost analysis. In general, this is a pragmatic look at self-employment, less quixotic than many "you can do it!" resources. Here, the primary emphasis is on the practicalities: understanding legal issues, business practices, conducting research, daily operations. For this reason, the book functions on two levels: as both an overview of (and thus an introduction to) the myriad facets of entrepreneurism and as a hand-holding, step-by-step guide. If you're interested in starting a traditional business (not a home-based or Web-based business), this is a good first stop. It'll give you an idea of what you're up against, as well as how to go about handling the formalities and beginner basics. The only significant drawback is that Anthony makes no mention of Internet or Web possibilities (brief mention is made of home-based businesses). It's an unfortunate omission, since even a traditional "store" start-up may want/need to take advantage of the Net. Still, for a workable start-up strategy and a straightforward view of what to expect, this is a solid choice.

Where To Find/Buy:
Bookstores and libraries.

How To Start & Manage Your Own Business

WORKING SOLO

★★★

Description:

So you want to go solo? It can be an intimidating—yet exciting—prospect. In this 4 part guide, Ms. Lonier offers potential entrepreneurs advice on the entire process, from choosing a business to "celebrating success." The first step, understanding the benefits of going solo and choosing the "right" business, is discussed in Part 1, "The Dream." (To help readers generate business ideas, Ms. Lonier provides a "Solo Business Directory," a list of over 1,000 "hot" prospects.) Part 2, "The Decision" addresses the basics of getting started: drafting a business plan, finding support (moral and financial), choosing your business structure (i.e. "Should I Incorporate?"), legal issues, and attracting clients/customers through marketing. Part 3 looks at "The Details:" making the most of technology and the Internet, bookkeeping, taxes, and insurance, time management, using goals, associates and employees, etc. Finally, Part 4 celebrates "The Delights" with tips for growth and expansion, i.e. how to "maximize the prosperity cycle" and how to "minimize the lean times." Technological trends, such as doing business electronically, are also investigated. A list of "Solo Resources" appears in the appendix.

Evaluation:

There is certainly a lot to think about if you want to start your own business! In most respects, Ms. Lonier does a good job of simplifying the process. She presents the basics (i.e. taxes, business structures) in everyday language that even a novice businessperson can understand. Actually, her book is at its best when dealing with "The Details." Though Part 5 does offer an educational, if brief, look at the possibilities of technology and technology's impact on the future of business, Part 4, which deals with practicalities of doing business (i.e. insurance, management) outdistances all other sections in both depth and usefulness. The first 2 parts are not as well done. Most of Ms. Lonier's advice on choosing the "right" business, which involves pages and pages of self-assessment-style questions, can be summed up in one sentence: do what you like. (On the whole, this is a better resource for readers who already have a business in mind.) And, though she offers some insightful "dos and don'ts" for writing a business plan, there aren't any step-by-step instructions or samples. Still, as a solid introduction to starting a business, and an excellent source for defining terms, this is a valuable book.

Where To Find/Buy:

Bookstores and libraries.

Overall Rating
★★★
A solid introduction to going solo with excellent tips on "the details"

Design, Ease Of Use
★★★
Explicit chapter headings and straightforward language; dense

1–4 Stars

Author:
Terri Lonier

Ms. Lonier is president of Working Solo, Inc. She advises such clients as Microsoft, Hewlett-Packard, and Claris on how best to access and communicate with the small business and SOHO (Small Office Home Office) market.

Publisher:
John Wiley & Sons

Edition:
2nd (1998)

Price:
$14.95

Pages/Run Time:
354

ISBN:
0471247138

Media:
Book

Principal Subject:
How To Start & Manage Your Own Business

Secondary Subject:
Ideas For Entrepreneurial Businesses

★★★

Overall Rating
★★★
Worthwhile for young entrepreneurs, online entrepreneurs, and financing

Design, Ease Of Use
★★
Be patient while navigating: there are hidden features the home page doesn't list

1–4 Stars

Author:
Inc. Online includes issues of *Inc.* and *Inc. Technology* magazines as well as additional resources and original content. *Inc.* was founded in 1979; the website was launched in 1996. *Inc.* and Inc. Online are owned by the Goldhirsh Group.

Publisher:
Goldhirsh Group

Media:
Internet

Principal Subject:
How To Start & Manage Your Own Business

Secondary Subject:
High-Tech And Internet-Based Businesses

Of Interest To:
Young Entrepreneurs

How To Start & Manage Your Own Business

INC. ONLINE
The Web Site For Growing Companies

Description:
When "Inc." and "Inc. Technology" go on newsstands, the full contents of both print publications are posted at Inc. Online. (There are 14 annual issues of "Inc."; 4 annual issues of "Inc. Technology.") But the online versions of these 2 magazines, plus an archive of issues dating back to 1988, aren't the only features you'll find at this site. There are original, site-only resources, such as Inc. Extra (an online zine), bulletin boards, and for-fee website creation. Inc. Extra focuses primarily on online businesses, in Online Entrepreneur, and on young entrepreneurs, in Zinc. Online Entrepreneur offers website profiles and articles, i.e. "Marketing Your Web Site," while Zinc offers peer-to-peer conversation, resource lists, and first-person articles from successful, young entrepreneurs. (A step-by-step guide to writing business plans is also provided.) To help you locate present and past articles on Internet business, financing, and Biz Tech, the online version of "Inc." offers Guides specific to these subjects. Each Guide has its own main page, complete with a menu and search interface, or you can browse a list of topics. Topics in the Internet guide include case studies, getting started, and server issues; topics in Finance include accounting, raising capital, and taxes.

Evaluation:
Young entrepreneurs, in particular, should visit this site, since it's rare to find an all-inclusive site with a feature (Zinc) specifically tailored to meet your needs. The articles in Zinc, especially the first-person articles on achieving a balanced lifestyle and facing the "bootstrapping" realities of starting out, are apt as well as engaging. Plus, Zinc's bulletin board should be a help in peer-to-peer networking. Online entrepreneurs will also benefit from this site. "Inc.'s" Guide to the Internet is chock full of information on everything from getting started to going global, and the article on online marketing (in Inc. Extra) is not to be missed. The Guide to Finance is another terrific feature, offering articles on banking (lines of credit, online banking), cash flow (accounts payable strategies, getting paid), and raising capital (ESOPs, IPOs, SCORs, valuing your business). The site has some unusual features, too: for-fee consulting, for-fee website building, and a free Customize Your View tool that allows you to edit the site's material to your specifications. There's no site map, so navigating can be problematic. Zinc and "Inc.'s" Guides, for instance, don't appear on the home page; Zinc can only be found in Inc. Extra and the Guides are accessible from "Inc." magazine's main page. Be patient when navigating; this is a worthwhile resource.

Where To Find/Buy:
On the Internet using the URL: http://www.inc.com

How To Start & Manage Your Own Business

STARTING ON A SHOESTRING
Building A Business Without A Bankroll

Description:

Goldstein teaches that in Shoestring economics, You Make Your Own Miracles. Checking Out Your Winning Idea includes advice for self-evaluation and market research. Starting Smart helps the reader develop realistic expectations of a business' financial needs, and an honest appraisal of boundaries for meeting those needs. Goldstein favors a corporate structure for the Shoestring business. He asks readers to Prepare a Winning Business Plan; the business plan both defines and supports issues of Finding the Money. Sources of borrowed funds may be obtained by Dealing with the Small Business Administration (SBA.) or Dealing with Venture Capital Firms. One chapter considers partnerships as a possible source of funds and/or expertise. In Setting Up Shop, Buying Advice at a Bargain Price, Full Shelves from Empty Pockets, and Promoting for a Pittance Goldstein shares many of his "Miserly" strategies for obtaining/stretching dollars. A Blueprint for Buying a Business shows that purchasing may be the least expensive route to business ownership. Pyramiding to the Top considers the momentum gained from the establishment of a successful business. Finally, a thirteen-plus page Index references these topics and more.

Evaluation:

Goldstein considers six myths (You Need Money to Make Money, Debt is Bad, etc.) that can undermine the "shoestring mentality." This philosophy is further clarified throughout the book in relation to topics such as determining a business idea, researching the idea, creating a business plan, financing the plan, and more. Goldstein shares his belief that the choice of a business is the most important one because the business idea must be a correct match for the entrepreneur's personality. He also values correctly timing the business start-up to coincide with the particular business cycle so that income will be immediately generated. This is important because Starting on a Shoestring means starting in debt. Regarding research, the recommendation is to make conservative estimates, and to be prepared for the unexpected by planning for the worst case scenario. In so doing, acquired funds will most likely be sufficient to provide for actual needs. A Good Business Plan Can Be your Roadmap to Success; Goldstein suggests that a business plan will point to problems before they become costly mistakes that unnecessarily drain funds. In summary, Goldstein offers suggestions and examples to teach entrepreneurs to identify every available dollar, and manage cash flow so that needs and obligations are met.

Where To Find/Buy:
Bookstores and libraries.

Overall Rating
★★★
Creative financing strategies are most applicable to product-oriented businesses

Design, Ease Of Use
★★
Topic coverage spread over multiple sections

1–4 Stars

Author:
Arnold S. Goldstein, PhD

Arnold S. Goldstein, PhD, is an attorney and a former senior partner of the Boston law firm of Goldstein, Chyten and Myers. He is the author of more than twenty books, including The Complete Book of Business Forms.

Publisher:
John Wiley & Sons

Edition:
3rd (1995)

Price:
$19.95

Pages/Run Time:
306

ISBN:
0471134155

Media:
Book

Principal Subject:
How To Start & Manage Your Own Business

III. Creating & Managing Your Own Business

How To Start & Manage Your Own Business

★★

Overall Rating
★★

Offers general business education which is basic to entrepreneurship

Design, Ease Of Use
★★★

Good use of examples to illustrate concepts

1–4 Stars

Author:
Joel Siegel and Jae K. Shim

Joel G. Siegel (Ph.D., CPA) is a self-employed accounting practitioner, and professor of accounting and finance at Queens College of the City University of New York. Jae K. Shim (PhD) is a financial and managerial consultant, and professor of business at California State University.

Publisher:
Barron's Educational Series, Inc.

Edition:
1991

Price:
$4.95

Pages/Run Time:
168

ISBN:
0812044878

Media:
Book

Principal Subject:
How To Start & Manage Your Own Business

KEYS TO STARTING A SMALL BUSINESS

Description:
Given that an entrepreneur might either buy an established business or start their own, Planning topics include: strategies for determining what to pay for a business, evaluating location, deciding whether to buy or create a business, and creating a business plan. Focusing on the topic of Finance (debt, equity, and lease/buy), Siegel advises readers to consider the factors of Availability, Cost, Flexibility, Control and Risk. The Management of Assets section deals with the topics of Working Capital, Cash Management, Inventory Management/Control, and Credit and Collections. Legal Considerations such as business structure, contracts, licenses, patents, trademarks and copyrights are discussed along with guidelines for Protecting Against Criminal Acts, Internal Controls, Accounting Records, and more. Tax implications are explained for the various business structures. Turning to revenue generation, advice is offered for Marketing Research and Planning, Product Introduction, Advertising, Sales Force, Pricing, Packaging, and Trade Shows. The Operations section focuses on management functions pertaining to the business itself—Insurance, Important Records, Computerizing, Recruitment Process, and Management of Employees.

Evaluation:
Siegel has offered the equivalent to an abbreviated business degree. His advice parallels the main points found in textbooks on accounting, finance, marketing, and operations/management. Siegel outlines the elements of Working Capital (Cash and Marketable Securities, Accounts Receivable, Inventory, Accounts Payable, Notes Payable, and Accrued Expenses,) and explains how these figures are compiled to create Financial Statements (Income Statement and Balance Sheet,) and Financial Statement Analysis (Liquidity Ratios, Activity Ratios, Leverage Ratios, and Profitability Ratios). Siegel puts the numbers to work by explaining how to evaluate and manipulate the accounting numbers until a balance is achieved that will facilitate management and marketing goals. In addition to the business teachings, Siegel advises entrepreneurs to consult with professional accountants, CPAs, and attorneys. In the sections on The Recruitment Process, Management of Employees, and Payroll Record-Keeping Siegel seems to direct his advice to entrepreneurs who plan to have a staff and facilities versus the work-at-home independent business person. The sections entitled Protecting Against Criminal Acts and Internal Controls are particular examples of advice that are most beneficial to "larger" small businesses.

Where To Find/Buy:
Bookstores and libraries.

How To Start & Manage Your Own Business

NO EXPERIENCE NECESSARY

Description:

Author Kushell is the 24-year-old owner of her own business. While her book contains guidelines of use to any entrepreneur, young entrepreneurs, or "YEPs," are her target audience. Part 1, "Introduction to Entrepreneurship," details the advantages and disadvantages to starting a business and the necessary skills. Part 2, "Planning: The Key To Success," examines the "Big Idea" and the "Big Bad Business Plan." Issues discussed include: "idea" selection, compatibility between "you and your business," tips on market/industry research (i.e. "become a customer of your competitors"). Current trends for "YEPs," such as high-tech companies and international trade, are also explored. For the business plan, each element of content is separately deconstructed: i.e. the executive summary, the business description, the management plan. Part 3, "Launching Your Business" tackles "the basics:" business credit, legal structures, taxes, and the "partnership decision." There is information on building a team, staffing, raising money (who and how), "image," publicity and advertising. Personal advice for "YEPs" (i.e. rallying support) and resource lists are also included.

Evaluation:

In today's job climate, where self-employment and entrepreneurism are on the rise for all age groups, the fact that there are guides for "YEPs" is neither revelatory nor surprising. In many ways, young people are more likely to embrace the possibilities and risks of going solo. YEPs may have fewer financial responsibilities, they tend to be more comfortable with technology, they are less likely to feel that going solo is disloyal to their current employer. For young entrepreneurs, a guide written by a fellow "YEP" is a real find, and Kushell's guide is a viable choice. She clearly explains and describes the entire process: from constructing a business plan to establishing business relationships. There are some unfortunate omissions, i.e. no sample business plans, but the "insider" tips are excellent and the list of "hot" business ideas are well worth perusing. Aimed at "YEPs" between the ages of 18 and 25, Kushell's strong suit is detailing the special situations in which her audience may find themselves. For example, she gives advice about what to order if, during a business meeting, everyone orders an alcoholic beverage and you're under 21. This may not be the most "sophisticated" guide to entrepreneurship available, but don't discount it. After all, Ms. Kushell's a success, isn't she?

Where To Find/Buy:

Bookstores and libraries, or directly from the publisher at 800-793-2665.

Overall Rating
★★
Practical information for "young entrepreneurs;" best for 18–25 age group

Design, Ease Of Use
★★★
Accessible; charts and tables provided but no samples

1–4 Stars

Author:
Jennifer Kushell

Ms. Kushell is the twenty-four-year-old founder and president of her own company, the Young Entrepreneurs Network, a support organization for young entrepreneurs from over forty countries. Her company has been featured on CNN and in the *Wall Street Journal*.

Publisher:
The Princeton Review

Edition:
1997

Price:
$12.00

Pages/Run Time:
226

ISBN:
0679778837

Media:
Book

Principal Subject:
How To Start & Manage Your Own Business

Of Interest To:
Young Entrepreneurs

III. Creating & Managing Your Own Business

★★

Overall Rating
★★
Informative, but lacks motivational tone

Design, Ease Of Use
★★★
Good use of tables and equations to support text, indexed

1–4 Stars

Author:
Stephen C. Harper

Stephen C. Harper is president of his own management consulting firm, a professor of management, a frequent speaker and seminar presenter, and the editor/coauthor of a book entitled *Management: Who Ever Said It Would Be Easy?* (1983.)

Publisher:
McGraw-Hill

Edition:
1991

Price:
$12.95

Pages/Run Time:
203

ISBN:
0070266875

Media:
Book

Principal Subject:
How To Start & Manage Your Own Business

STARTING YOUR OWN BUSINESS
A Step-By-Step Blueprint For The First-Time Entrepreneur

Description:
In Creating a New Business, Harper concludes that Starting a Business Is Survival of the Fittest. Here, he focuses on the preparedness of the individual entrepreneur who he encourages to meet market needs. As a reflection of entrepreneurial potential, Harper describes eight characteristics that are typical of successful entrepreneurs. In addition, two Entrepreneurial Qualities Self-Tests are supplied along with guidelines for scoring and evaluating responses. Moving the focus to market considerations, six steps are outlined for Identifying New Business Opportunities. Having facilitated an analysis of the individual and the market, the next topic is Preparing Your Business Plan to successfully grow a business. This section includes: The General Overview and Legal Structure, Selecting the Right Target Market, Product-Service Strategy and Price Strategy, Promotional Strategy and Physical Distribution Strategy, Determining Your Initial Capital Requirement, and Projecting the Financial Status for the First Years. Both text detail and numerical examples are used to convey these points. The concluding section relates to obtaining financing, purchasing an existing business, and franchises.

Evaluation:
Harper's view that entrepreneurship is risky business comes across in every chapter. He strives to help readers reduce the risk encountered by focusing on entrepreneurial qualities, market considerations, and a solid business plan. Attributing the failure of many businesses to poor management, only scores above 50% on the first Entrepreneurial Qualities Self-Test are advised to further consider starting a business. In addition to the right mix of personal characteristics, Harper focuses on market needs to determine a business idea, stating that "the greatest mistake people make when starting a new business is that they try to sell products they like." The largest section of instruction pertains to Preparing Your Business Plan. As the book's title implies, this is very much a Step-By-Step Blueprint. While Harper advises hiring an accountant and attorney, he explains that a firm grasp of financial accounting concepts must be achieved to effectively run the business, and to know the right questions to ask. In addition to this text, Harper strongly supports gaining experience in the same/similar field to the business idea being pursued; rationalizing that "the marketplace does not reward trial-and-error learning on the job." Overall, Harper's blunt, procedural style will appeal to readers looking for a streamlined presentation.

Where To Find/Buy:
Bookstores and libraries.

How To Start & Manage Your Own Business

THE FIELD GUIDE TO STARTING A BUSINESS

Description:

Pollan has personally experienced entrepreneurship as an attorney, banker, venture capitalist, business entrepreneur and consultant to entrepreneurs. He has also interviewed professors, deans, accountants, attorneys, venture capitalists, entrepreneurial advisors and entrepreneurs themselves to gain further insight. Information from these various viewpoints is presented in two sections. Book I contains information that Pollan considers to be the essentials for all entrepreneurs. He begins by looking at the individual personality in relation to business ownership. Then he discusses the concept of a business idea, the customer market, and location. Pollan devotes one chapter to Cultivating the Right Image for Your Business. This first section concludes with the topics of financing, opening for business, and growth. Book II features advice for determining a business plan and a business structure, the two foundational elements which guide the overall financial management of a business. This section also includes specialized information that reaches beyond the basics such as How to Pick a Partner, Buying an Existing Business, or Buying a Franchise, Tactics for Retail Business, Tactics for Service Business, Tactics for Home Businesses, and The Secrets of Success.

Evaluation:

Although Pollan has experience as both an investor and an entrepreneur, the advice presented here comes primarily from the vantage point of an investor. Having sifted through hundreds of business plans as a venture capitalist, Pollan has an insider's insight into how entrepreneurs can maximize financing. In his discussion of The Entrepreneurial Personality, Pollan describes personality traits such as honesty and preparedness that he has observed among successful seekers of financial backing. Pollan strongly encourages entrepreneurs to personally create their business plan, rationalizing that this process is a valuable learning experience. And in fact, the same exhaustive preparation which results in a good presentation to prospective lenders also increases the likelihood of overall business success. However Pollan does not provide an in-depth analysis of business plan preparation. Generally, the author provides thorough treatment of the financing process (from a lender's perspective), but less depth is available on topics such as pricing, marketing, and tactics for retail/service/home businesses.

Where To Find/Buy:

Bookstores and libraries.

Overall Rating
★
Does not deliver the thorough step-by-step indicated by title and introduction

Design, Ease Of Use
★★★
Clearly organized, Indexed

1–4 Stars

Author:
Stephen M. Pollan and Mark Levine

Stephan M. Pollan, financial consultant, has been seen on *Good Morning America* and *Today*, and is the coauthor of *The Field Guide To Home Buying In America*, also with Mark Levine. Both authors live in New York.

Publisher:
Fireside (Simon & Schuster)

Edition:
1990

Price:
$11.00

Pages/Run Time:
255

ISBN:
0671675052

Media:
Book

Principal Subject:
How To Start & Manage Your Own Business

How To Start & Manage Your Own Business

Overall Rating
★
Upbeat and full of ideas; lacks practicality

Design, Ease Of Use
★★
Straightforward format

1–4 Stars

Author:
Joel and Lee Naftali
Joel and Lee Naftali are the heads of Naftali Marketing in Santa Barbara.

Publisher:
Ten Speed Press

Edition:
1997

Price:
$11.95

Pages/Run Time:
240

ISBN:
0898158974

Media:
Book

Principal Subject:
How To Start & Manage Your Own Business

Of Interest To:
Young Entrepreneurs

GENERATION E
The Do-It-Yourself Guide For Twentysomethings & Other Non-Corporate Types

Description:

To help "twenty-somethings and non corporate types" create a small, viable business, the Naftalis designed a guide for people who "have no money, no business experience, and no idea what sort of business you'd start even if you did." Divided into 4 parts, the authors tackle all aspects of going solo, from choosing a business idea to handling taxes. Part 1 begins the journey to independence by providing advice and interactive, brainstorming exercises to help you "find your passion." Chapters address finding your guiding principle, discovering your hidden resources, and developing an outline of your ideal business. In Part 2, over 300 businesses you can start or customize are detailed in the "Business Idea Directory." The Directory groups ideas by category (i.e. animals, computers, health), and includes such businesses as doggie day care, event planner, and computer consultant. Part 3 moves you from "passion to profit" with advice on market research, forming a customer profile, financial planning, business structures, and cost analysis. There's also a Marketing Tool Kit. Finally, Part 4 offers a Quick and Easy Guide to Accounting and Taxes.

Evaluation:

If you have "no money, no business experience, and no [business] ideas," self-employment is not going to be as easy as the Naftalis suggest in their upbeat guide. The Business Directory of supposedly viable businesses, for example, is full of possibilities that require a great deal of hard work and preparation; more preparation than the paragraph-length description implies and more preparation than the rest of the book provides. If you love animals, the book says, you could be an animal breeder or an animal trainer. If you can write "understandable prose," you could be an editor or grant writer. Or, you could organize fund-raisers, be a topiary designer, or consult. While it is true that you can be any of those things, it isn't true that you can start "tomorrow." Plus, in many cases, some type of experience or training is required. Yet the second half of the guide, which offers general guidelines for starting a generic business, i.e. market research techniques, isn't going to get you from concept to reality (or to a regular paycheck). Also, there's no discussion of networking, a glaring omission when many of the business ideas require networking to succeed. You can't go from accountant to exotic animal breeder "just like that," despite the book's contrary opinion. This is a dream book for a dream world; not the real one. At best, it may inspire ideas.

Where To Find/Buy:

Bookstores and libraries.

How To Start & Manage Your Own Business

THE ENTERPRISING WOMAN
An Inspirational And Informational Guide For Every Woman Starting, Running, Or Redefining Her Business

Description:

By 2000, it's projected that women-owned businesses will constitute half of all businesses in the U.S. Yet, despite the enormous strides women have taken and the greater number of possibilities now available, women entrepreneurs still face challenges their male counterparts do not. Thus, Florence designed her guide to both inspire women and to provide basic information on going solo. The text is divided into 10 chapters; each chapter looks at one industry, presents profiles of successful women in that industry, and imparts advice on one or more general aspects of starting/managing a business. For example, Chapter 1 examines women in Arts & Entertainment specifically and start-up, estimating costs, and securing capital in general. Other chapters include Finance & Consulting, Health Care, Media & Public Opinion, Retail, and Science & Technology, and cover such subjects as venture capital, bank loans, insurance, networking, hiring, and going public (IPO). There's also a chapter on Labor & Manufacturing which addresses working in non-traditional fields, and a chapter on Service which discusses franchises. An appendix of resources and a foreword by Debbi Fields (Mrs. Fields Cookies) round out the book.

Evaluation:

Florence's guide is a perfect example of a good idea poorly executed. With more and more women entering into entrepreneurial enterprises, the need for resources that directly address their experiences and particular challenges is surely growing. That Florence tries to fill that niche is admirable; her effort, however, is flawed. First, the book is ill constructed. By scattering the how-to advice among chapters dedicated to specific industries, the reader is forced to flip through pages of industry information that doesn't concern her to find the general information that does. There's also a problem here with consistency. While some chapters do offer valuable insights into the industries they depict, other chapters fall short. Science & Technology, for instance, spends its first half discussing the discrimination against women in science from elementary school through graduate school then jumps to a few vague tips on choosing software and technology products for your business and handling IPOs. There aren't any strategies for combating the discrimination that, Florence implies, is a serious obstacle for women entrepreneurs in these fields. Basically positive and up-beat, this guide is somewhat inspirational, but it doesn't fulfill its promise to teach women "how to do it." This is a supplemental resource at best.

Where To Find/Buy:
Bookstores and libraries.

Overall Rating
★

A supplemental resource for women; includes too many how-to generalities

Design, Ease Of Use
★

Poorly formatted; readers must flip through pages to find needed information

I–4 Stars

Author:
Mari Florence

Ms. Florence is a small business owner.

Publisher:
Warner Books

Edition:
1997

Price:
$19.95

Pages/Run Time:
309

ISBN:
0446672750

Media:
Book

Principal Subject:
How To Start & Manage Your Own Business

Of Interest To:
Women

Overall Rating

★

Some interesting links, but the text is too general to be of help in and of itself

Design, Ease Of Use

★

Practical, no-frills format; reads like a pamphlet or outline

1–4 Stars

Author:

Laurie Litman

Written and designed by Laurie Litman, this document was prepared by the San Joaquin Delta College Small Business Development Center in cooperation with the Orange County Small Business Development Center at Rancho Santiago College.

Publisher:

InfoWright

Media:

Internet

Principal Subject:

How To Start & Manage Your Own Business

HOW TO START A BUSINESS

Description:

To help entrepreneurs, this online book attempts to cover the spectrum of nuts-and-bolts issues involved in starting a business. The first "chapter," Business Ownership, looks at entrepreneurial options: starting from scratch, buying a business, franchising, and MLM. Laying the Groundwork follows with segments on business plans (an outline is included), legal structure, insurance, home-based business, accounting, and financing. Subsequent "chapters" address Finding Your Market and conducting market research, Management (i.e. employees), and Resources (i.e. websites). Like a print book, you can choose to read the text in a linear fashion, by clicking on "next" at the bottom of each page, or you can use the hyperlinked table of contents to find specifics. Individual topics are also arranged alphabetically in the hyperlinked index, for easy searching. (Both the table of contents and the index are accessible from each page.) Links to off-site resources are scattered throughout the text, providing additional information; for example, in Taxes, there are links to the IRS site, the U.S. Tax Code, and IRS publications. A complete list of the links used in the text can be found in Net Resources. A Spanish translation is available.

Evaluation:

Online books are a relatively new source of information for most people, even those that frequent the Web. Eventually, online books will doubtless evolve into a medium of their own, but at this time most of them, including this one, suffer from an identity crisis. The basic format mimics a book, with a table of contents, index, no graphics, text-based, etc., but because, hey, this is the Web, the developers throw in lots of links to off-site resources. Unfortunately, the result is that the authors of this online book are allowed to skimp on content by relying too heavily on the off-site links, which, if used with any regularity, are distracting. What you'll find at this site is the equivalent of a pamphlet or outline of the complex process of starting a business that continually requires you to seek in-depth information elsewhere. The problem is, once you've gone off-site to find market research or IRS data, you probably won't bother to return here—the composition is so dry and lacking in personality, it won't hold your attention. An example: "Doing research can cost time and money so work it into your budget. This is one of the keys to a successful business." Don't bother with this read; the Net Resources can be browsed separately and they're the site's best feature.

Where To Find/Buy:

On the Internet using the URL: http://www.inreach.com/sbdc/book/index.html

HOW TO START AND OPERATE YOUR OWN BUSINESS

Description:

Small businesses are popping up with greater frequency than ever, but few survive beyond infancy. Although no one can guarantee a long life span for your business, thorough planning and research at the start can make the difference in the end. In this video, this type of "initial preparation" is the primary focus. The video is a combination of dramatic vignettes and "how to" commentary from a host. The vignettes follow a fictional couple who have an idea for a start-up. Scenes of the couple are interspersed with scenes of the host, who explains the action to the viewers and provides explanations and advice. "Preparation" begins with defining your business by identifying objectives and pinpointing your "distinct advantage," the thing that makes your business unique. The next step is conducting market research and "building a team," i.e. bringing in "experts" to compensate for "weaknesses." For example, the video couple brings in a third partner for finance know-how. Assessing your financial needs is also discussed. Tips on creating a comprehensive business plan, getting financing, and daily operations, i.e. choosing a computer system, follow. A bonus video on sales, "Everyone in Your Company is a Salesperson," is included.

Evaluation:

If you think you can learn to start and operate a business in 45-minutes, you have at least one of the entrepreneur qualities this video exhorts: optimism. However, you also have one of the "warning signs" of failure: unrealistic expectations. While the 25 minute segment on "initial preparation" is a useful look at what planning a business entails, the video compresses its treatment of such important subjects as business plans, getting financing, and daily operations into 20 minutes of "highlights." These "highlights" comprise little more than buzzwords and tips. For example, the segment on "getting financing" briefly lists the types of loans available and then tells viewers to contact the SBA or SCORE. (See the SBA Online and SCORE reviews.) Viewers are also told to "customize" their approach to each lender, but no explanation of how to do so is provided. Similarly, the segment on daily operations offers this advice on choosing a computer system: choose the software that will do what you need first, then choose the hardware. Period. And don't expect any guidance on creating a business plan; you have to buy another video for that. For a look at the entire start-up process (without a lot of detail), this resource may be a good choice; at least it's quick. For real "how to," look elsewhere.

Where To Find/Buy:

Bookstores and libraries.

Overall Rating
★
Provides a quick overview of the start-up process and what to expect; lacks detail

Design, Ease Of Use
★
Easy to watch, but you'll have to pause, rewind, etc. to take notes

1–4 Stars

Author:
Richard Diercks

Publisher:
The Richard Diercks Company

Edition:
1992

Pages/Run Time:
45 minutes

Media:
Videotape

Principal Subject:
How To Start & Manage Your Own Business

Overall Rating

★

Only an introduction to the topic, alternately oversimplified/incomplete

Design, Ease Of Use

★

Terms defined in margin not always pertinent to section-unnecessary distraction

1–4 Stars

Author:

Linda Pinson and Jerry Jinnett

Linda Pinson and Jerry Jinnett are co-authors of six books on small business. They are consultants and often attend and/or direct many workshops and conferences Ms. Pinson has developed a user-friendly business plan software program.

Publisher:
Upstart Publishing

Edition:
3rd (1996)

Price:
$22.95

Pages/Run Time:
242

ISBN:
1574100386

Media:
Book

Principal Subject:
How To Start & Manage Your Own Business

STEPS TO SMALL BUSINESS START-UP
Everything You Need To Know To Turn Your Idea Into A Successful Business

Description:

Writing to the "new small business entrepreneur," the authors supply information, forms and worksheets which incorporate feedback from readers of their previous publications. The first topic encountered is the characterization of the individual entrepreneur. Next, the options of business creation, purchase, or franchise are explained. Types of location such as shopping center, business incubators and enterprise zones, are evaluated along with lease provisions. The authors include a chapter devoted to Developing a Home-Based Business as well. Legal considerations related to Choosing a Legal Structure, Protecting Your Business, Securing a Business License, Registering a Fictitious Name, and Obtaining a Seller's Permit are also covered. The topic of Presenting Your Business includes Graphic Identity, Business Cards, Promotional Materials and Choosing a Printer. Matters of Insuring, financing (records keeping), and advertising the business are also addressed. Business Planning: The Key to Your Success is the concluding topic of discussion.

Evaluation:

While the authors include many steps to small business start-up, some portions of the process are covered more thoroughly than others. Getting Started guides an entrepreneurial evaluation that primarily serves to clarify individual personality characteristics, while Researching Your Market emphasizes the research activity as a means to determine profiles for competition and the target market. Potential business ideas are not covered. Yet the sections pertaining to legal, accounting, and marketing considerations of a business start-up are fairly thorough. The legal topics tend to be especially detailed and are typically accompanied by a sample form. Keeping Your Books is another section which benefits from the inclusion of sample forms, although the detail here is unlikely to prepare an entrepreneur to the extent that an accountant's services can be omitted. Although the business plan is pertinent to every topic in this book, the authors intention is "to convince you that you need to write a business plan and to give you some basic information." The information provided in the business plan section includes citing another book by the authors entitled Anatomy of a Business Plan, and the software equivalent entitled Automate Your Business Plan. This book does not seem to have a consistent range or audience.

Where To Find/Buy:

Bookstores and libraries.

IDEAS FOR ENTREPRENEURIAL BUSINESSES

Gather a group of entrepreneurs together in a room (one with four walls or an Internet chat room) and soon talk will turn to how they ended up doing what they do. Some will confess that they didn't shop around for a business, but rather, "the business found them." Some will say they stumbled upon a great idea that "somebody ought to do" and decided that somebody was them! Others methodically researched their options—franchising, building from scratch, creating a product, offering a service—before choosing their business.

However most successful entrepreneurs have this in common; their business feels like a natural extension of who they are. Their work incorporates a talent, skill, interest or hobby, and this makes the long hours enjoyable, even meaningful.

So how do you go about choosing a business? Be aware of the "need gaps" that you encounter in daily life. Pay attention when you overhear someone say, "I wish there was a . . ." Need translates into demand. It is much easier to sell a product or service that people realize they need, or want, than to create a product and then try to convince a market into existence.

Entrepreneurs "see" the world differently. Most people focus on getting through instances where they are frustrated by the lack of a certain product or service. Entrepreneurs assess the situation and consider whether it represents an opportunity for a new business.

Realize, too, that you don't have to create a new business. Research successful entrepreneurial business models, those with plenty of market left to share are particularly attractive, and consider if one fits you.

Seize The Opportunity In Bouncing Chicken

When microwave ovens were first introduced, I was very curious about them, because they used magnetrons just like I had used to help navigate the fighter airplanes I used to fly in WWII. So I ordered a microwave oven for my home.

The minute it arrived, I opened the carton, swung open the door of the microwave and saw that the manufacturer had included a new cookbook. One of the recipes, "How To Cook A Chicken" popped off the page. The recipe said to get a glass dish, put two coffee saucers on top of it, put the chicken on top of the saucers and cook it for 30 minutes. I carefully followed the instructions.

When the time was up, I opened the oven's door and an inch of chicken fat ran down the kitchen counter. The chicken was deathly white and when I brought it out of the oven it slipped out my tongs and bounced on the floor!

That's when I thought, "What a terrible way to cook a chicken" and decided to design cooking utensils especially for microwave ovens. Because microwave ovens were so new, I had to learn how they worked. I knew I needed to determine how and where the oven developed heat, so I could create cookware to best take advantage of it.

The only device available at the time was an electronic thermometer, but it was far too expensive, so I thought of a way to test the oven's heat by using popcorn. I did my test by putting popcorn kernels on plastic sheets in the oven and watching and learning where the first kernels popped and where the last kernels popped. We moved the sheets up in the oven by two inches at a time. As the popcorn on the sheets began to pop, I counted which popped, which didn't, and noted which ones popped first. My tests worked!

The heat pattern that developed was an onion shape, about one inch wide at the bottom of the oven, widening into a circular shape. So I designed the cookware to take advantage of where the heat was the strongest.

I eventually designed 21 different types of cookware in clay and tested it many times. I called the company "Masonware" and trademarked the name. It was a very successful venture and we eventually had three factories making high quality potteries.

SCOUTING BUSINESS IDEAS

No one can list all the different kinds of business opportunities available to you, for the possibilities are endless. And you are the only one who knows your assets, strengths, skills, interests, availability and experience well enough to do the hard work of selecting the right business for you. But I can offer some unconventional ways to uncover potential businesses:

- Study the yellow pages in your phone book. It's filled with descriptions of existing (and therefore at least temporarily viable) businesses.

- Visit the colleges in your city. Be sure you don't overlook the technical schools. Speak with the career services center during their slow season to get a pulse on local and regional growth markets.

- If you find an idea that intrigues you, but you lack experience in the area, take classes to learn more. Many colleges offer evening or even distance learning classes. Don't be afraid if you are younger or older than other students are, you can learn.

The resources we review in the following two chapters can help you research potential new businesses. The first chapter contains general business ideas, the following high tech and Internet-based businesses. Section V contains a chapter on ideas for home-based businesses, so be sure to look there if you're considering working out of your home.

101 BEST BUSINESSES TO START

Description:

The authors introduce each business by defining: Startup Investment, Time Until Break Even, Annual Revenues, Annual Pre-tax Profits, and Staffers Needed for Startup. Then, readers are told why each business is timely by describing what "gap" is being filled by its product/service. For each idea, the successful experiences of a featured entrepreneur indirectly illustrate a variety of business topics such as financing, business organization, marketing, and growth. Each suggestion concludes with sources for additional information. While over three hundred interviews were conducted, the Best had to deliver wealth, independence, fun, and/or ease of entry and operations to be selected. Some of the suggested businesses require employees, professional office and/or special training while others do not. Comprising over 500 pages, the list of businesses is divided among the following categories: Business Services, Child Care And Education, Communications, Computers, Environment-Related Businesses, Food and Drink, Health Care and Fitness, Household Services, Personal Services, Real Estate, Retailing, Sales and Marketing, and Travel and Entertainment.

Evaluation:

Whereas the focal point of many sources for business ideas is either the individual entrepreneur or the business itself, the central theme here pertains to gaps that have opened in the marketplace due to ever-changing trends. For example, as a result of the rising number of dual-income households, many Child Care, Household, and Personal Services are needed. Technological advances have spawned businesses such as Desktop Publishing and Video-editing. Environmental awareness is transforming cultural values and fueling the new industries of Ecotourism, Environmentally-Sound Entertainment, and Recycler. In addition to the big picture rationale, particular needs of the target market are considered for each business idea. For example, Auditing Specialist features an entrepreneur who advises readers to find a lucrative market among "fields infamous for rate confusion because billing differs depending on usage, package deals, or date of installation." Along with the general trend/customer analysis for each business, experiences of the featured entrepreneur reflect what readers might find in the way of industry norms and competition, office setup, and business operations such as product/service activity.

Where To Find/Buy:

Bookstores and libraries.

Overall Rating
★★
Offers rationale as to viability of ideas, further research likely before startup

Design, Ease Of Use
★★★
Format provides comprehensive information

1–4 Stars

Author:
Sharon Kahn and The Philip Lief Group

The Philip Lief Group is a New York-based book-producing company that has packaged a wide range of books for small businesses, including *The 220 Best Franchises To Buy*, *Moonlighting*, and *The Best Home-Based Franchises*. Sharon Kahn is a regular feature writer for *Venture* magazine.

Publisher:
Doubleday (Bantam Doubleday Dell Publishing Group, Inc.)

Edition:
2nd (1992)

Price:
$17.50

Pages/Run Time:
529

ISBN:
0385426232

Media:
Book

Principal Subject:
Ideas For Entrepreneurial Businesses

★★

Overall Rating
★★
Many listings, little depth

Design, Ease Of Use
★★★
Logical/concise layout, good
highlights

1–4 Stars

Author:
Katina Jones

Katina Jones is the author of several
books, including *Succeeding With
Difficult People*. An entrepreneur
herself, she is the founder of Going
Places Resume Service.

Publisher:
Adams Media

Edition:
1996

Price:
$14.95

Pages/Run Time:
643

ISBN:
1558506020

Media:
Book

Principal Subject:
Ideas For Entrepreneurial
Businesses

Secondary Subject:
Ideas For Home-Based
Businesses

Ideas For Entrepreneurial Businesses

BUSINESSES YOU CAN START ALMANAC

Description:
Jones conducted hundreds of interviews to research her book. She has
included excerpts from some of these interviews in Advice from the
Experts. In Legal Issues for Small Businesses, she highlights situations
that call for consultation with an attorney such as Avoiding Legal
Trouble, Agreements, Contracts, Copyrights, and Trademarks. Putting
Together a Solid Business Plan contains comments on the various
portions of the business plan such as Executive Summary, Company
Profile, Product or Service Analysis, Market Analysis, Marketing
Plan, Financial Analysis and Management and Advisory Team. Jones
precedes the business listings with an overview of Why Some Start-
Ups Fail (And What You Can Do To Survive.) The list of 500
Businesses You Can Start is comprised of part-time/full-time
opportunities most of which can be operated from a home office.
The list is comprised of both "blue-collar" and "white-collar"
endeavors. Businesses are listed alphabetically and arranged under
the following categories: Start-up for under $1,000, Start-up between
$1,000 and $5,000, Start-up between $5,000 and $15,000, Start-up
Between $15,000 and $40,000, and Start-up over $40,000. Appendices
serve as categorical and alphabetical Indexes to businesses.

Evaluation:
Over 90% of this book is dedicated to business listings. For each
idea, Jones begins by quoting an estimate/appraisal of Start-up
costs, Potential earnings, Typical fees, Advertising, Qualifications,
Equipment needed, Home business potential, Staff required,
Handicapped opportunity and Hidden costs. Then she provides a
short narrative to describe Lowdown, Start-up, and Bottom line
Advice for the particular listing. Some listings also include more
Advice From the Experts that is relevant to the particular business
idea. Nonetheless, the 500 Business Ideas do not tend to be covered
at great depth. Jones says that "the majority of businesses highlighted
here are based on the assumption that you already have some area of
interest, or skill, that you would like to apply to your own business."
Further, she points out that this book emphasizes the potential for
many businesses to become offshoots of others, and she highlights
the value of searching the index to find a companion-type business
that can be merged with another part-time opportunity. Each section
seems to offer only "blips" of useful information. Although Jones does
not elaborate on marketing and research anywhere in this text, these
topics would be an essential step towards the establishment of a
business generated from these ideas.

Where To Find/Buy:
Bookstores and libraries.

THE IDEAL ENTREPRENEURIAL BUSINESS FOR YOU

Description:

Desmond looks to The Forces of Change in determining business opportunities. He favors service-oriented startups that require little capital and are characterized by a flexible approach to satisfying market needs. A chapter entitled Location and Risk also includes risks associated with competition, litigation, demographics, seasonality, sensitivity to recession, regulations, salability, adaptability, cash versus billing, cyclical factors, complexity, permits/licenses, and more. Your Winner's List of Ideal Entrepreneurial Businesses lists businesses that have met the criterion set out in the introductory section. There are fifteen classifications; each begins with research information and contains a list of Hottest Prospects and More Hot Prospects. Businesses to Approach with Caution contains businesses that Desmond perceives as negatively affected by The Forces of Change. Desmond encourages readers to work with a broker If You Decide to Buy. The Relocation Possibilities section includes Recent Sales, Demand, Financing and General comments as reported in a telephone survey of business brokers all over the country. In Before You Make Your Decision, Desmond asks questions and summarizes Some Basic Small Business Dos and Don'ts.

Evaluation:

Desmond declares that he is qualified to write this book based on his experiences as an entrepreneur and as a business appraiser. Many of The Forces Of Change that he outlines are still apparent: new technologies, health care costs, overpopulation/traffic, demographics of aging population, corporate downsizing/layoffs, and environmental concerns. But Desmond wrote this book when recession threatened, and a strong economy has since prevailed. The observations/advice, which were based upon The Forces Of Change and the economic climate at the time of publication come across as outdated. For example, current publications differ with his advice to steer clear of SBA/banks opting instead for credit cards or friends/family as sources of funds. Although prudent, recent publications are also unlikely to contain Desmond's Sensitivity to Recession as a risk factor. While insightful to predict that service-based startups would thrive, Desmond contributes little more than to divulge "The Secret? Service!" Only a short description, initial investment, and contact information is stated for Hottest Prospects. More Hot Prospects is even more slight; this section simply names the business and initial investment. It would require further research to startup any of these suggestions.

Where To Find/Buy:

Bookstores and libraries.

Overall Rating
★
Outdated perspective, rigid advice

Design, Ease Of Use
★
Lacks detail

1–4 Stars

Author:
Glenn Desmond and Monica Faulkner

Glenn Desmond is a business consultant, lecturer, author and professional business appraiser. He is also the founder of many companies, including business appraisal firms, a publishing company, and a seminar company. Faulkner is a writer and editor.

Publisher:
John Wiley & Sons

Edition:
1995

Price:
$12.95

Pages/Run Time:
261

ISBN:
0471118125

Media:
Book

Principal Subject:
Ideas For Entrepreneurial Businesses

HIGH-TECH & INTERNET-BASED BUSINESSES

As a schoolboy of fourteen, I began work in the afternoons and evenings as a page in the Trenton, NJ public library. I was enamoured with the great knowledge represented by the million or so books on their shelves and in their stacks. In today's world, the Internet represents a billion such "books" of information—all at the beck and call of you and your potential customers.

If your plans call for entering Internet-based businesses, remember that your customer or client base will be international with people outside of the United States eager to talk to you and perhaps even buy from you. Though the U.S. leads the world in citizens' access to the Internet, there is a strong rate of growth in both the developed and developing world. Some of the most exciting opportunities in business today lie in taking advantage of this newly-enabled global market.

On a recent trip to California I passed a place outside of Los Angeles which was formerly desert but is today covered with shiny new automobiles of all makes and models for as far as the eye can see. This place is where many new cars are sold in the Los Angeles area, primarily via the Internet. Dealers are selling cars and buyers are purchasing cars by simply clicking through a Website. Financing is handled online as well. In fact, the only personal interaction is when the buyer goes to their local dealer to sign the papers and pick up the keys.

"Netpreneurs" are not only adding new products to the online market (everything from houses to time-shares can now be purchased via the Web), but they are inventing new ways of buying and selling products and services.

My consulting firm was retained to help work out a unique system of selling travel insurance. Our partner was very experienced in both the insurance and travel industries. (This was a key consideration in our going forward with the project. It is essential that you or your partner are an expert in the subject area in which you are interested).

We decided that the best way for him to succeed was to devise a unique system of supplying a service for his clients and patenting it, similar to what Priceline.com did very successfully. While many businesses sell travel on the Internet, Priceline.com patented a system of doing business that no other company can use for the life of the patent. They are also providing a service to their customers by facilitating inexpensive travel and to the airlines by filling seats that would otherwise remain vacant.

For those of us who have been around long enough to remember when pocket calculators were the hot electronic gadget of the day, today's technical innovations may rate a high F.U.D. (fear, uncertainty, doubt) factor. However businesses ignore technological advances at their own peril. You can be sure that your competition is exploiting technology to boost productivity. It can be as simple as investing in a headset telephone (freeing your hands during phone time will make you more productive and reduce neck kinks) or as involved as taking a course in electronic databasing.

Free or low cost technology courses are offered at many libraries, schools, adult colleges and through university extension courses. UCLA has been a pioneer in online coursework, sometimes called "distance learning." Their catalog includes extension courses in hundreds of areas of interest to the self-employed community.

The books and websites reviewed in this chapter range from hand-holding Web guides for Net newbies to dense texts for serious cyber-savvy entrepreneurs. Web sites covering other topics are reviewed in their respective chapters.

High-Tech & Internet-Based Businesses

Overall Rating
★★★★
Packed with information on funding high tech start-ups; very expensive

Design, Ease Of Use
★★
Dense and unfriendly, but overflowing with data, graphs, case studies,

I–4 Stars

Author:
John L. Nesheim

Mr. Nesheim is president of Saratoga Venture Finance, an engineer, and a Silicon Valley financial officer.

Edition:
1997

Price:
$49.95

Pages/Run Time:
303

ISBN:
0914405713

Media:
Book

Principal Subject:
High-Tech & Internet-Based Businesses

HIGH TECH START UP
The Complete How-To Handbook For Creating Successful New High Tech Companies

 Recommended For:
High-Tech & Internet-Based Businesses

Description:

Chances are, if you want to start your own high tech company, you're going to need substantial financial backing. Most likely, you're going to need venture capital (VC). To help you get the VC you need, form the company, and eventually manage the initial public offering (IPO), Nesheim's guide combines advice, research data and statistics with 23 learn-by-example case studies. Chapters 1–2 begin with an introduction to start-ups and their funding and an historical overview of high tech entrepreneurial capital formation. Chapter 3 divides The Process of Forming the Company into 14 stages, including getting the idea, creating the business plan, filling the management team, raising seed capital, incorporation, launching the first product, raising working capital, and the IPO. (Nesheim estimates that the "entire process," from conception to IPO, takes 4–8 years.) Aspects of this process—legal issues, preparing the business plan, creating the core management team, raising capital—are examined in greater depth in Chapters 4–7. Chapter 8 explores personal rewards and costs. The final 6 chapters address sources of capital: venture capitalists, leasing, bankers, corporate sources. Wall Street and the IPO is also discussed.

Evaluation:

One thing's for sure: this book will test your dedication to your high tech start-up dream! If you're not absolutely serious about your venture, you'll never make it through Nesheim's litmus test; this is not a fun book to read. It's tedious and tiresome, but it also provides almost exhaustive coverage of its primary subject: acquiring (and negotiating) capital, particularly venture capital. If you're an engineer or techie with little business experience, especially if you're an idea person rather than a financial whiz, this guide is the introduction to high tech start-ups you need. Hopefully, you have someone on your management team with a greater understanding of VCs, raising capital, and IPOs, but if you want to participate fully in your company, a basic familiarity with these business facets is a must. Although Nesheim's vocabulary isn't "general audience," he explains venture capitalists (i.e. where they get their money), corporate sources of VC, and the role of investment bankers and institutional investors with relative clarity. (If you have absolutely no familiarity with such subjects, re-reading will be required.) He covers business plans and the cycles of raising capital well, too. This is the sort of guide that you'll be grateful for after you've finished; ultimately informative, it's worth the effort, and the hefty price tag.

Where To Find/Buy:

Bookstores and libraries.

High-Tech & Internet-Based Businesses

STRIKING IT RICH.COM
Profiles Of 23 Incredibly Successful Websites You've Probably Never Heard Of

★★★

 Recommended For:
High-Tech & Internet-Based Businesses

Description:

To demonstrate that online businesses aren't just a fad, Easton carefully chose the 23 web-based enterprises profiled. She deliberately excluded the well-known giants and sites that sell computer-related products/ services or adult materials (because it's "too easy" to sell such things online). Instead, Easton selected 23 successful websites that offer a diverse (and uncommon) array of products/services. Every type of enterprise is represented: information sites that rely on advertising revenues, subscription sites, online retailers, business-to-business sales. Sites range from Gamesville, a content site where visitors play games and win prizes, to FragranceNet, a perfume seller, to Motorcycle Online, an online publication. There are also profiles of businesses, such as Long Island Hot Tubs and Discount Games, that put existing catalogs/stores online and, in doing so, increased their bottom line by hundreds of thousands of dollars. As well as providing insights from the founders, the profiles contain details about starting up and learn-by-example advice on such issues as attracting visitors, choosing a host, building a site, marketing, and getting top ranking in search engines. URLs and a glossary of Internet terms are also included.

Evaluation:

Easton has two objectives in writing this guide: to prove that "there is indeed wealth in the Web" and to "teach by example." Her first objective is admirably fulfilled. The 23 web business profiles demonstrate that online entrepreneurial bliss is obtainable, as a reality of today, not a dream for tomorrow. Since Easton covers every type of online enterprise—from content sites to retailers—and a wide variety of businesses, she also demonstrates that there are entrepreneurial possibilities online for anyone: salespersons, consultants, field experts, writers, current business owners. The text is exceptionally well organized; you can "pick and choose" which profiles to read based on the business type, and the profiles themselves are educational, inspirational, and confidence-building. For an engaging, thought-provoking introduction to online entrepreneurism, this is a terrific choice. ("Updates" on the profiled sites can be found at Easton's site, StrikingItRich.com.) However, Easton's second objective is never fully realized. While the profiles are insightful and do, in many places, offer advice, there's no cohesive how-to instruction. The reader picks up general lessons based on specific examples, but these lessons are scattered throughout the profiles. For the nuts and bolts of starting-up (i.e. building the site), you'll need a supplementary resource.

Where To Find/Buy:

Bookstores and libraries. On the Internet using the URL: http:// www.StrikingItRich.com

Overall Rating
★★★
A terrific introduction to web-based enterprises

Design, Ease Of Use
★★★★
Organization allows for "picking and choosing;" includes glossary of terms

1–4 Stars

Author:
Jaclyn Easton
Ms. Easton is a columnist and feature writer for *The Los Angeles Times*; she has been reporting on Internet commerce since "the beat" began in 1994.

Publisher:
McGraw-Hill

Edition:
1999

Price:
$24.95

Pages/Run Time:
249

ISBN:
007018724X

Media:
Book

Principal Subject:
High-Tech & Internet-Based Businesses

Secondary Subject:
Stories From Successful And Not-So-Successful Soloists

III. Creating & Managing Your Own Business

★★★

High-Tech & Internet-Based Businesses

CAREERS FOR CYBERSURFERS & OTHER ONLINE TYPES (SERIES)

Overall Rating
★★★
Introduces readers to the myriad possibilities of the Net; valuable website addresses

Design, Ease Of Use
★★★
Explicit language; uses diagrams to illustrate difficult concepts

1–4 Stars

Author:
Marjorie Eberts and Rachel Kelsey

Ms. Eberts is the author of more than 60 books; she also has a nationally syndicated newspaper column, "Dear Teacher." Ms. Kelsey has extensive experience with computers and has written several software programs. Both are graduates of Stanford University.

Publisher:
VGM Career Horizons

Edition:
1998

Price:
$14.95

Pages/Run Time:
147

ISBN:
0844222968

Media:
Book

Principal Subject:
High-Tech & Internet-Based Businesses

Description:

Divided into 10 chapters, Chapter 1 begins with a brief introduction to the Internet. (Though the authors assume at least a familiarity with the medium, "background" information is provided for many of the profiled jobs. For example, in one chapter a diagram illustrates the Internet's "traffic pattern," and network access points and "major backbone operators" are explained.) Chapters 2–9 describe various types of Internet-related jobs, including start-up and independent ventures as well as jobs with established companies. There are chapters on providing Internet access, outfitting companies/individuals with proper hardware, developing software, and helping companies get online. Working as a webmaster, providing a "unique service" on the Net, and operating an online business are also discussed, along with advice for "starting up." Chapter 9 explores other freelance options, such as researchers and writers. Each chapter shares a similar format: a general overview of the job area, followed by profiles of companies or individuals for illustration, advice, and examples. Addresses to pertinent websites are found throughout; a glossary of terms completes the book.

Evaluation:

This is a small book, dedicated to introducing readers to the job possibilities of the Internet; it isn't the "final destination," nor is it best for people who have a great deal of experience with the medium. For example, if you already know that you want to start an Internet-related consulting company (and you know what such a company would do), this isn't the guide for you. However, if you like the idea of working out of your home in an Internet-related capacity but need ideas, or if you need a brief overview of Net opportunities, this is a valuable, quick "first step." The authors cover a variety of careers, from the well-known, i.e. access providers and Webmasters, to the lesser known, such as webcasting and "information brokers." Although the guide's wide scope precludes an in-depth analysis of any one field, it does a fine job of promoting enthusiasm for and awareness of "what's out there" in cyberspace. The chapter on "Becoming an Internet Entrepreneur," though guaranteed to start the mind's wheels spinning, can't compare with a resource solely dedicated to the subject. Nor will the chapters on freelance and consulting options provide enough information to really help you start up. Still, for brainstorming and finding new ideas, this book is a little gem.

Where To Find/Buy:

Bookstores and libraries.

INTERNET BUSINESS START-UPS

Description:

Actium's informational website introduces users to the basic issues involved in starting an online business. Comprised primarily of excerpts from the publishing group's print resources (i.e. "121 Internet Businesses You Can Start From Home" and "How to Succeed in Internet Business By Employing Real-World Strategies"), the site is formatted like an online book, with "chapters" on Planning Your Online Business, Sources For Working Capital, and Methods Of Marketing. The segment on Main Types of Online Businesses discusses options like online retailers, consulting, self-services, and money-makers based on advertiser fees or subscriptions. Subsequent segments address Promotion, The 5 Most Important Things To Remember About Running A Business Online, and Methods Of Payment On The Internet. Hyperlinks to supplemental resources are interspersed throughout the text, and there's a separate Q & A segment for additional help. There's also a page of tips from online entrepreneurs, whose advice is based on their own experiences "on the front-line." The site includes a list of server services, links, articles, and a glossary of Internet-related terms.

Evaluation:

Since the bulk of the material found at this site is excerpted from Actium's print resources, it's difficult not to make comparisons between the two. For example, by virtue of length and depth, "How To Succeed in Internet Business By Employing Real-World Strategies" is a better step-by-step guide for true Internet novices; a few excerpts cannot compete. (See review.) That said, however, the site does have its merits. First of all, the excerpts that comprise the main segments, such as Planning Your Online Business and Main Types Of Online Businesses, are quite effective in and of themselves. Where other sites offer excerpts as "teasers," Actium offers excerpts that are complete mini-guides; they don't end before important points are made, just to get you to buy the book. Planning, in particular, is especially good, as is the portion on Methods Of Payment On The Internet. Secondly, the site can provide "bonus" features that only a website can: links, a database of articles, Q & A. The tips posted from other online entrepreneurs are insightful and well worth reading (though they apply to currently operating businesses, not start up concerns), and the list of server services is helpful. Finally, of course, the real advantage to Actium's site over its products is the cost: it's free. This is a solid introduction to online business and a good first stop.

Where To Find/Buy:

On the Internet using the URL: http://www.actium1.com

Overall Rating
★★★
A solid introduction to online business

Design, Ease Of Use
★★★
Simple online book format

1–4 Stars

Author:
Actium is the publisher of several print resources on Internet businesses, including *121 Internet Businesses You Can Start From Home* and *How To Succeed in Internet Business By Employing Real-World Strategies.*

Publisher:
Actium

Media:
Internet

Principal Subject:
High-Tech & Internet-Based Businesses

★★★

Overall Rating
★★★
Represents the Internet as a business tool

Design, Ease Of Use
★★
At times repetitive; on-line references and examples supplement text

1–4 Stars

Author:
Daniel S. Janal

Daniel S. Janal (B.S. and M.S. in journalism) is President of an Internet marketing and public relations agency, a key note speaker and seminar leader, an author of several books, a co-developer of Publicity Builder software, and a teacher at UC, Berkeley.

Publisher:
ITP (International Thomson Publishing Company)

Edition:
1997

Price:
$29.95

Pages/Run Time:
471

ISBN:
0442026080

Media:
Book

Principal Subject:
High-Tech & Internet-Based Businesses

Secondary Subject:
Ideas For Entrepreneurial Businesses

101 SUCCESSFUL BUSINESSES YOU CAN START ON THE INTERNET

Description:
Janal introduces seventeen reasons Why You Should Open a Business on the Internet, and warns of Six Challenges To Running An Internet Store. Internet Basics answers questions such as "what is the Internet," "what equipment do I need," and more. Internet Business Basics considers "netiquette," new paradigms for online marketing, steps to opening your online store, site effectiveness, and some general business practices. Janal summarizes Thirty Killer Business Models that could be applied to a range of business ideas. Case Studies are offered for Consumer Products; Housing and Real Estate; Job Hunting Online; Information Services; Writers and Books; Dramatic Arts; Visual Arts; Music; Food and Dining; Professional Services; Travel and Tourism; Software and Consultants; Internet Technical Services; Internet Sales, Advertising, and Publicity; Internet Creative Marketing Services; Bulk Mail Services; Network Marketing; Tradespeople; Speakers, Agents and Seminars. Wacky and Wonderful case studies include Astrology Chart Business and Fan Club. All case studies contain all/part of the following: Overview, Rewards, Risks, Special Marketing Considerations for the Home Page, Hot Site, and a Q/A exchange with a business owner taken from e-mail interviews.

Evaluation:
Janal teaches Internet business ideas and practices by building upon the reader's foundation of knowledge related to Main Street businesses. For example, the Internet's Digital Mall is compared to Main Street's strip mall, and the World Wide Web is equated with the portion of a city that is zoned for commercial activity. In an effort to influence readers to restrict marketing efforts to the Web rather than invading mailing lists and newsgroups, Janal paints the picture of an unwelcome life insurance salesperson who chooses to seek clients in the steam room of a health spa. Janal considers Internet store setup similar to that on Main Street where entrepreneurs may choose to do it all, or hire professional help such as the a plumber or carpenter. Defining the Internet as a place to market both product-based and service-based businesses relatively inexpensively, Janal suggests Web site design that will serve customers by offering information, saving time, and/or creating access to desired products/ services. More than once, Janal warns against overuse of time-consuming visuals. The 101 Businesses suggested are real examples of how the Internet is facilitating doing business in the modern economy. Overall, readers will gain an appreciation for the possibilities and may latch onto a specific plan.

Where To Find/Buy:
Bookstores and libraries.

High-Tech & Internet-Based Businesses

HOW TO SUCCEED IN INTERNET BUSINESS BY EMPLOYING REAL-WORLD STRATEGIES

★★★

Description:

Chapter 1 begins with the story of Abe, who started an online hardware retail business. Abe built an attractive, well-organized site, registered it with every search engine and link-exchange service he could find, and promoted his opening in newsgroups and online magazines. Despite all that, no customers came; his business failed. Why? Because his marketing strategies addressed only the online market; he forgot about the "real world." He didn't promote his site offline, he didn't advertise his site locally, and he didn't employ any of the standard marketing techniques, such as direct mail, that are vital to any business. To help web entrepreneurs succeed, this guide combines how-to advice for starting an Internet enterprise with the basics for offline promotion and marketing. Chapter 2 covers the "Internet Basics" with explanations of how the Net, and such tools as e-mail and the Web, work. Chapters 3 and 4 examine choosing a product/service and starting-up: server services, domain names, site building, etc. Online promotion (i.e. search engines, links), conventional promotion (i.e. networking, press, media), and advertising techniques comprise Chapters 5–7. Appendices, including useful links, appear at the end.

Evaluation:

OK, so this is an unattractive book that reads like a high school textbook. Gielgun is a dry, humorless, and far from dynamic writer. But he knows his stuff, and his stuff—the practical end of online entrepreneurism—is exactly the basic information that all Internet entrepreneurs must know. He is explicit in his descriptions, which is a plus if you're unfamiliar with the Net or unsure of how everything works (providers, server services, search engines, and the like) or if you're unfamiliar with standard marketing strategies. (One of the appendices outlines marketing methods such as selling to distributors/ wholesalers, multi-level marketing, and drop-shipping. Another appendix provides a glossary of Net terms.) For expert cybersurfers, Gielgun's tendency to "define it all" may seem taxing, just as latter chapters may seem pedestrian to seasoned marketers, but if you're a novice in either area (or both), perseverance will payoff. Gielgun does a fine job of creating a whole picture, rather than a lopsided one, of what doing business online entails; for that alone, this is a valuable book. Gielgun's ideas are sound, if not exactly innovative, and the practical importance of combining online and offline business strategies is inarguable. This is one for the reference shelf; you may want to supplement it with a more enjoyable read, like "StrikingItRich.com."

Where To Find/Buy:

Bookstores and libraries.

Overall Rating
★★★
Covers the practicalities of Internet business start-up and promotion

Design, Ease Of Use
★
Explicit but not entertaining; reads like a high school textbook

1–4 Stars

Author:
Ron E. Gielgun

Mr. Gielgun is the editor of an online magazine for Internet entrepreneurs, an Internet marketing consultant, and the author of *121 Internet Businesses You Can Start From Home*.

Publisher:
Actium

Edition:
1998

Price:
$19.95

Pages/Run Time:
201

ISBN:
0965761762

Media:
Book

Principal Subject:
High-Tech & Internet-Based Businesses

Secondary Subject:
Success Strategies

★★

Overall Rating
★★
Computer Business ideas lack action tools; general use topics are more informative

Design, Ease Of Use
★★★
Cannot locate Business Appendix, otherwise information is clearly presented

1–4 Stars

Author:
Paul and Sarah Edwards
Sarah and Paul Edwards, authors of the Working From Home book series, provide informative and inspirational advice on self-employment through their radio and television shows, their on-line venues, and their column in *Home Office Computing* magazine.

Publisher:
Tarcher/Putnam (Penguin Putnam)

Edition:
2nd (1997)

Price:
$15.95

Pages/Run Time:
391

ISBN:
0874778980

Media:
Book

Principal Subject:
High-Tech & Internet-Based Businesses

Secondary Subject:
Setting Up And Running A Home-Based Business

High-Tech & Internet-Based Businesses

MAKING MONEY WITH YOUR COMPUTER AT HOME
The Inside Information You Need To Know To Select And Operate A Full-Time, Part-Time, Or Add-On Business That's Right For You

Description:
The authors address Using Your Computer as a Business, Forty-seven Questions You Need to Answer to Start Making Money with Your Computer, and Using Your Computer in Business. Listed alphabetically, one hundred businesses that use a computer are profiled. Text for each business is preceded by icons that describe various characteristics of the business at a glance. Types of businesses included are Word, Numbers, Database, Graphics, Computer service, Communications, Multimedia, or Multiple Application Businesses. Income potential is indicated as substantiating the business as a Full-Time, Part-Time, or Add-On endeavor. All of the ideas are for businesses that are either conducted At-Home or From-Home. Some may also have a Noteworthy Characteristic such as Idea Business, High Income Potential, Evergreen, Recession-Resistant, Up and Coming, or Low Start-Up Costs. Lastly, resources for additional information are cited. Using Your Computer in Business includes applications for money management, business administration, marketing, and going online to find customers, collect money, and get information. Additional online advice is offered in two appendixes.

Evaluation:
The Using Your Computer as a Business section offers overviews of business ideas, but often skimps on the details. For example, in the business profile for Event and Meeting Planner, contest organizing is highlighted as an aspect of the business. Readers are advised to be familiar with state laws regarding contests and to have a statistical/mathematical foundation to design successful contests, but no further details or sources of information are provided. With such scant information, it would be difficult to even know where or how to learn more about the opportunity. The authors more thoroughly address the topic of establishing a business in the Q/A section. One question acknowledges the importance of determining a market's supply/demand for a particular business product or service. A follow-up question prompts a description of methods for determining if an oversupply/undersupply is indicated within a particular market. The final section, Using Your Computer in Business, does a better job of preparing readers to take action, but you are still left itching for more substantial guidance. This guide may be helpful for someone with little computer or technical experience, but it's not sophisticated enough for technically savvy readers.

Where To Find/Buy:
Bookstores and libraries.

High-Tech & Internet-Based Businesses

ENGINEERING YOUR START-UP
A Guide For The Hi-Tech Entrepreneur

Description:

So you want to start your own high tech company. What does such a venture entail? What are your chances of success? The lure of excitement, freedom, and wild riches—as well as a genuine devotion to The Idea—has lead many an engineer astray; to keep you on track, Baird's guide functions as a map to the road ahead. Divided into 5 parts, Part 1 explores start-up opportunities, the technology-oriented professional as company founder, and "life in your start-up." Part 2 deals with "concepts that could make or break your start-up," including developing marketing skills and learning finance-related terminology. The basics of starting-up are detailed in Part 3. Chapters outline the ingredients for success (i.e. leadership) and provide instructions for creating your management team, evaluating markets, defining your product/service, and writing a business plan. Funding, such as raising seed capital and subsequent funding rounds, is also discussed. Part 4 covers remuneration issues, focusing primarily on balancing salary and equity rewards. Final thoughts on making the start-up decision and suggested resources comprise Part 5. Figures and tables are used throughout as examples and illustrations.

Evaluation:

It is truly unfortunate that Baird didn't find a writer to help him with this book because the content, which is undoubtedly worthwhile, is overwhelmed and obfuscated by the awkward language and style of the text. Baird is an engineer and businessman, not a writer. Unfortunately, his expertise in the first two categories is muddied by his weakness in the latter. The overabundance of charts, graphs and tables helps somewhat; at least the illustrations clarify some of the more convoluted explanations. Despite its shortcomings, however, this guide does offer a realistic, pragmatic overview of the nuts-and-bolts of starting a high tech company. On the subject of raising capital and initial public offerings, it is less exhaustive than "High Tech Start Up" (see review), but it does hit the "highlights:" cost analysis, finding capital, remuneration practices, stock options. One thing Baird does do well is address the needs of his target audience: entrepreneurial engineers. Chapters on "life in your start-up" and handling the CEO's management/leadership role are specially tailored to the technology-oriented professional, as is the emphasis on such considerations as marketing (a necessity many engineers, Baird fears, may overlook). As an introduction to the demands and necessities of a high tech start up, this is a viable option. Treat it like homework.

Where To Find/Buy:

Bookstores and libraries.

Overall Rating
★★
Pragmatic look at the nuts-and-bolts of starting a high tech company

Design, Ease Of Use
★
Poor writing, but includes plenty of diagrams, charts, illustrations

1–4 Stars

Author:
Michael L. Baird
Mr. Baird is the Chief Technology Officer for Snap-On Incorporated, a $1.5 billion company. He is also the author of *Starting a Hi-Tech Company*.

Publisher:
Professional Publications

Edition:
1997

Price:
$28.95

Pages/Run Time:
294

ISBN:
0912045485

Media:
Book

Principal Subject:
High-Tech & Internet-Based Businesses

High-Tech & Internet-Based Businesses

Overall Rating

★

Free materials include a few good articles for Web-based businesses and helpful links

Design, Ease Of Use

★★

Clear format with no tricks; for free info, start with Learn To Succeed

1–4 Stars

Author:

SmartAge Corporation offers a suite of Internet-empowering services to small and growing businesses.

Publisher:

SmartAge Corp.

Media:

Internet

Principal Subject:

High-Tech & Internet-Based Businesses

SMARTAGE

Description:

While SmartAge designed its site primarily to showcase and promote its fee-based services and products, such as software to help you create a site and/or build an online store, it also provides an array of free and informational resources for burgeoning Internet entrepreneurs. A list of the free resources can be found by clicking on Learn To Succeed on the homepage. The list is divided into 4 subject categories, Build & Maintain, Promote, Sell, and Small Business, and each subject category is subdivided into resource-type: Articles, Resources & Links, and Books. In Build & Maintain there are introductory articles on Starting A Website, Finding A Host, and Content & Design, links to off-site articles and tools for Writing & Design, Web Designers, and Web Business, and details on books for Building Your Own Website. Promote includes articles on advertising, search engines, and tracking and measuring site activity, while Sell covers questions about e-commerce, selling online, and collecting money on the Web. Case studies and Essentials for Small Business Sites are among the subjects addressed in the Small Business articles. Users can also learn about SmartAge's membership benefits, i.e. the free weekly newsletter.

Evaluation:

Many of the how-to sites for Internet entrepreneurism are commercial sites that toss in free material as a lure but really hope to hook you with their fee-based products and services. This description is an apt one for SmartAge's site, which focuses primarily on showcasing its own services (including help with creating and building a website). But don't discount this site entirely. For one thing, the bait—the articles, resources and links—is worth browsing. For the most part the in-house articles tend to be pithy introductions to their subjects, rather than in depth reports, but the annotated links to off-site articles from such sources as "Inc." and "Fast Company" allow you to find pertinent resources with ease. In Writing & Design, for example, there are links to articles on writing for the Web, the "best features" of the Web, and Five Fatal Flaws Of Web Design. There are also links to Web Design tools and Web Designers, which are good places to begin your research. Another noteworthy element of this site is that, while it is commercial, it isn't tricky. Some for-profit sites use misleading section headings and other sneaky tactics to make it difficult to circumvent the advertising. Not so here. The free materials are neatly contained in the segment Learn To Succeed, so you can chose to learn more about SmartAge's products without feeling ambushed.

Where To Find/Buy:

On the Internet using the URL: http://www.smartage.com

High-Tech & Internet-Based Businesses

WEBWORKER

Description:

WebWorker is an expansive site with more than one agenda; it includes segments on RV Lifestyle and commercial information on the consultancy Ads Plus WebWorker. For Internet entrepreneurs, there are 2 main areas of interest: the directories of Top 10 lists and Web-u-Start, a free online guide to starting a Web business. To familiarize yourself with the site's contents, users can view the site map from the home page, browse the entire master index of Top 10 directories, or search the site for specific information. There are Top 10 directories for web page design and creation, web page promotion, Internet resources, and web businesses. To access Web-u-Start, the online guide, click on Web Business Resources (on the home page), then click on Overview, and scroll to the bottom of the next page (the page titled Web Business Builder Resources Directory for Web Developers & Promoters). Formatted like an online book, Web-u-Start has its own table of contents and is divided into 4 "phases." Phase 1 examines why you need a website, Phase 2 discusses organizational set-up, Phase 3 details web page creation (i.e. design, ISPs, WSPs), Phase 4 covers promotion. Hyperlinks to additional resources appear throughout the text.

Evaluation:

It's a shame that this website isn't better designed because there are several worthwhile features here for aspiring Internet entrepreneurs. The best feature is Web-u-Start, which, if you can find it, is a good quick introduction to creating a business website. (You can go directly to Web-U-Start at www.webworker.com/ww/webustart.html) Phase 2, Organizational Set-Up, offers pertinent guidelines for preparation, and Phase 3 contains hyperlinks to web building sites along with advice on using such services. The Top 10 lists are valuable too, since they provide research vehicles for learning more about website creation and promotion, as well as lots of business ideas (not just MLMs). For example, there's a list of Top 10 Web Business Builder Reports and a list of Top 22 Submission Secrets To Search Engines. The problem at this site, aside from its poor navigational aids (you won't find Web-u-Start on the site map), is the bizarre mix of information it contains. Alongside the web-based business resources are segments on RV Lifestyle, best-selling book lists (i.e. general fiction), and metaphysical/spiritual matters. Co-founders Bryce and Lisa Jackson created WebWorker to suit their needs; unfortunately, their disparate interests have rendered this site an eclectic mess. This one's for the patient Internet entrepreneur only.

Where To Find/Buy:

On the Internet using the URL: http://www.webworker.com

Overall Rating

★

Includes some helpful resources, if you can find them

Design, Ease Of Use

★

In desperate need of a more user-friendly format; hard to navigate

1–4 Stars

Author:

Co-Creators Bryce and Lisa Jackson started the WebWorker website in 1996. Ads Plus WebWorker offers Internet Consulting, Web Developing, ISPS, Virtual Web Hosting and Internet Marketing services for home based businesses.

Publisher:
WebWorker

Media:
Internet

Principal Subject:
High-Tech & Internet-Based Businesses

High-Tech & Internet-Based Businesses

ABOUT DOMAINS.COM

Non-Rated Resource

Description:
Just as the name suggests, this site is all about domain names: how to find out if a name is available, how to "park," "reserve," and "register," how to secure a domain name that's on "hold," etc. There's also information on InterNIC, proposed extensions (i.e. arts.), and selling domain names, as well as a list of domain-related service providers.

Publisher:
AboutDomains.com

Media:
Internet

Principal Subject:
High-Tech & Internet-Based Businesses

Where To Find/Buy:
On the Internet using the URL: http://www.aboutdomains.com

CYBER BUSINESS NETWORK

Non-Rated Resource

Description:
Users will find a variety of helpful free resources at this site for cyber business, including a colorful, in depth article on Internet business success strategies, a directory of classified business opportunities, and information on "CBN's" services and training programs. There are also web guides to how-to and educational websites and online tools and services.

Publisher:
Cyber Business Network

Media:
Internet

Principal Subject:
High-Tech & Internet-Based Businesses

Where To Find/Buy:
On the Internet using the URL: http://www.cyber-biz.net

E-COMMERCE WEEKLY

Non-Rated Resource

Description:
Formerly known as "Entrepreneur Weekly," this online newsletter focuses on online sales, marketing, and e-commerce strategies. Users can browse 78 back issues, which include start-up articles, success stories, book excerpts, and tips on promotion. Advertising, posting to Usenet newsgroups, HTML, and programming tips are among the subjects discussed.

Publisher:
E-Commerce Weekly

E-Commerce Weekly is the weekly newsletter formerly known as Entrepreneur Weekly.

Media:
Internet

Principal Subject:
High-Tech & Internet-Based Businesses

Where To Find/Buy:
On the Internet using the URL: http://www.eweekly.com

High-Tech & Internet-Based Businesses

GARAGE.COM

Non-Rated Resource

Description:
While there are general-access features, most of Garage.com is password-protected. Its primary purpose is to match member investors with member, technology-related start-ups in need of seed capital. To become a member, start-ups must meet the site's criteria and pass a screening process; details are provided in "FAQs" under Start Here (on the home page).

Publisher:
Garage.com

Garage.com was founded by Craig Johnson (Chairman of Venture Law Group), Rich Karlgaard (Publisher of *Forbes* magazine), and Guy Kawaski to help high-technology companies obtain seed capital.

Media:
Internet

Principal Subject:
High-Tech & Internet-Based Businesses

Where To Find/Buy:
On the Internet using the URL: http://www.garage.com

INTERNET MARKETING CENTER

Non-Rated Resource

Description:
This information source for online business marketing offers Internet entrepreneurs web promotion tips (including a profile of the average Internet buyer), success stories, a free monthly newsletter and links to Research Resources. In Research Resources there are links to how-to sites, web builder sites, software sites, and other start-up necessities.

Publisher:
Internet Marketing Center

Media:
Internet

Principal Subject:
High-Tech & Internet-Based Businesses

Where To Find/Buy:
On the Internet using the URL: http://www.marketingtips.com

MICROSOFT SMALLBIZ

Non-Rated Resource

Description:
Microsoft's small business site offers an array of resources for entrepreneurs, including limited tech advice, help finding tech consultants, and information on Microsoft products. Other features include success stories, links, articles on such subjects as e-commerce and taxes, and how-to information and tools for putting your business on the Net (Creating Web Sites).

Publisher:
Microsoft

Since its inception in 1975, Microsoft has become the major player in small business software development. Its products include operating systems for personal computers, server applications, client/server environments, interactive media programs, and Internet platform an development tools.

Media:
Internet

Principal Subject:
High-Tech & Internet-Based Businesses

Where To Find/Buy:
On the Internet using the URL: http://www.microsoft.com/smallbiz

High-Tech & Internet-Based Businesses

TRIPOD

Non-Rated Resource

Description:
Tripod, part of the Lycos Network, offers tools for web building, such as the QuickPage Builder, Freeform Editor, Filemanager, homepage help and design tips. There are also chat rooms for networking and sharing ideas, millions of Tripod homepages to explore, and details on membership and membership benefits. (Membership is free.)

Publisher:
Lycos

Tripod, Inc., is the flagship online community company of the Lycos Network.

Media:
Internet

Principal Subject:
High-Tech & Internet-Based Businesses

Where To Find/Buy:
On the Internet using the URL: http://www.tripod.com/tripod/map

WEB MARKETING INFORMATION CENTER

Non-Rated Resource

Description:
Mr. Wilson's site is overflowing with resources for business owners interested in doing business on the Web. There are links to hundreds of articles on subjects ranging from "Banner Ads" to "E-Mail Marketing." There's also an "E-Commerce Research Room" with links to information on web store design, online transactions, and international exporting.

Author:
Ralph F. Wilson

Dr. Wilson is Director of Wilson Internet Services, which offers services in website design and consulting.

Publisher:
Wilson Internet Services

Media:
Internet

Principal Subject:
High-Tech & Internet-Based Businesses

Where To Find/Buy:
On the Internet at http://www.wilsonweb.com/webmarket/

Working As A Freelancer Or Consultant

Working As A Freelancer Or Consultant

Technological advances and faster communications have only begun to impact the way that Americans do business, yet the first waves of that impact are already reverberating throughout the labor market. Technology driven increases in productivity have enabled many corporations to streamline their operations, cutting out middle managers and downsizing, or rightsizing, their permanent employees. The skeletal work force that remains expands and contracts by adding and releasing contract workers, many of them professional consultants. By outsourcing all but their core competencies, enterprises pay for expertise or production on an as-needed basis, rather than paying (and providing expensive benefit packages for) full-time employees.

Small businesses have thrived as new technologies (fax machines, powerful desktop computers, e-mail, the Internet) enable them to compete for more of the market. While many large companies are shrinking, small and micro-businesses are booming. The 23 million small businesses currently operating in this country generate more than half of the nation's gross domestic product and employ more than half of the private workforce.

Small businesses often survive the cyclical nature of business by hiring consultants for specific projects, and scaling back in the interim. Growth markets have become increasingly sophisticated, specialized, and complex. Few small organizations can afford to hire full-time employees with the skills or experience necessary to handle all aspects of their business. They turn to consultants, freelancers, and contract workers to complete projects or to do work that they do not have the time or ability to do themselves.

I decided I would keep my business small yet I am able to take on large projects using consultants from all over the country. When I take on a new contract I gather experts on the various subjects to work for me on a fee-for-service basis. This method has helped to keep costs down for our clients.

When You *Are* The Company

Consultants come in all shapes and sizes and perform a wide variety of tasks. There are management consultants, financial consultants, image consultants, even leisure consultants. In fact, consulting is the fastest growing profession in the 90s, with an annual growth rate of 20%. The opportunities for consulting are increasing, but you're not the only hopeful who has taken notice. As the profession grows, so does the competition. To succeed as a consultant, you will need clients. Which means you will need referrals. Which means you'll need a marketing plan. And that's just the tip of the iceberg.

Starting a consulting practice, like starting any business, requires extensive preparation and research. Many consultants fail because they begin with the mistaken assumption that, because they have the expertise, their service will sell itself. Not so. At least, not in the beginning. Your first step, as with any new business, is to conduct market research. You need to determine whom your clients will be, what your specialty will be, and how you can sell your specialty in the existing market. Next, you'll set up shop: find and equip an office, create a business plan, secure financing. Then there's marketing, your second full-time job. In a competitive marketplace, the right marketing strategy is all that separates the survivors from the casualties. You'll need to position yourself in the market, raise your public image, and fashion yourself as an authority in your field. Above all, you'll need to network. Constantly.

The resources in this chapter help with every aspect of becoming a consultant, from starting out to making millions. These books cover the spectrum in tone and subject matter, from practical to philosophical, cautionary to idealistic. Some concentrate on business basics: taxes, business structure, accounting, bookkeeping. Others focus on the intangibles: attitude, comportment, interaction with clients. We've found books that provide models for completing projects and books that help you transition from your current job. Almost all of the resources discuss marketing. The authors (all consultants themselves) take radically different approaches; the evaluations will help you choose which resources will work best for you.

Some of the resources we review are geared for freelancers. The term "freelancer" comes from the Middle Ages, when warriors who had no overlord sold their sword (or lance) to the highest bidder. Freelancers were, in effect, mercenaries, with allegiance to no one but themselves. Today, the term is most often used to describe self-employed writers, photographers and artists, but any type of work can be freelanced. You may be a freelance designer, card-maker, cartoonist, accountant, bookkeeper or tech writer. The term is commonly applied to any type of work done on a contract or contingency basis.

In this chapter, most of the resources for freelancers are aimed at creative, communications-related work (i.e. writing, design). There are several websites to visit where you can appraise current freelancers' work and learn start-up tips. There are also resources for "portable executives," a growing group of highly skilled professionals who perform executive-level work on a contract basis. The resources for consultants will also be of help, since they tackle the relevant issues of marketing, billing clients, networking, and creating an image for yourself and your business.

We also include resources for temporary workers. Although "temping" through a temporary service agency isn't self-employment in the conventional sense (you are paid by the agency), it is a way to remain independent and consistently employed, on your own terms and in the manner that best suits your life style. The advantages of temping have attracted enough workers into the fold to build Manpower, Inc., one of the first on the temp agency scene, into one of the nation's largest employers.

In today's rapidly evolving marketplace, adaptability is key. If you have developed a high-demand, portable skill set, you can create a niche for yourself that may provide greater job security than traditional corporate positions. By becoming an independent contractor, you will have the freedom and flexibility to adapt to market changes. Follow your dream. The future for freelancers, consultants, and contract workers looks very, very bright.

THE COMPLETE GUIDE TO CONSULTING SUCCESS

 Recommended For:

Working As A Freelancer, Consultant or Contract Worker

Description:

Interactive worksheets, sample business letters and contracts support the informational text in this step-by-step guide for entry level consultants. Divided into 10 chapters, Chapter 1 begins by introducing readers to the varied field of consulting, addressing the demand for consultants, qualities of a successful consultant, and the 3 "big myths." Next, readers take the first step toward creating their practice by choosing a business form and developing a skills inventory, brochure, and Internet presence. Chapter 4 explains where to look for consulting opportunities, and Chapter 5 helps readers turn those opportunities into profits. Marketing, including ideas for low cost/no cost marketing and direct marketing, is discussed in Chapters 6 and 7. Learning to sell services through interviews, presentations, and written proposals follows. Readers will also learn how to visualize a project as a whole by constructing a Functional Flow Diagram. (A Typical Functional Flow Diagram is provided for illustration.) Setting fees, contracts, and client-consultant relationships are the subjects of Chapters 9 and 10. There is an Appendix of additional samples, i.e. Sample Fixed-Price Service Contract, and a reference bibliography.

Evaluation:

There is a tendency among how-to-consult authors to construct their work as if it were a high school or community college course book: big, bold headings, simple language, little presumption of prior knowledge. That is not the case with this guide. Franklin's updated version of the original Nicholas and Shenson text reads more like a business school text, or, at least, it presumes far more professional and business acumen than most of its peers. It does an exceptional job of explaining the practicalities of starting a consultancy, from initial preparation to proposals, contracts, and marketing techniques. It offers sophisticated, adaptable work models, which many guides do not, and it provides a solid introduction (complete with sample home pages) to consulting websites, another rarity. Beyond the basics, this book contains some stand-out inclusions, such as an examination of Newly Educated Markets and advice on identifying opportunities therein. It features a comparative chart which reports the median incomes of specialty consultants in a wide variety of areas, i.e. aerospace, health care, quality control. The language is denser in this book than in quickie Q&A books; digesting the information requires a fair amount of "chewing." But the extra work pays off. This is a sophisticated, high-value resource.

Where To Find/Buy:

Bookstores and libraries.

Overall Rating
★★★★
Written for sophisticated professionals just starting out on their own

Design, Ease Of Use
★★★★
Includes explicit contents, a table of figures, and plenty of worksheets and samples

1–4 Stars

Author:
Howard Shenson and Ted Nicholas, with Paul Franklin, Consulting Editor

The late Mr. Shenson helped more than 100,000 consultants worldwide improve their practices. Mr. Nicholas owns and operates 4 corporations and is a best-selling author. Mr. Franklin is a Certified Professional Consultant and founder of National Training Center.

Publisher:
Upstart Publishing

Edition:
3rd (1997)

Price:
$29.95

Pages/Run Time:
243

ISBN:
1574100556

Media:
Book

Principal Subject:
Working As A Freelancer, Consultant or Contract Worker

★★★★

Overall Rating
★★★★
Provocative, simultaneously idealistic and realistic; a real treat

Design, Ease Of Use
★★★★
Includes dynamic models you can use in your own consultancy

1–4 Stars

Author:
Geoffrey M. Bellman

Mr. Bellman started his own consulting business in 1977, offering services in both the public and private sector. He is also the author of *The Quest for Staff Leadership* and *Getting Things Done When You Are Not in Charge.*

Publisher:
Jossey-Bass

Edition:
1990

Price:
$20.00

Pages/Run Time:
238

ISBN:
1555424112

Media:
Book

Principal Subject:
Working As A Freelancer, Consultant or Contract Worker

Secondary Subject:
Reflective Guides To Creating The Work And Life You Want

THE CONSULTANT'S CALLING
Bringing Who You Are To What You Do

 Recommended For:
Working As A Freelancer, Consultant or Contract Worker

Description:

In his introduction, A Quest For Meaning Through Work, Bellman says "I see consulting as my opportunity for self-discovery, rather than just a way to make a living." While he helps readers become (better) consultants by advising them on business practices, his book has a greater goal: to impart a philosophy for achieving balance between life and work through consulting. Part 1, Balance & Being, begins by exploring the personal: consulting as a way of living and how work fits into your whole life. Part 2, Opening The Organization, focuses on the work itself. Here, Bellman provides models that illustrate how consultants' work is done, explains how organizations work, and offers insights for helping organizations change. In Part 3, Power & Partnership, he turns his attention to the client-consultant relationship, discussing the formula for creating strong partnerships, what consultants can bring to clients, and ethical considerations. Most of the practical, how-to information is contained in the final segment, Part 4, Money & The Marketplace. Self-marketing and self-presentation are addressed, and there are guidelines for writing, setting fees, contracting, and preparing to "make the leap" to consulting.

Evaluation:

Bellman's book is vastly different from traditional how-to consulting books. He doesn't offer step-by-step guidance in the form of "get this permit, buy that office equipment" directives. Yet, he does provide explanations of, and insights into, the work consultants do, offering dynamic work models for completing projects and adaptable techniques for building client-consultant relationships. There are sales tips and advice for positioning yourself in the marketplace, as well. While you may need another resource for the A-B-Cs of getting started (how to write a proposal, legal forms), Bellman presents readers with something less tangible but no less valuable: how to be a consultant, behave like a consultant, think like a consultant. He paints a vivid portrait of the consulting life—a life he sees as a means toward balance between work and family—and avoids tottering toward idealism by sharing many of his own, less-than-ideal experiences. His proclivity for values rich, philosophical-laden text is enjoyable and resonant. He's as frank about the negatives (i.e. fear, discouragement) as he is eager to proselytize. For consultants of any ilk, this is a provocative, earnest, and inspiring read. It's a treat.

Where To Find/Buy:
Bookstores and libraries.

CONSULTING ON THE SIDE
How To Start A Part-Time Consulting Business While Still Working At Your Full-Time Job

 Recommended For:

Working As A Freelancer, Consultant or Contract Worker

Description:

Starting a consulting business while still employed has its advantages; for one thing, you have the safety net of your current income. But there are drawbacks, too, such as long hours and ethical issues which can arise from consulting in the same field as your current job. To help, Cook created her guide to teach you how to start and operate a part-time consultancy. Chapter 1 begins with preparation: planning your business, budgeting, networking, market research. Chapter 2 addresses the Logistics Of Balancing Two Jobs (i.e. time and stress management), while Chapter 3 discusses the ethical issues involved (i.e. non-compete agreements, codes of conduct). Identifying Your Best Area For Consulting, via self-assessment, is examined in Chapter 4. Financing is covered in Chapters 5–6 (i.e. cost analysis, fee setting, loans), Chapter 7 offers advice on setting up your SOHO, and Chapter 8 provides marketing and sales strategies. Legalities, accounting, insurance, and taxes are reviewed in Chapter 9. The 6 Key Areas Of A Part-Time Consultant and knowing when to leave your full-time job are detailed in the last 2 chapters. Appendices of resources, i.e. resources for women and minorities, and a reference list appear at the end.

Evaluation:

Consulting opportunities are on the rise. With many companies turning to contract workers and outsourcing everything but their core competencies, and with increasing numbers of workers interested in self-employment, the stars seem aligned for consulting-business success. But, while the potential for success exists, the everyday reality is not reassuring: it will probably take over a year for your consultancy to produce a healthy income. You may find Cook's advice—to start a part-time consultancy while still employed at your full-time job—works for you. While there are lots of books on becoming a successful consultant, Cook's is one of the few to focus on the option of gradual transition. She does a good job of communicating both the how-to practicalities and the less than attractive realities (i.e. long hours, stress, handling your current employer). She's also quite candid about her own experiences as a consultant, and, in a refreshing twist, she uses her own brochures, business cards, etc., as examples. Although this guide was written for a general audience, the fact that Cook's personality shines so clearly in her work is a plus for women, who have fewer choices when it comes to choosing a consulting mentor. For practical how-to, valuable insights, and a part-time focus, this is a terrific resource for future consultants.

Where To Find/Buy:

Bookstores and libraries.

Overall Rating
★★★★
Packed with important details for juggling a part-time consultancy and full-time job

Design, Ease Of Use
★★★★
Conversational tone; includes lots of samples, examples and forms

1–4 Stars

Author:
Mary F. Cook

Ms. Cook is President of Mary F. Cook & Associates, a human resource consultancy and Director of Human Resources for M.D.C. Holdings, Inc. She is also the author of *The Human Resources Yearbook* and *The Complete Do-it-Yourself Personnel Department.*

Publisher:
John Wiley & Sons

Edition:
1996

Price:
$19.95

Pages/Run Time:
242

ISBN:
0471120294

Media:
Book

Principal Subject:
Working As A Freelancer, Consultant or Contract Worker

Of Interest To:
Women

★★★★

Overall Rating
★★★★
A real find for executives who want to go solo! Inspiring and realistic

Design, Ease Of Use
★★★★
Well written and engaging; includes interviews and interactive exercises

1–4 Stars

Author:
John A. Thompson and Catharine A. Henningsen

Mr. Thompson is the founder of IMCOR, the nation's first interim management firm. Ms. Henningsen is a writer and consultant whose articles have appeared in The Atlantic and The New York Times.

Publisher:
Fireside

Edition:
1997

Price:
$12.00

Pages/Run Time:
320

ISBN:
0684818914

Media:
Book

Principal Subject:
Working As A Freelancer, Consultant or Contract Worker

THE PORTABLE EXECUTIVE

 Recommended For:
Working As A Freelancer, Consultant or Contract Worker

Description:
The economy is doing great, so why are so many executives facing downsizing and "no-fault termination," or being asked to accept early retirement? The fact is, the work world is changing; it's outsourcing, hiring more contractors and fewer full-time employees. To flourish in this new job market, and to discover the satisfaction and freedom of self-employment, many executives are taking their skills on the road. They're becoming "portable executives," and in this guide, entrepreneur John Thompson shows readers how to join their ranks. Preliminary chapters explore the "new reality" of business, profile the "portable executive," and discuss breaking the corporate "habit." Readers then assess their portable skills, "invent" their business, learn to network, and form an "action plan." (Interactive exercises are included.) "Maintaining your skills," marketing and sales, setting up a business, and pricing are addressed next, while the final chapter takes an in-depth look at 5 individuals who are "Portable, and Loving It!"

Evaluation:
If you always thought of freelancing as the realm of writers and artists, think again; by 2005, it's estimated that over half a million self-employed workers will be managers, administrators, and executives. This is a terrific resource for upper level employees who are leaving or who want to leave corporate America. While there are many guides to freelancing, consulting, and contingency work, few are as insightful and authoritative as this one. Mr. Thompson was a corporate executive before he began his own business and knows first hand the advantages and disadvantages of both positions. In his book, Thompson cleverly weaves quotations, advice, warnings and stories from "portable" executives, creating an inspirational and informative tone. His enthusiasm for going solo is balanced by practical exercises and clear directions. In many respects, this is a book that all executives should read, even if those not planning to leave. "Job security" is becoming an oxymoron, and this guide provides the tools, confidence, and know-how for surviving and blossoming in the new work world. Turn a seeming defeat, whether its being fired, downsized or coaxed into an unwanted early retirement, into a victory: read this book.

Where To Find/Buy:
Bookstores and libraries.

MILLION DOLLAR CONSULTING
The Professional's Guide To Growing A Practice

 Recommended For:
Working As A Freelancer, Consultant or Contract Worker

Description:

The "era of corporate downsizing," Weiss believes, heralds a new frontier for consultants of any ilk. Now, he says, is the time to develop your practice into a lucrative, million-dollar business; his 3-part guide is dedicated to showing you how. Part 1, Strategy: Establishing Your View Of The Profession, begins by analyzing the current (and projected) marketplace for consultants. Weiss goes on to explain how "jobs get in the way of careers," and how to establish ideal goals and re-vamp your consultancy (by abandoning certain clients). Prerequisites for growth are enumerated, a surefire growth strategy is detailed, and the 10 basic principles of "million dollar consulting" are presented. Part 2, Tactics: Implementing Your Vision Of Your Firm, focuses on action: networking, establishing and raising fees, forging strong client relationships, and avoiding or surviving business declines. Weiss uses one chapter to explore the benefits of integrating technology. He provides tips for marketing online and for using e-mail and graphic designs. In Part 3, the central topic is Success. Ethics, contracts, and managing capital are discussed, plus there are techniques for intensifying your firm's profile and attracting clients by becoming a "star."

Evaluation:

As the subtitle suggests, this is a "professional's guide" to consulting. That is to say, this is one of the more sophisticated offerings in the genre. It's a better choice for seasoned business people, the audience for whom it was written and for whom the style, language, and format was conceived. There is a presumption of business knowledge and acumen here that is absent from the beginner-oriented, step-by-step books. This is a smart, cutting edge, occasionally cutthroat guide. Weiss provides (relatively) up-to-date information about the consulting market, including a savvy section on using the Net (a rarity), and offers perceptive insights into client-consultant relationships. He adds realism to his theories by using examples from his own work experience. He evokes confidence with his firm, take-a-stand tone. Not every reader, however, will find him appealing. His firmness can be viewed one of two ways: positively, as for-your-own-good insistence, or negatively, as almost-Machiavellian. For example, part of his strategy to re-vamp your consultancy is to help you weed out clients who pay less as you cultivate "better" ones. In such circumstance, the implication is: you're not in business to build relationships, you're in business to make money. If you want gung-ho guidance on taking your practice to the next financial level, look here.

Where To Find/Buy:

Bookstores and libraries.

Overall Rating
★★★★
Cutting-edge business savvy for taking your consultancy to the next level

Design, Ease Of Use
★★★
Incorporates diagrams, charts, and figures for illustration

1–4 Stars

Author:
Alan Weiss

Alan Weiss, PhD, is founder and president of Summit Consulting Group, Inc., an organization and management firm whose clients include GE, Hewlett-Packard, and *The New York Times*. He is the author of *Money Talks*, *Making It Work*, and *Managing For Peak Performance*.

Publisher:
McGraw-Hill

Edition:
2nd (1998)

Price:
$14.95

Pages/Run Time:
292

ISBN:
0070696284

Media:
Book

Principal Subject:
Working As A Freelancer, Consultant or Contract Worker

★★★

Overall Rating
★★★
Step-by-step instruction for the business end of consulting; for beginners

Design, Ease Of Use
★★★★
Easy to personalize/use the files on the disk; contains lots of forms, samples

1–4 Stars

Author:
Elaine Biech
Ms. Biech is President and managing principle of Ebb Associates Inc. She is the author of more than a dozen articles and books, and has been in the consulting business for over twenty years. She has designed training and performance packages for a variety of industries.

Publisher:
Jossey-Bass/Pfeiffer

Edition:
1999

Price:
$39.95

Pages/Run Time:
246

ISBN:
0787940216

Media:
Book + Software

Principal Subject:
Working As A Freelancer, Consultant or Contract Worker

THE BUSINESS OF CONSULTING
The Basics And Beyond

Description:
Designed to be a one-stop resource for effectively running a consulting business, Biech covers the basics of starting up, day-to-day management, and growing your practice. Interactive worksheets, forms, and samples appear throughout the guide's 11 chapters. These exhibits are also contained on the enclosed disk (for IBM; Microsoft Word 6.0/95), and can be personalized to help you tabulate expenses, keep records, and create letters. Chapters 1–2 explore what it is to be a consultant and what it takes to succeed (skills, personal characteristics). The next 3 chapters detail the start-up process: selecting a pricing structure, setting fees, writing a business plan, developing your niche/image, marketing. Chapter 6 analyzes the cost of doing business; Chapter 7 offers advice on building strong client relationships. Instructions for doing "everything you can" to grow your business follow in Chapter 8. Chapter 9 discusses ethical considerations, such as the ethics of subcontracting. Biech examines ways to exude professionalism in Chapter 10, which includes tips for managing your time and achieving balance in life and work. The last chapter describes "a week in a consultant's life" based on Biech's own experience.

Evaluation:
With the exception of legal/tax issues, which receive only minimal attention from Biech, this guide offers basic step-by-step instruction on the business end of consulting. The important word being basic. It seems ironic that future consultants would need advice on such basics as tallying start-up costs or choosing a business structure. If your consulting specialty is management- or finance-related, you probably don't need this type of beginner help. If, however, your specialty lies in another area, this resource may be suitable. It's straightforward, explicit, easy to understand, and it comes with an assortment of samples, exercises, and tools. All of the samples/tools appear both in the text and on the enclosed disk (Microsoft Word). They can act as examples and records, and may help you decide what type of record-keeping you will need, but they won't/can't take the place of accounting or financial management software. Despite Biech's telling account of a week in her life (A Week In A Consultant's Life), this is a book about running a consulting business, not about being a consultant. Biech herself makes that distinction; so for insight beyond business basics, you'll have to look to another resource.

Where To Find/Buy:
Bookstores and libraries.

THE COMPLETE BOOK OF CONSULTING

★★★

Description:

To give potential consultants step-by-step guidance, each of 10 chapters contains both explanatory text and several related forms, such as samples and worksheets. (Tips for using/customizing the forms appear at the bottom of the page.) Chapter 1 explores What It Takes To Be A Consultant, offering a series of forms to help you assess your skills and define your services. In Chapter 2, Setting Up Your Business is discussed: business structure, location, choosing a name, creating a business plan. Forms include a Mission Statement Worksheet and a Business Plan Outline. Next, there are tools for setting fees and determining costs, i.e. Daily Fee Calculation Worksheet. Various means of marketing, direct and indirect, are presented in Chapters 4–5. Here, you'll find sample follow-up, sales, and networking letters, as well as press release samples and Book/Article Proposal Worksheets. Chapter 6 discusses interviewing prospects and provides interview questions. Developing proposals and preparing contracts, along with instructive forms, are detailed in Chapters 7–8. Final chapters examine credit, collections, and record keeping. All 150 forms can be found via title/subject indices in the back.

Evaluation:

The main attraction in this guide is its extensive collection of marketing tools and samples. There are telemarketing scripts for 4 different scenarios, including management training and marketing, and there are 11 different sample sales letters to prospective clients, including letters for computer training, financial planning, and engineering. There are also letters for building business with current clients, examples of ads and brochures, and an assortment of promotional samples: press releases, seminar ads, newsletters. Aside from marketing, there are several other fine inclusions. The guidelines for interviewing prospects are relatively in depth, and there are enough proposal samples to appease even the nervous beginner. What's missing here is greater attention to the less tangible aspects of consulting: self-assessment, conducting the work, building strong client-consultant relationships, persevering when morale is low. Still, if it's forms and samples you're looking for, this is an excellent place to find them. (An order form in the back of the book enables you to purchase the forms in a software program that uses Windows 3.1 or Windows 95 and higher, for $92.90. Or you can call to order (203) 438-6303).

Where To Find/Buy:

Bookstores and libraries.

Overall Rating
★★★
A reliable learning tool for practicalities; offers a range of marketing samples/ideas

Design, Ease Of Use
★★★★
Informational text followed by samples, forms, examples

1–4 Stars

Author:
Bill Salmon and Nate Rosenblatt

Mr. Salmon has been a consultant, writer, and educator for nearly 30 years, helping companies in the areas of development and training. Mr. Rosenblatt is a sales and marketing professional.

Publisher:
Round Lake

Edition:
1995

Price:
$19.95

Pages/Run Time:
300

ISBN:
0929543440

Media:
Book

Principal Subject:
Working As A Freelancer, Consultant or Contract Worker

★★★

Overall Rating
★★★
Smart, fast know-how for management consultants

Design, Ease Of Use
★★★★
Written in a question-and-answer format

1–4 Stars

Author:
Lawrence W. Tuller

Mr. Tuller is a C.P.A. who has owned and operated 13 companies. He is also the author of *Exporting, Importing and Beyond* and *Small Business Valuation Book.*

Publisher:
Adams Media

Edition:
2nd (1999)

Price:
$9.95

Pages/Run Time:
296

ISBN:
1580621058

Media:
Book

Principal Subject:
Working As A Freelancer, Consultant or Contract Worker

THE INDEPENDENT CONSULTANT'S Q & A BOOK

Description:

Tuller, who is himself a management consultant, focuses primarily on that field in this 15 chapter guide to starting and operating a consultancy. Written in a Q & A-style format, Tuller poses frequently asked questions and then provides answers, incorporating both general advice and insights gleaned from his own experience. Chapter 1 explores common questions about consulting, i.e. competency and expertise, and discusses the basics of preparation: choosing the right market, research, public image, planning. Chapters 2–4 explain how to get clients (tips on networking, cold calls, and subcontracting are included) and how to advertise and promote the business. The ethics of management consulting are explored next, followed by guidelines for writing effective proposals and setting fees. Chapters 8–10 offer techniques for making your business "look bigger than it is," creating reports and presentations, and keeping clients happy. Billing concerns, such as getting paid, are examined in Chapter 11, while Chapter 12 helps readers handle administrative chores (i.e. taxes) profitably. Final chapters look at sources of financing, how to end an engagement gracefully, and selling your business when it's time to retire.

Evaluation:

A management consultant sells business (management) advice to private- and public-sector companies; it's an umbrella term that includes both project work and general management work, both specialty areas and more general areas of expertise. Although many portions of this guide are applicable to any consulting field, readers interested in management are the primary audience here, and Tuller himself is a management consulting guru. (Chances are, if you're interested in selling business or project management advice, this guide will apply to you.) It's an easy read, simply formatted as quick-but-informative Q & A briefs, and it's smart and reliable. Tuller is extremely pragmatic, offering realistic advice on financing, promotion, client-relations, and billing. The techniques for self-promotion, e.g. creating a public image (an important facet of running a consultancy), are especially on-target and educational. Tuller advises potential consultants to raise their public image before starting up by "becoming an authority," "taking a stand," or "becoming a supporter," and provides tips for getting attention through "promotional freebies." He's good with the logistical details too; this is a good choice for fast reminders about need-to-know basics. For a practical resource that's a quick read, look here.

Where To Find/Buy:
Bookstores and libraries.

STREETWISE INDEPENDENT CONSULTING

Description:

To teach you to be a "streetwise" (a.k.a. savvy and successful) independent consultant, Kintler and Adams tackle the basics involved in starting and managing a practice. The 12 chapters begin with "Getting Started," a preparatory chapter which introduces the field, lists "hot growth areas," and helps you define your business, objectives, and target market. Practicalities such as setting up a home or commercial office and choosing office equipment are also discussed. Chapter 2 is dedicated solely to business plans: explanation and development. Strategies for finding and winning clients are detailed in Chapters 3–5, which include tips for generating leads, selling yourself, using direct mail, and attracting clients with free publicity. Chapter 6 helps you price your services. Chapters 7–8 help you write and present proposals. There's a "Seven Step Process" for writing proposals, plus several sample proposals/templates. Chapters 9–10 cover legal issues (i.e. business structure, incorporation, contracts) and financial issues (i.e. cash flow, fees, taxes). Lastly, Chapter 11 reviews the "steps" to consulting success, while Chapter 12 offers additional forms, samples, and templates (invoices, sample letters).

Evaluation:

Snazzy graphics, bold print, straightforward language, interactive exercises, and plenty of samples give this guide a "text book" feel. For consultants just starting out, a textbook treatment of the subject may be exactly the style you need. While many guides purport to offer step-by-step instruction, few do. This is the exception. This book provides as much hand-holding as possible, walking you through every logistical detail, from choosing office equipment to choosing your business structure. If it's help with the practicalities you need, this is a fabulous resource. There are enough samples, examples, and templates to assist you with most (if not all) start-up paperwork. While seasoned financiers and business persons may view the chapter on Understanding Finance as pedestrian, beginners and consultants whose expertise lies elsewhere will find it highly rewarding. It teaches the basics of accounting exceptionally well. Kintler and Adams treatment of legal issues is similarly valuable for novices; here too, little foreknowledge is expected. Since this is a detail-oriented book, rather than theory-oriented, you'll need to look elsewhere for advice on the "art" of consulting. For a basic primer on the fundamentals, however, you need look no further.

Where To Find/Buy:

Bookstores and libraries.

Overall Rating
★★★
Step-by-step help with the practicalities; best for novices

Design, Ease Of Use
★★★★
Format is reminiscent of a textbook: interactive exercises, snazzy graphics, samples

1–4 Stars

Author:
David Kintler with Bob Adams

Mr. Kintler is president and founder of SalesWinners, Inc., a marketing consulting firm. Bob Adams, MBA, is president of Adams Media Corporation.

Publisher:
Adams Media

Edition:
1998

Price:
$16.95

Pages/Run Time:
378

ISBN:
1558507280

Media:
Book

Principal Subject:
Working As A Freelancer, Consultant or Contract Worker

★★★

Overall Rating
★★★
Irreverent but insightful;
temping as a "lifestyle choice"

Design, Ease Of Use
★★★★
Straightforward format, very
well written; full of humor
and anecdotes

1–4 Stars

Author:
Brian Hassett

Mr. Hassett lives in the highest-
income ZIP code in the U.S.—
10021, in New York City—and he
hasn't held a real job in fifteen
years.

Publisher:
Carol Publishing Group

Edition:
1997

Price:
$11.95

Pages/Run Time:
211

ISBN:
080651843x

Media:
Book

Principal Subject:
Working As A Freelancer,
Consultant or Contract
Worker

THE TEMP SURVIVAL GUIDE
How To Prosper As An Economic Nomad Of The Nineties

Description:
Mr. Hassett has made a lucrative career (implied) out of temping, and, as he says in his book, if you can type, you can too. Using lots of humor, anecdotes, and pop-culture references, Mr. Hassett explains the advantages of "A Temping Life," "The Way the Business Works," and the "ins & outs" of getting started: the necessary skills, choosing an agent, "acing" the interview, etc. He then prepares you for "Your First Day" with advice on arriving prepared, tackling "massive complicated documents" (and bosses), and adjusting to office "culture;" he also details the "philosophy of temping" and the "Radar O'Reilly Temporary Hall of Fame." There are strategies for "Making the A-Team" (i.e. "collecting rave reviews," "getting yourself booked back") and "Survival Techniques" for avoiding such temp pitfalls as feeling subservient, patronized, etc. Other chapters include tips on raises, taxes, new agencies, "Milking the Cows," and "Going Permanent." The "Temp Commandments" and appendices of resources are provided.

Evaluation:
From page one of this engaging guide, it's clear that this isn't an average career resource. (Among the reasons cited in favor of "A Temping Life" is the temp's opportunity to appraise the "singles scene" at various businesses; the sub-chapter is called "Sex and Where to Get It.") Mr. Hassett is the denizen of a temp underworld, a world in which creative, insouciant, dynamic individuals like himself use temping to flit into the "real world of work," "milk the cows," and escape unscathed (a.k.a. take the money and run and never get your hands dirty). The underlying theme of this guide? If you want to work as little as possible and you have the smarts/personality to make everyone else think you really care, temp. Sure, it sounds great; with his irreverent humor and terrific writing, Hassett makes it sound even better. But is it realistic? Most people who possess the skills needed to get the high-paying temp jobs would just as soon get a job or work for themselves. On the other hand, temping can be a kind of half way house for people who don't want to be pinned down to a "real" job yet don't have either the discipline or the desire to be fully self-employed (and therefore completely responsible). For such talented "nomads," this is the book!

Where To Find/Buy:
Bookstores and libraries.

THE CONCISE GUIDE TO BECOMING AN INDEPENDENT CONSULTANT

Description:

Containing 4 fewer chapters than "How To Succeed As An Independent Consultant," this abridged version of that text begins with an introduction to today's consulting marketplace. In the first 5 chapters, Holtz prepares the reader for start-up by examining such issues as what consultants do, choosing a specialty, and consulting as a second career. He also analyzes why consultants fail and presents the "keys" to success. The details of launching and managing a consultancy follow in Chapters 6–20. Business plans, finances, and taxes are discussed, as is the "art" of finding clients. Several chapters look at marketing techniques, as well as various market segments. For example, there are separate strategies for marketing to the government vs. marketing to the private sector. Instructions are provided for creating proposals and final reports, selling yourself in initial meetings, and handling negotiations, fees, and contracts. Consulting procedures and processes are addressed, and Holtz offers advice on developing such necessary skills as writing and giving presentations. Finally, Chapter 20 explores the use of new technologies: modems, software, fax machines, etc.

Evaluation:

To be explicit: the primary difference between this "Concise" guide and its original version, "How To Succeed As An Independent Consultant," is that there are four chapters in the original that do not appear in "Concise." Those four chapters include a reference guide (lists of books, associations, people), a discussion of ethics, and details on supplementary methods of earning income, such as public speaking and writing. The text here is less dense, making it a quicker read, but all of the important sections remain virtually intact and just as valuable. (It is a pity that Holtz didn't take the opportunity to update and expand his chapter on new technologies, which still contains little mention of the Internet. See the "How To Succeed" review for details.) Holtz offers excellent advice on consulting skills, especially proposals and presentations, as well as practical, insightful guidance on finding, getting, and keeping clients. Particularly laudable inclusions (in both books) are the chapters on marketing addressed to varying markets, private sector vs. government, for example. Like the original, this guide tends to address an audience of mature readers and retirees. For "concise" help in beginning a consultancy, this is a fine choice.

Where To Find/Buy:

Bookstores and libraries.

Overall Rating
★★★
Concise and valuable consulting theory plus practicalities

Design, Ease Of Use
★★★
Shorter paragraphs and less dense prose than the original

1–4 Stars

Author:
Herman Holtz

Mr. Holtz has been a consultant to IBM, GE, Chrysler, and many other Fortune 500 companies. He is the author of more than 20 books on consulting, including *The Concise Guide To Becoming An Independent Consultant.*

Publisher:
John Wiley & Sons

Edition:
1999

Price:
$19.95

Pages/Run Time:
302

ISBN:
0471315737

Media:
Book

Principal Subject:
Working As A Freelancer, Consultant or Contract Worker

★★★

Overall Rating
★★★
Self-analysis for "transitioning" to freelance, consulting or temporary work

Design, Ease Of Use
★★★
Easy-to-read, clear topic headings

1–4 Stars

Author:
William Bridges

William Bridges, PhD is a consultant on work transitions. He travels widely to speak, lead workshops and consult with corporations. He is also the author of *Job Shift* and *Transitions*.

Publisher:
Addison-Wesley

Edition:
1997

Price:
$22.00

Pages/Run Time:
184

ISBN:
0201419874

Media:
Book

Principal Subject:
Working As A Freelancer, Consultant or Contract Worker

CREATING YOU AND CO.
Learn To Think Like The CEO Of Your Own Career

Description:
Dr. Bridges' guide is dedicated to helping you discover which skills and interests you can exploit in the "new" workplace. The basic idea is that technological advances, which enable companies to downsize, rightsize, and cut back on middle management, are "de-jobbing" America. As many companies move away from the idea of traditional, full-time jobs, they're turning to outside sources to complete projects; they're outsourcing. Bridges believes that by changing your career game plan, you can learn to thrive in this "new" job market. Rather than fearing downsizing, he advocates taking advantage of the freelance, consulting, and contract work available. In Part 1, "Why You Need You & Co.," he explains this premise and the evolving work force. To help you evaluate your resources for dealing with these transitions, Bridges introduces the concept of determining your Desire, Abilities, Temperament, and Assets (D.A.T.A.). In Part 2, "Mining Your D.A.T.A.," you explore these concepts using introspective questions and worksheets. The final part, "Turning Your D.A.T.A. Into A Product," focuses on reinventing your career and formulating a plan for career development based on your self-analysis.

Evaluation:
The Information Age, with its technological advances, is fast overwhelming the Industrial Age; "jobs" as we know them, so says Dr. Bridges, are an endangered species. While the idea of facing the "instability" implied in a mobile work force of freelancers, temps, consultants, etc., can be frightening to those who are unprepared and who don't understand what's happening, the growing demand for such "independents" is great news for aspiring soloists. And if you're an aspiring soloist, Bridges is behind you one hundred percent! The best thing about this book is that it goes a long way in increasing optimism and confidence. Not only will it inspire a "hey, I can do this!" response, it also emphasizes the "positives" of "going solo," i.e. greater satisfaction, control, etc., over the perceived negatives. The only problem is that Bridges is (deliberately) short on specifics. This is, despite its title, not about the daily grind of freelancing or the "how to." It's a self-assessment book designed to inspire creative career ideas. For that reason, this is a better choice for inspiration than for pragmatic problem solving. It's also a better choice for people who aren't sure which skills and talents they want to use in a solo venture; if you already know what type of work you want to do, this guide isn't necessary.

Where To Find/Buy:
Bookstores and libraries.

GOING SOLO
Developing A Home-Based Consulting Business From The Ground Up

Description:

There are 17 chapters in Bond's guide to building a home-based consultancy, beginning with an introduction to specialty consulting and client expectations. Chapter 3 helps you organize your home office, with advice on supplies and equipment. Tips for matching your specialty to your clients and finding clients follow, along with chapters on selling your services and securing your first meeting with a potential client. Chapter 8 deals with Presenting A Knockout Proposal At The Contracting Meeting and includes techniques for setting up the meeting, creating the proposal, and setting fees. The next three chapters offer instructions for handling a client's answer ("yes" or "no"), for completing the client's work, and for presenting your findings (i.e. creating presentations and reports). Chapters 12–13 teach the basics of marketing and public relations with segments on developing a cohesive marketing strategy and raising your public image. Final chapters discuss management, communication skills, and profitable "spin offs" (i.e. paid public speaker); the last chapter provides a summary. Ideas for increasing sales, a list of specialty fields, start-up pointers, and basic contract forms can be found in the Appendices.

Evaluation:

Bond hits a triple with his primer for home-based consultants. He addresses the important fundamentals, from the (seemingly) simplistic, such as choosing office equipment and keeping your family from interfering with your home office, to the more complex: developing your own "marketing mix," generating publicity, delivering effective presentations. He even details an array of contingencies in dealing with clients, i.e. what if they want an oral agreement, what if they say "no." Bond's approach relies heavily on motivational aids; he frequently uses words like "visualize" and "the consulting process." His step-by-step plan for completing the work suffers from this tendency, providing "go get 'em!" inspiration rather than a workable model. (A more practical model can be found in "The Complete Guide To Consulting Success," see review.) Bond is an able educator, however, and for specialty consultants, particularly those not involved in management consulting, this may be the introductory resource you're looking for. It isn't especially sophisticated, and may bore the more experienced business person, but novices will find it informative and helpful.

Where To Find/Buy:

Bookstores and libraries.

Overall Rating
★★★
A primer for home-based consultants; a straightforward introduction

Design, Ease Of Use
★★★
Uses case study-like examples for illustration; includes forms, samples

1–4 Stars

Author:
William J. Bond

Mr. Bond has been studying, researching, and writing about successful home-based businesses for 30 years. He is the author of a series of Home-Based Business guides.

Publisher:
McGraw-Hill

Edition:
1997

Price:
$14.95

Pages/Run Time:
248

ISBN:
0070066426

Media:
Book

Principal Subject:
Working As A Freelancer, Consultant or Contract Worker

Secondary Subject:
Setting Up And Running A Home-Based Business

Overall Rating
★★★
Candid and inspirational downsized-to-riches story

Design, Ease Of Use
★★★
Conversational tone, engaging read

1–4 Stars

Author:
Hubert Bermont

Mr. Bermont has served as a consultant to more than 70 corporations and trade associations, including the U.S. Chamber of Commerce, McGraw-Hill, and the Smithsonian Institute. He is the author of 8 books about consulting.

Publisher:
Prima Publishing

Edition:
3rd (1997)

Price:
$13.00

Pages/Run Time:
212

ISBN:
0761511008

Media:
Book

Principal Subject:
Working As A Freelancer, Consultant or Contract Worker

Secondary Subject:
Stories From Successful And Not-So-Successful Soloists

HOW TO BECOME A SUCCESSFUL CONSULTANT IN YOUR OWN FIELD

Description:
At 43, Hubert Bermont was a successful but unfulfilled executive who, suddenly, found himself the victim of downsizing. Knowing that he never again wanted to work for someone else, he used his accumulated knowledge to become a successful—and much happier—consultant in his own field. In his book, Bermont describes both the path that led him to consulting as well as his life as a consultant, combining candid revelations with practical advice. In the chapters Expertise, Getting Started, Growing, and The Life, he discusses getting started (he began as a contract worker via outsourcing), gaining confidence, using contacts, and setting up shop. In The Fee and Money, he explains how to set fees and get paid, and how his own income developed over time (from $18,000 the first year to $102,000 by the fifth year). Subsequent chapters explore the wide range of consulting work, ethics and practices, and provide guidelines for writing proposals and reports. Other sections address competition, getting clients, case histories, and handling government work. Bermont also analyses the psychology of consulting and offers tips on How To Mass Market Your Advice. Answers to frequently asked questions and an appendix of Bermont's clients complete the text.

Evaluation:
Many people suffer from a mid-life malaise which, in Bermont's view, is often the product of a life lived within the confines of the "rat race." His solution—to go solo—has gained great popularity over the years, making Bermont something of a forerunner. (It was well over 10 years ago that he was downsized from his corporate job and thus began his consultancy.) The most delightful aspect of this book is Bermont's own story, which he tells with candor, charm, and a pleasing modesty. He isn't self-effacing—he speaks with a reliable confidence—but neither is the story weighed down with bravado. His persona is that of a skilled, industrious, intelligent everyman, imbued with all of the qualities it takes to succeed. His book is an inspiration precisely because it allows you, the well-trained, good-at-your-job executive, to see yourself in Bermont's place: capable and able to succeed. (This is a particularly applicable choice for middle-aged readers, the obvious intended audience.) This isn't a how-to book, though there is advice on setting fees, writing proposals and reports. Bermont takes pains to keep his information general; he reveals little about his own industry, which is occasionally frustrating for the intrigued reader. The lack of detail renders this a supplemental resource, but as such, and for inspiration, it is an engaging book.

Where To Find/Buy:
Bookstores and libraries, or by phone at 916-632-4400.

HOW TO SUCCEED AS AN INDEPENDENT CONSULTANT

Description:

In addition to proffering advice on launching and managing a successful consultancy, Holtz provides a multiple-chapter analysis of the field and of what it takes to be a consultant. To begin, there's a general introduction to consulting, which looks at how consultants specialize and how the consulting market has grown. Chapters 1–5 continue this preliminary discussion by addressing what consultants do, consulting specialties vs. marketing needs, consulting as a second career, why consultants fail, and the "keys" to success. Start-up and management details follow in Chapters 6–24. Holtz offers instruction for establishing your practice (i.e. business organization), handling finances and taxes, creating marketing materials, and "finding leads and closing them." There are chapters on various strategies for marketing to both private and public sectors, as well as on proposal writing, meeting with clients, negotiations, fees, and contracts. Consulting procedures and processes are reviewed, as are final reports, presentations, and other avenues of income, such as writing for profit. Final chapters explore the use of new technologies and ethical considerations, and describe references.

Evaluation:

This is a particularly good resource for older readers, retirees or long-time business persons who are looking to consulting as a possible second career. Holtz seems to be addressing such persons specifically; his style, examples, and presumption of long-term experience are tailored to a mature audience. His business values and ethics, too, are consistent with an older audience. On rare occasions (even though he updated this book in 1993), his viewpoint downplays some of today's business developments. The chapter on integrating new technology, for example, touts fax machines as a great new communication tool, rather than e-mail. (As would be expected of a book updated in '93, little mention is made of the Internet.) Also, there was a projected recession in 1993 that influenced the market-analysis portions of this guide. Keep in mind when reading these sections that the late 1990s have seen a growth in consulting opportunities. These minor criticisms aside, Holtz does provide in depth—and still relevant—advice on the practicalities: logistics of starting up, marketing, networking, forging strong client-consultant relationships. Especially helpful are the chapters on consulting skills: writing, giving presentations, public speaking. This is an insightful, extensive, mature look at consulting and all it entails.

Where To Find/Buy:

Bookstores and libraries.

Overall Rating
★★★
Mature, relevant and rewarding; a few specifics are slightly outdated

Design, Ease Of Use
★★★
Densely written; not a book for browsing

1–4 Stars

Author:
Herman Holtz

Mr. Holtz has been a consultant to IBM, GE, Chrysler, and many other Fortune 500 companies. He is the author of more than 20 books on consulting, including *The Concise Guide To Becoming An Independent Consultant*.

Publisher:
John Wiley & Sons

Edition:
3rd (1993)

Price:
$34.95

Pages/Run Time:
397

ISBN:
047157581X

Media:
Book

Principal Subject:
Working As A Freelancer, Consultant or Contract Worker

IV. Working As A Freelancer Or Consultant

★★★

Overall Rating
★★★
Sensible advice for generating more income; no surprises

Design, Ease Of Use
★★★
Written with humor; includes faux conversations for illustration

1–4 Stars

Author:
Robert W. Bly

Mr. Bly is the director of the Center for Technical Communication, a consulting firm providing on-site seminars in business and technical writing to such clients as IBM, GE, and AT&T. He is the author of over 40 books, including *Selling Your Services*.

Publisher:
Upstart Publishing

Edition:
1998

Price:
$29.95

Pages/Run Time:
326

ISBN:
157410120X

Media:
Book

Principal Subject:
Working As A Freelancer, Consultant or Contract Worker

THE SIX-FIGURE CONSULTANT
How To Start (Or Jump Start) Your Consulting Career And Earn $100,000+ A Year

Description:

In this time of expanding opportunities and corporate downsizing, Bly reports that many consultants in solo and small practices earn $100,000–$300,000+ annually. To teach you how to earn top dollar and "jump-start" your consultancy, Bly combines start-up tips with advice on marketing, attracting clients, and generating sales. To begin, chapters explore what consultants do and how to start a successful practice. Bly then explains how you can become a leading authority in your specialty, generate more sales leads than you can handle, and design a "promo kit." Techniques for wooing prospects, making presentations, and "closing the sale" follow. Next, Bly concentrates on client-consultant relationships. He discusses how to achieve profitable relationships and presents his "proven" strategies for keeping clients satisfied. Practicalities, such as time management, organizational skills, and ways to resolve problems quickly and efficiently, are also addressed. The last two chapters look at ways to boost your consulting income (and raise your profile): creating information products, taking advantage of the training and speaking market. Appendices of resources, forms, and sample documents are included.

Evaluation:

Only one chapter in this guide is dedicated to start-up. Logistical details such as setting up an office, legal and accounting issues receive back-burner treatment (when treated at all). On the front burner are client-consultant relations and methods for generating sales. Bly's advice on client-consultant relationships, which covers everything from following up with prospects to making the sale and addressing client dissatisfaction, is perceptive and logical. He's a believable role model. His suggestions for generating sales and commanding high salaries, which include tips for becoming an authority, are sensible "classics." Bly isn't alone in encouraging consultants to heighten their profile (and image as an authority) by writing books and giving speeches; almost all consulting guides encourage such activities. There are no surprises or innovations here. The book is filled with tried and true methods. Since the guide focuses so intently on its money-making areas, offering no real beginner basics, this is a better resource for consultants with some experience, or as a supplement to novice-oriented books.

Where To Find/Buy:

Bookstores and libraries.

TEMPING: THE INSIDER'S GUIDE
Find The Career That's Right For You

★★★

Description:

Mr. Rogers' "Insider's Guide" to temping has two primary concerns: to explain the growing role and function of temporary employment in America's "changing workscape" and to explore the benefits of temping for today's job seeker. To accomplish the first of these tasks, Mr. Rogers dedicates a third of his guide (Chapters 1–4) to answering such questions as "Temping—What is It?" and "Who Does It and Why?" Once "The Role of the Temporary Help Service" (Chapter 4) is understood, readers learn how to choose the "right" temp service/agency, how to "sign up" (i.e. testing, the interview), and how the employee-agency relationship works (i.e. responsibilities, dos and don'ts). Going "on assignment" is next discussed, i.e. how to dress, how to negotiate for money, "ice breakers," etc. The final third of the guide examines the "pluses and minuses" of "career temping," "Temping Your Way to Full-Time Employment," and "High-End Temping." Insights from temping professionals are incorporated throughout the text.

Evaluation:

This is a straightforward guide to temporary employment, a virtual "how to" manual that explains simply and succinctly how temping works, why it may (or may not) be right for the reader, and how to go about "getting started." Although Rogers does address himself to an audience of job seekers, that is, people who presumably want eventual, full-time employment, his book works just as well for those readers who want to temp for any reason, be it part-time employment, seasonal employment, or as a career. It provides all the "need to know basics" and a few insights (though most of the advice is common sense); altogether, it's a fine resource for anyone contemplating temp work. Readers will learn what to expect upon entering a temp service, what the possibilities are for continued employment, and exactly how the relationship between temp agency and client really works, both practically and legally. Although the benefits of the "nouveau" "temp lifestyle" are discussed, this book is more "mainstream" than its counterpart, "The Temp Survival Guide" (see review). Mr. Rogers' guide is a more appropriate choice for those interested in using temp work in the "traditional" ways: as a "steppingstone" in one's career path, as an expedient way to make money, etc.

Where To Find/Buy:

Bookstores and libraries.

Overall Rating
★★★
A straightforward guide to the "need to know" basics of temping

Design, Ease Of Use
★★★
Simple, direct language, easy to use

1–4 Stars

Author:
Richard Rogers

Publisher:
Arco

Edition:
1996

Price:
$14.95

Pages/Run Time:
202

ISBN:
0028610601

Media:
Book

Principal Subject:
Working As A Freelancer, Consultant or Contract Worker

★★

Overall Rating
★★
A good place to get a feel for freelancing and freelancing opportunities

Design, Ease Of Use
★★★
Simple, straightforward format; easy to use

1–4 Stars

Author:
Freelance Online is a professional online service for freelancers in the publishing and advertising fields. It serves as a directory for employers and as a resource and information center for freelancers.

Publisher:
Freelance Online

Media:
Internet

Principal Subject:
Working As A Freelancer, Consultant or Contract Worker

FREELANCE ONLINE

Description:

Created to help freelancers in communications make "matches" with employers in the publishing and advertising industries, this self-titled "Resource Center" features its own database of jobs and a "Directory" of freelancers' profiles/biographies. There's a member fee of $15 (per annum) to post a profile, but non-members and "newbies" can use the rest of the site, including the job bank, free for six months. (Before the job listings are made available, users will be asked for their member number/code; as a non-member, don't enter anything, just click on "submit." The listings then appear for free.) Job listings are arranged by type, i.e. "art-related," "editorial-related," etc. Each listing contains contact information and a description of the position. Information for new freelancers can be found in the "FAQs" segment, which covers such topics as necessary equipment, finding work, and what to charge. The site also offers message boards for networking and links to additional resources, i.e. related sites, professional organizations, newsletters, etc.

Evaluation:

While there are other "matchmaker" sites out there for freelancers, most are much more expensive than this one. (The member fee is $15.) Thankfully, the operators of this site are kind enough to let non-members explore for free (for six months), which is just what you should do if you're interested in art/editorial-related freelancing. It's not an expansive, enormous site; the job bank is comparatively small and there aren't many participants in the networking forums. But that's not the point. If the idea of freelancing is appealing to you but you're not sure how to proceed, this is the perfect introduction. The "FAQs" are brief but educational (there are links in the text for further information), especially for writers, proofreaders and editors, and browsing the job listings is a terrific way to get a feel for "what's out there." You can see what other freelancers are up to by taking a look at the "Directory," and the "Resources" list of links is worth bookmarking. This is a site worth visiting.

Where To Find/Buy:

On the Internet at http://www.freelancersonline.com/index2.html

SIX-FIGURE CONSULTING
How To Have A Great Second Career

Description:
To help you decide whether consulting is right for you, Goodman starts with an examination of The Consulting Lifestyle and The Psychology Of Consulting. In these 2 chapters (Chapters 1 and 2 of 5), the author uses examples from his own life to give you an idea of what to expect. He analyzes consultant character traits, describes experiences and skills that will prepare you, and discusses potential earnings. He explores why clients hire consultants (officially and unofficially) and explains the importance of understanding your own objectives. Chapter 3 begins the practical how-to section of the guide with advice on marketing your services. Indirect and direct marketing, generating publicity, and telemarketing are addressed, and there are pointers for setting appointments by phone, face-to-face selling, and creating an effective sales letter. In addition to consulting, there are other forums through which you can deliver your knowledge: training workshops, audio and video tapes, articles, books, newsletters. These are detailed in Chapter 4. Steps for making the transition to consulting are laid out in Chapter 5; a 12-week start-up plan is provided. An Addendum on crafting "perfect" promotional articles is also included.

Evaluation:
Goodman (whose PhD is in Communications) focuses on the intangibles of the business: Are you temperamentally suited for consulting? What kind of lifestyle can you expect? He covers teaching marketing techniques and self-promotion strategies, but the book's strength is its focus on whether consulting is the right field for the reader. He communicates some of the general lifestyle and psychological elements of consulting, but with too few details to paint a truly vivid portrait. His outline includes the usual elements: lots of travel, fluctuating income levels, plenty of time spent alone. One notable section is the 12-week start-up plan, which, inexplicably, appears in the last chapter. Divided into weekly segments, Goodman outlines a number of "to do" activities for each week. For example, Week 1's agenda includes picking a business name, ordering letterhead and at least 2 phone lines, and compiling a list of 100 companies to target. The plan is a nice, tidy overview of the start-up process. It doesn't address all aspects, but it hits the critical points. It cannot, by any stretch, compete with a true, step-by-step guide. If you want precise instruction, you won't find it here. What you will find is some valid, if not exciting, marketing pointers and an insider's look at the consulting life.

Where To Find/Buy:
Bookstores and libraries.

Overall Rating
★★
Valid, traditional strategies for marketing and self-promotion; not detailed how-to

Design, Ease Of Use
★★★
Lots of anecdotes; short, to-the-point segments encourage quick reading

1–4 Stars

Author:
Dr. Gary Scott Goodman

Dr. Goodman is president of Goodman Communications. He is a consultant to Fortune 1000 companies, a lecturer, and writes for several periodicals. His other books include *Selling Skills For The Nonsalesperson* and *You Can Sell Anything By Telephone*.

Publisher:
AMACOM

Edition:
1997

Price:
$17.95

Pages/Run Time:
179

ISBN:
0814479588

Media:
Book

Principal Subject:
Working As A Freelancer, Consultant or Contract Worker

★★

Overall Rating
★★
Rudimentary but smart ideas
for sustaining business in a
tight economy; no details

Design, Ease Of Use
★★
Short paragraphs and plain
language; table of contents is
ambiguous

1–4 Stars

Author:
Marsha D. Lewin
Ms. Lewin, MBA, is President
of Marsha D. Lewin Associates,
Inc., a management consultant
firm specializing in project
management and information
system implementation. She is
also the author of *The Overnight
Consultant*.

Publisher:
John Wiley & Sons

Edition:
1997

Price:
$24.95

Pages/Run Time:
220

ISBN:
0471160792

Media:
Book

Principal Subject:
Working As A Freelancer,
Consultant or Contract
Worker

THE CONSULTANT'S SURVIVAL GUIDE
14 Ways To Sustain Your Business In A Tight Economy

Description:
In a cyclical economy, the ability to survive economic downturns
is imperative. As an independent consultant who has practiced
for more than 30 years, Lewin has endured her share of cycles.
In this guide, she reveals the strategies she and other experienced
consultants use to sustain themselves in tough times. The first
couple chapters introduce the need for strategic planning. There's
an analysis of the marketplace and its "threats" to consultants
(i.e. growing competition) as well as advice on staying in control and
surmounting fear. Next, Lewin emphasizes the importance of creating
a demand for your services and explains how to develop a cohesive
personal plan by combining strategies. Each subsequent chapter
examines one specific strategy. Lewin details techniques for trimming
expenses, for maintaining your billing rate in hard times (Don't
Lower Your Fees), and for writing "precisely ambiguous" proposals.
Other hard-time tactics, such as adapting your specialty to the
market, selling big projects as a series of smaller ones, and teaming
with other consultants, are also presented. Final chapters offer tips
for doing good work and discuss ethics and (strategic) volunteering.

Evaluation:
An equally appropriate subtitle for this book would be "What To
Do When Times Are Tough." Although most of Lewin's strategies
are simply smart business strategies, such as doing good work and
keeping in touch with clients/contacts, she treats them as tactics for
surviving in a recessive economy. Many of these tactics are intriguing
and logical; some are quite persuasive. For example, one reason that
consultants have fewer assignments in a tight economy is that clients
are less willing and able to spend money on consulting services.
In such a situation, Lewin suggests that you (the consultant) can
overcome a client's reluctance by breaking large projects into smaller
pieces "at the end of which the client can decide to go ahead with
the next piece or hold off until they see more optimism in the
future." Other sensible strategies include various ways to trim
expenses, teaming with other consultants, and keeping your spirits
(and profile) up by volunteering. The problem is that while Lewin's
ideas are interesting and probably effective, she does little more than
introduce each one. By not expounding on her ideas, she leaves the
details of follow-though up to the reader. That may be fine for the
seasoned pro, but why (presumably) would a seasoned pro need this
book? This is basically a list of survival strategies, albeit a useful one.

Where To Find/Buy:
Bookstores and libraries.

HOW TO START AND RUN A SUCCESSFUL CONSULTING BUSINESS

Description:

The ins and outs of becoming a consultant are systematically outlined and discussed in the Kishels' guide to starting and running a successful consultancy. Chapters 1–4 cover the initial steps, beginning with an introduction to consulting trends and practices, and tips for picking your field. (A list of possible consulting fields is included.) There are guidelines for setting up your business (i.e. forming a business plan, obtaining licenses, permits, supplies) and for setting fees. Chapters 5–7 discuss basic business strategies, such as promotional methods, networking, meeting with clients, and preparing proposals, contracts, and reports. Techniques for time management and for keeping clients satisfied are presented in Chapters 8–9, while Chapters 10–11 deal with handling ethical matters and selling your services to the government. Going International is the next subject addressed, with pointers on assessing the global marketplace and overcoming cultural barriers. Chapter 13 offers an array of ideas for generating additional income, such as public speaking and giving seminars. The final 2 chapters include advice on record keeping and tax issues, as well as information on using/contacting outside support services (i.e. the SBA).

Evaluation:

Reading the Kishels' guide is a little like reading a lengthy brochure on consulting: each chapter is a series of short paragraphs arranged under boldface headings. For example, Chapter 3, Setting Up Your Business, offers 3 paragraphs and a list of questions you should answer to help you Start With A Plan, introduces options for offices in 3–4 paragraph blurbs (i.e. home office, private office), then provides shorter blurbs outlining permits, licenses, copyrights, trademarks, and business forms (i.e. sole proprietorship). There are samples of several forms, and the information is helpful, but the text is so short, bland, and general it's difficult to stay engaged. The book functions best as an outline to the practicalities: supplies, legal details, etc. This is not the choice for inspiration or ideas. The Kishels make poor mentors, offering none of their own experiences for comparison or background. There's no personality here, no taste. For readers who want information without commentary or creative insights, this is a good choice. It will, at least, acquaint you with the banalities. For a more engaging "quick" guide (for management consultants), "The Independent Consultant's Q & A Book" is similar but superior.

Where To Find/Buy:

Bookstores and libraries.

Overall Rating
★
Pat information on the basics; no creativity or personality

Design, Ease Of Use
★★
Short paragraphs with bold-faced headings dominate the text; easy to browse

1–4 Stars

Author:
Gregory Kishel and Patricia Kishel

The Kishels are business consultants and coauthors of *How to Start, Run, and Stay in Business* and *Start, Run, and Profit from Your Own Home-Based Business*. They both have MBA degrees and teach college courses in management, marketing, and finance.

Publisher:
John Wiley & Sons

Edition:
1996

Price:
$17.95

Pages/Run Time:
212

ISBN:
0471125458

Media:
Book

Principal Subject:
Working As A Freelancer, Consultant or Contract Worker

Overall Rating

★

Incomplete how-to with a few good samples

Design, Ease Of Use

★★

Simple writing and standard organization

1–4 Stars

Author:

Marsha D. Lewin

Ms. Lewin, MBA, is President of Marsha D. Lewin Associates, Inc., a management consultant firm specializing in project management and information system implementation. She is both a Certified Management Consultant and a Certified Systems Professional.

Publisher:

John Wiley & Sons

Edition:

1995

Price:

$19.95

Pages/Run Time:

234

ISBN:

0471119458

Media:

Book

Principal Subject:

Working As A Freelancer, Consultant or Contract Worker

THE OVERNIGHT CONSULTANT

Description:

Exhibits, sample letters, business forms, charts and inventories, are interspersed throughout Lewin's 3-part guide to starting and managing a consultancy. Part 1, Getting Started, begins with an introduction to the field, including the topics: types of consultants, ways to practice, and generalists vs. specialists. Start-up and work basics are also detailed: finding clients, preparing proposals, writing contracts, conducting and completing the assignment. Part 2 explores The Business Of Management Consulting in chapters on organizing your business, choosing a business structure, and setting fees. Other chapters in this section address marketing techniques, selling yourself, and qualifying potential clients. Using computers effectively is discussed as well, with pointers for generating client invoices, maintaining mailing lists, and using the Internet. The final third of the book focuses on Survival Issues In Consulting. Lewin offers guidelines for managing and recognizing stress, growing your business, and handling ethical issues. The last chapter in this section provides a Recap, reviewing what makes an assignment successful and the characteristics of successful consultants.

Evaluation:

While Lewin herself is a successful consultant, she isn't the best mentor for inexperienced persons. There are some helpful exhibits in her guide—sample business cards, invoices, and such—but she either skips over important fundamentals or gives them too little attention for this to be an effective stand-alone resource. For example, in the short segment on finding clients, she tells readers to make a list of contacts and then explains that "there are many wonderful and comprehensive books on the marketing of consulting services. . . . [so] there's no reason to repeat the sage advice in those tomes." Instead, she directs readers to her bibliography, which lists a few of these "wonderful" guides. Other segments are similarly abrupt, providing only a few general details. Using Your Computer Effectively is another example. In this chapter, there's a list of computer equipment you'll need and a quick introduction (one short paragraph each) to what such equipment can do: mailing lists, accounting, etc. That's it. No software details or user tips are included, and her Internet instructions amount to an exhortation to get/use e-mail. That Lewin addresses stress management is laudable, few guides do, but a single admirable inclusion can't save this book. There are far better how-to resources than this one.

Where To Find/Buy:

Bookstores and libraries.

CREATIVE FREELANCERS ONLINE

Non-Rated Resource

Description:
Creative Freelancers Online is in the business of connecting freelance talent with the people who hire freelancers. Although there is a $300 annual fee to post your portfolio, non-members can view job listings for free and take a peek at other people's portfolios, for information and/or research. (Or just to check out the competition.) Users can search for job postings by category, i.e. writer, and/or post a brief resume.

Publisher:
Creative Freelancers

For 20 years, Creative Freelancers has provided freelance talent to advertising agencies, publishers, major corporations and small businesses.

Media:
Internet

Principal Subject:
Working As A Freelancer, Consultant or Contract Worker

Where To Find/Buy:
On the Internet at http://www.freelancers.com

JOURNAL OF MANAGEMENT CONSULTING

Non-Rated Resource

Description:
At the JMC site, users can search a database of back articles on all aspects of management consulting. Regular departments (collections of articles) include Practice Development Practice Management, Technology Applications, The Consulting Process, and Professional Ethics. There are also profiles of Best Practices and Recommended Reading lists.

Publisher:
Journal of Management Consulting

The Journal of Management Consulting is a nonprofit educational organization that has served the management consulting profession since 1981. The print version of JMC is published twice a year for a circulation of 8,600 consultants, consulting firms, libraries and universities.

Media:
Internet

Principal Subject:
Working As A Freelancer, Consultant or Contract Worker

Where To Find/Buy:
On the Internet using the URL: http://www.jmcforum.com

NATIONAL ASSOCIATION OF TEMPORARY AND STAFFING SERVICES

Non-Rated Resource

Description:
The NATSS site offers visitors interested in temporary and staffing services an online directory of member agencies. (There are more than 1,600 members.) To find an agency, users can search by location, company name, or by service/skill segment (i.e. health care). Search results frequently contain a link to the company's website as well as contact information.

Publisher:
NATSS

NATSS, the National Association of Temporary and Staffing Services, represents more than 1,600 staffing companies that operate approximately 13,000 offices throughout the U.S.

Media:
Internet

Principal Subject:
Working As A Freelancer, Consultant or Contract Worker

Where To Find/Buy:
On the Internet at http://www.natss.com

WORKING FROM HOME: THE HOME-BASED REVOLUTION

Setting Up & Running A Home-Based Business

Americans are leaving the traditional corporate world and heading home in droves. Not to retire, but to build their own business. With the advent of facsimile machines, high-powered desktop computers, video conferencing, email and the Internet, home offices can achieve the functionality required to conduct local, national and even global business.

A home-based business has several appealing advantages. Because of lower overhead, it often costs less than a traditional start-up. It offers flexibility, especially in deciding when, where and how you will work. The time and expense of commuting is avoided. Location is not a limiting factor; you are only a modem away from being plugged into the world. A not so insignificant benefit for some is the comfort of being able to conduct business in sweats and slippers. And many entrepreneurs report that operating a home business allows them to spend more time with their family.

Is A Home-Based Business Right For Me?

While these advantages explain why a home business is an appealing option, keep in mind that it is not an *easy* option. Few home businesses develop into the profitable ventures their creators envision. Many remain mired in the hobby-sphere and never transform into viable, sustainable enterprises. When evaluating whether a home-based business is right for you, keep in mind the drawbacks inherent in working from home.

The same flexibility that allows you to work at the computer in the morning, take a break while you mow the lawn, and then get back your work, can make it difficult to remain focused on business related tasks during your work time. The convenience of not commuting also means that your work is only a room away. Will unfinished tasks beckon from the home office when you're trying to enjoy family or leisure time? Creating and equipping a home office can be expensive. Is your family willing to yield an area of the house to your business needs? How does your family feel about the notion of a home-based business being established in their home? Are they supportive of your vision?

If you decide to move forward with your dream of starting a business at home, do your homework first! The resources in this chapter are written for a general audience, while those in the following chapter are specifically addressed to either women, parents or couples. The final chapter of this section reviews resources designed to give you ideas for choosing which home-based business is right for you.

TIPS FOR RUNNING A SUCCESSFUL HOME BUSINESS

- Working for yourself can be the ultimate dream, but only if you are able to work consistently and establish deadlines and structure.

- Create clear physical boundaries that define your work area. Communicate to family members that when you are in your work area, you are not to be disturbed.

- To manage time effectively, create a routine and stick to it. Schedule vital tasks that don't seem to get done, such as cold calling for clients.

- Be a life-long learner. Stay on top of technical advances in your field. Read a trade journal or other professional resource on a regular basis.

- Be aware of emerging technologies that can help you be more productive. Take advantage of free or low-cost technology courses offered by libraries and adult colleges.

- Working from home can be isolating. Stay connected to others in your field through venues such as networking websites, professional associations or entrepreneurial clubs.

★★★★

Overall Rating
★★★★
A dizzying array of home-based business tools

Design, Ease Of Use
★★★★
Offers ease of navigation and excellent search engines; great to browse or search

1–4 Stars

Author:
Home Business Magazine Online is the online product of the print publication of the same name.

Publisher:
Home Business Magazine

Media:
Internet

Principal Subject:
Setting Up & Running A Home-Based Business

HOME BUSINESS MAGAZINE ONLINE

 Recommended For:
Setting Up & Running A Home-Based Business

Description:

Despite the title, "HBM" is not an online version of the print magazine of the same name. Visitors to the site can view the current print issue's table of contents, but the contents aren't available at the site. Rather, this site is an entity unto itself, offering a wide range of tools for the home-based business entrepreneur. The home page provides access to "HBM's" major sections, which include Today On HBM (new daily stories), News & Reviews, Timely Highlights (tips related to current events), and a series of Channels. The Channels are segments dedicated to such subjects as Business Start Up, Business Management, Home Office, Marketing & Sales, Webmastery, and Technology. Each segment has its own main page and features. For example, Business Start Up contains articles on financing, insurance, and motivation, Webmastery and Marketing & Sales provide tutorials, and Home Office details home office equipment. For more information, users can search (by keyword) the HBM Library, an archive of hundreds of resources, divided into 3 categories: Articles & Reports, Business Letters, and Legal Forms. (The letters and forms are samples.) The site also features celebrity interviews, classifieds, and an e-zine.

Evaluation:

For potential SOHO entrepreneurs, the real boon at this multi-faceted site is the HBM Library. While archives of hundreds of informational and how-to articles have become somewhat common at larger sites like this one, the inclusion of the enormous database of sample legal forms and business letters is rare. Samples can be one of the best learning tools for new business owners, particularly for those with limited business experience; they teach by example and are often invaluable introductions to subjects that are difficult to explain in abstract. The Library's large quantity and wide topical range of both articles and samples is an extra bonus. Chances are, whatever you're looking for, you'll find it. For example, there are 300 matches for "Start Up" in Articles & Reports and 300 matches for "Marketing" in Business Letters. In legal forms, the keywords "Partnership AND Agreement" produce such documents as a Joint Venture Agreement, a Declaration of Irrevocable Trust, and a Declaration of Revocable Trust. Of course, there's more to this site than the Library. The Channels offer helpful featured articles and tutorials, the new daily stories and frequently updated Timely Highlights make each visit different, and the celebrity interviews are just plain fun. For home-based businesses, this is one to bookmark!

Where To Find/Buy:

On the Internet using the URL: http://www.homebusinessmag.com

Setting Up & Running A Home-Based Business

HOMEMADE MONEY
How To Select, Start, Manage, Market And Multiply The Profits Of A Business At Home

 Recommended For:
Setting Up & Running A Home-Based Business

Description:
Brabec has written this book so that readers won't "have to learn everything the hard way." Similar to many other books on this subject, Brabec begins with a discussion of "going solo" trends, pros, and cons. While the first four chapters focus on the broad considerations regarding the decision to become self-employed, the remainder of the book is dedicated to more specific concerns/decisions of being self-employed. In chapter five, Brabec offers information pertaining to the creation of a successful business image. Chapter six is an "A-to-Z Crash Course" in Business Basics" that may be indexed by its own table of contents. Chapter seven offers time management advice. Chapters eight through twelve address various topics related to the marketing of your business: marketing plan, pricing strategies, networking opportunities, publicity, and reaching new markets. In "Adding a Computer to Your Life," the reader is offered many points-of-view in regards to computers and their impact via a "Computertalk" Networking Session. In chapter fourteen, Brabec shares examples of challenges that others were able to turn into positives. An "Epilogue" and "U.S. and Canadian Resources" are concluding chapters.

Evaluation:
In writing her book, Brabec has drawn upon her own long history of self-employment experiences. Having had the early influence of a self-employed father, Brabec entered the "arts and crafts revolution" in the mid-1960s and thereafter began publishing a quarterly newsletter. In it she wrote about her experiences selling handcrafts at local shops and fairs. Through these early endeavors, Brabec gained "experience and contacts that would neatly position (her) as a pioneer and leader in the (self-employment) industry." While this is not a "how to" book; it is a presentation of tips and questions that will support readers embarking on the adventure of starting/growing their own business. Each chapter is guided by an underlying theme. For example, her section on "Assessing Your Situation" conveys her belief that you must have a "clear understanding of yourself, your capabilities and your limitations" to create a successful business. The reader will appreciate Brabec's attention to detail; in her section on legal advice, she cites her sources by name/credentials. In the "Computertalk" discussion, Brabec offers the lone business owner the camaraderie of a peer group. The philosophies, insights and examples that Brabec shares have broad application to many types of businesses; and they address the issues faced by dreamers, beginners and established small business owners.

Where To Find/Buy:
Bookstores and libraries.

Overall Rating
★★★★
Information, resources, and strategies

Design, Ease Of Use
★★★★
Well thought-out, written and indexed

1—4 Stars

Author:
Barbara Brabec

Self-employed virtually all her adult life, Brabec is one of the country's best-known home-business writers and speakers. She has published a newsletter for 15 years, authored five books and spoken at numerous home-based business conferences throughout North America.

Publisher:
Betterway Books
(F & W Publications)

Edition:
5th (1997)

Price:
$21.99

Pages/Run Time:
392

ISBN:
1558704663

Media:
Book

Principal Subject:
Setting Up & Running A Home-Based Business

Setting Up & Running A Home-Based Business

★★★

Overall Rating
★★★
Good balance between individual and informational focus

Design, Ease Of Use
★★★★
Well outlined and cross-referenced

1–4 Stars

Author:
Barbara Weltman

Barbara Weltman is a nationally-known expert on business and tax planning. She is a home-based attorney who has authored several books on succeeding in your own business.

Publisher:
Alpha Books

Edition:
1997

Price:
$16.95

Pages/Run Time:
329

ISBN:
0028615395

Media:
Book

Principal Subject:
Setting Up & Running A Home-Based Business

THE COMPLETE IDIOT'S GUIDE TO STARTING A HOME BASED BUSINESS

Description:

Fifteen years ago, Weltman decided to work from her home due to the interplay between an increased commute and her need to be available for her young children. Similar to other books on the market, her guide begins with "The Home-Based Business Revolution" and "Why Start from Home?" Then in "Finding Your Perfect (Business) Match," questions are posed to guide the reader to consider their unique talents, skills and interests in relation to business opportunities. Also in this section, readers are offered details regarding legal issues (partnerships, incorporating, etc.) to consider when establishing their business. In "Raising Dollars with Sense," Weltman includes "Writing Your Business Plan: 101" where she provides the outline for a business plan; she also directs the readers to other sections of the book for help "When Numbers and You Don't Mix." The section on setting up your office considers zoning, space, and equipment. In "Running Your Business," Weltman focuses on money-related issues such as marketing, collection, employees, insurance, accounting, taxes and write offs. The book concludes with "Up Close and Personal Issues" where consideration is given to the unique and personal aspects of time management, isolation, image, and growth.

Evaluation:

Although Weltman is an attorney, the information she conveys is not restricted to the legal ramifications of self-employment. In the introduction she praises the opportunities for personal growth that she has enjoyed since choosing to go solo. She then dives into information that is either explicit and detailed (creating a business plan, determining operating expenses), or more general (creating a business concept, acquiring financing.) Both the explicit and the general information work to define a step-by-step process. For example, chapters one through three offer guidance and encouragement by using questions and comments that prompt the reader to (1) evaluate their present situation, (2) consider the opportunities at hand, and (3) to prepare for launching a home-based business. Throughout the book, Weltman conveys the attitude that the job at hand is to seek information and to prepare as needed. The broad topics covered in this step-by-step manner necessitate a cover-to-cover reading of the book to get the big picture being presented. As a quick reference, each chapter contains "The Least You Need to Know." Weltman's advice is at times obvious—presumably for those potential entrepreneurs who don't have a substantial amount of knowledge or experience to build upon prior to reading this book.

Where To Find/Buy:

Bookstores and libraries.

Setting Up & Running A Home-Based Business

YOUR SMALL BUSINESS.COM
Helping Your Small Business Become Successful

★★★

Description:

Created to help entrepreneurs with any type of small business—from SOHO to Web-based—this online "resource center" contains a number of special interest departments, a database of 250+ articles, and a wide range of tools and tips for Internet Businesses. Departments include Starting a Biz (articles and links to related articles), Women in Biz (primarily links to outside resources), Home Biz Dept (articles and office supplies), Marketing Ideas and Money Issues. In Starting a Biz, users will find how-to articles, 50 Business Start-up Reports, and Q & A. For more assistance, users can browse the 250+ in-house articles, arranged by subject category, i.e. Advertising, Computer Related, Sales, and Websites. The Website articles cover a variety of topics, from start-up to making "cyberprofits." Plus, there's a Website Owner department and information on web hosting, e-commerce, and site promotion. Users can navigate the site's main sections via the side menu on the each page, or click on the appropriate icon for the extensive Site Navigation Bar. (For a complete list of Web-based business tools, use the Bar.) Message boards, magazine and book lists, news items, and updates on office supplies are also featured.

Evaluation:

Although there are plenty of relevant and helpful articles and reports here for SOHOs of any type, this site is especially beneficial for Web-based entrepreneurs and small or home businesses that want a Web presence. In that category, there are lots of terrific resources: start up articles, details on e-commerce, website building information, etc. The resources aren't organized in a beginning-to-end, step-by-step manner; you'll need to take this tip from here, that instruction from there, and so forth. But that isn't unusual, nor should it be a deterrent. It's par for the course at a site designed for both start-ups and current businesses, for both novices and the more experienced "cyber" pro. Thus, your first visit will be one of fact-finding: determining which tools you need now and which you'll return for later, once you're up and running. The only problem is that the navigation is tricky. The Site Navigation Bar (the best way to find all of the Web-related resources) uses ambiguous titles, concealing whether or not the information is free or a for-fee service/product. Plus, the site employs a split screen technique to separate the Bar from the main pages. If your computer screen is small, the Bar may squeeze the main pages off your screen, forcing you to scroll to the right to read the end of sentences. Nuisances aside, this one is still worth a visit.

Where To Find/Buy:

On the Internet using the URL: http://yoursmallbusiness.com

Overall Rating
★★★
Good for SOHO and small business; especially good for web-based businesses

Design, Ease Of Use
★
Navigation can be tricky

1–4 Stars

Publisher:
Your Small Business.com

Media:
Internet

Principal Subject:
Setting Up & Running A Home-Based Business

Secondary Subject:
High-Tech And Internet-Based Businesses

Of Interest To:
Women

Setting Up & Running A Home-Based Business

★★

Overall Rating
★★
Informative, but directive
rather than stimulating

Design, Ease Of Use
★★★★
Clearly presented, yet
comfortably informal

1–4 Stars

Author:
Karen Cheney and Lesley
Alderman

Karen Cheney is a staff writer at
Money Magazine who writes
extensively on home businesses,
taxes, and health care. Lesley
Alderman is the originator and
author of *Money Magazine*'s
"Worklife" column. She also
answers personal finance questions
on Money's CompuServe Site.

Publisher:
Money Magazine
(Warner Books)

Edition:
1997

Price:
$10.99

Pages/Run Time:
212

ISBN:
0446673161

Media:
Book

Principal Subject:
Setting Up & Running A
Home-Based Business

HOW TO START A SUCCESSFUL HOME BUSINESS

Description:
Cheney targets an audience that is ready to work 12 hour days
in an effort to make big money in their own business. She takes
full advantage of her network of contacts at Money Magazine, and
calls upon the many professionals and associations connected with
the publication to provide information. Chapter one includes a
discussion of self-employment trends, the entrepreneurial spirit,
finding a market niche, market research, and a brief discussion
of legal protections. Chapter two highlights "Ten Home Business
Winners" following the same format to present each business:
"Skills You Need," "Work-Life Snapshot," "Special Costs," "Income
Potential," and "For More Information." Chapter three outlines the
process for getting a financial forecast in writing, and includes ideas
for obtaining personal/commercial sources of funds. Chapter four
offers perspective on home office setup and insurance needs.
Chapter five addresses tax issues. Chapter six shares sales tips and
some insider information regarding journalistic PR opportunities.
Chapter seven deals with topics of lifestyle transition. Chapter eight
considers the components of change as a business evolves/grows.
The "Best Home Based Resources" includes Associations, books,
government and online resources, and magazines.

Evaluation:
Considering that this book was created by Money Magazine, it is
not surprising that it reads like a piece of investigative reporting.
Although the writing is informal, Cheney is entrenched in practicality
and does not venture much beyond providing information. The
reporting tone is especially evident in "Ten Home Business Winners"
where research on the "Winners" is presented in a succinct format.
In the discussions related to defining and testing your market niche,
a problem-solving perspective is emphasized. Chapter five delivers a
valuable section entitled "Recouping Your Start-up Costs" that is
not found in most books on this subject matter. Prudently, readers are
further advised to talk with a "tax pro." The journalistic influences on
marketing/sales strategies are evident in a section entitled "Catch the
Media's Attention" where readers are advised to "pitch a story, not
your business." As a seasoned reporter, Cheney offers additional
resources for nearly every topic covered in this book for further
research. While the journalistic style employed throughout this book
is informative, Cheney does not provide a springboard for creative
thinking on the reader's part. This book will appeal to the practical
minded who are investigating the choice to start a home-based
business as their full-time employment.

Where To Find/Buy:
Bookstores and libraries.

Setting Up & Running A Home-Based Business

THE KITCHEN TABLE MILLIONAIRE

★★

Description:

To become a Kitchen Table Millionaire, Cochrane believes it is necessary to make money, save, and invest. In Part One, he addresses some choices related to the establishment of your business such as identifying, naming, and protecting the business. Both product-based and service-based businesses are an option. For the product-based choice, Cochrane offers advice for obtaining a manufacturer. He outlines legal and financial aspects of establishing and operating a business that could apply to both business types. In Part Two, Cochrane details Dynamarketing Strategies such as mail order, newspaper classifieds, catalogs, trade shows, flea markets, and industry publications. Per Inquiry (PI) advertising, a relatively new marketing tool, is also included as are insights on free publicity. Cochrane suggests sources beyond friends, family and the bank to provide needed funds. The Million-Dollar Home Based Businesses found in Part Three include self-publishing, 900 numbers for selling information/entertainment, buying/selling with consignment/auctions, buying/selling "paper," and cybermarketing. Part Four is entitled Protecting Your Assets and begins with Reframing Your Belief Systems followed by personal financing advice.

Evaluation:

The Home-Based Money-Making Strategies to Build Financial Independence Today are not specific business ideas, but rather marketing channels that can serve to promote an array of business ideas. Cochrane encourages readers to take action by highlighting the stories of some successful business ideas such as the Pet Rock and Happy Face. He does not walk readers through the process of choosing a business, although he does encourage a "can do" attitude and shares some practical advice on topics such as registering your business, spending, taxes, and home office set-up. The advice given often helps to convey tasks as a doable activity. For example, Cochrane suggests protecting your idea in the short-run by describing your business in letter form and sending a copy to your lawyer before establishing a standard right such as a patent. Tips for turning your dream into a reality are offered with a focus on marketing. The section on Internet marketing exemplifies the scope of information offered for each strategy. Here, Cochrane provides an overview by offering a glossary of specific terms and advising readers to stay on the "main road" of the massive Internet so as not to get lost. Although this book is written for the business beginner, the broad range of traditional and progressive marketing channels could also serve the seasoned business owner who seeks to reach a wider market.

Where To Find/Buy:

Bookstores and libraries.

Overall Rating
★★
Good marketing insight, but lacks depth on other business particulars

Design, Ease Of Use
★★★
Resource directory includes descriptive information; thorough index

1–4 Stars

Author:
Patrick Cochrane

Patrick Cochrane is an entrepreneur, speaker, and home-based-business consultant. He has taught business strategy classes and has appeared on television, radio, and in print throughout North America.

Publisher:
Prima Publishing

Edition:
1997

Price:
$12.00

Pages/Run Time:
233

ISBN:
0761509291

Media:
Book

Principal Subject:
Setting Up & Running A Home-Based Business

★★

Overall Rating
★★
Good introduction/overview, but not a definitive guide

Design, Ease Of Use
★★
Multiple formatting and presentation styles

1–4 Stars

Author:
Mel Cook

Mel Cook is a retired CEO of a New Jersey company and has extensive business experience with such companies as *The New York Times*, the Times Mirror Company, and ITT, as well as in management consulting. He received his MBA and his PMD.

Publisher:
Macmillan (Simon & Schuster Macmillan Company)

Edition:
2nd (1998)

Price:
$14.95

Pages/Run Time:
320

ISBN:
0028622529

Media:
Book

Principal Subject:
Setting Up & Running A Home-Based Business

Secondary Subject:
High-Tech And Internet-Based Businesses

HOME BUSINESS BIG BUSINESS
The Definitive Guide To Starting And Operating On-Line And Traditional Home-Based Ventures

Description:
In Part One, Cook introduces some role models with Making It Big: Profiles of Home-Based Ventures That Become Million-Dollar Companies (such as Discovery Toys). He also highlights eight tips for fast-tracking which relate to market considerations and management skills. Part Two addresses a range of topics such as The Essentials of Successfully Starting, Operating, and Expanding a Home Business by posing questions that an entrepreneur is likely to ask and providing a here's-what-you-do response. Cook focuses on getting the most from your efforts by saving and earning as much money as possible. Part Three highlights business opportunities based on crafts, foods, personal services, business services, mail-order, unique talents, manufacturing, selling, repairs, and educating/instructing. Internet opportunities are discussed in Part Four, and Part Five is comprised of Special Information Chapters. This last section considers franchises, work-at-home opportunities for retirees and the disabled, and offers some home-business legal advice. A Resource Guide lists Recommended Books, Help Organizations, Small Business Magazines, Library Reference Books, Government Publications, and The Fifty Most Useful Web Sites for Home-Based Business.

Evaluation:
Aptly titled, this book emphasizes that home-based start-ups can grow BIG. The question/answer format that is used to explain The Essentials of Successfully Starting, Operating and Expanding a Home Business may be tedious for readers who are eager to get to the heart of a topic. But this book seems to be intended for the inexperienced entrepreneur, and the text flows nicely for readers who have little or no business experience. While the cumulative Q & A format used in Part Two leads to an adequate presentation of the "big picture," it does not provide a thoroughly specific/detailed strategy on topics such as the business plan, marketing, or financial accounting. And a firm grasp of these topics is essential for entrepreneurial success. In Part Four, Cook delivers a well-balanced overview of Profitable Cybermarketing: Using the Internet to Launch and Grow Your Home Business. This concise overview conveys both the big picture and many specifics related to online opportunities. Although most of the book is geared for the novice, this section delivers valuable information to both novice entrepreneurs and those who have already gained experience in the traditional marketplace and want to research online opportunities.

Where To Find/Buy:
Bookstores and libraries.

Setting Up & Running A Home-Based Business

HOW TO MAKE MONEY PUBLISHING FROM HOME
Everything You Need To Know To Successfully Publish: Books, Newsletters, Greeting Cards, Zines, And Software

Description:

Shaw begins with an account of some of the pros and cons to running a home-based publishing business. In turn, she asks readers to evaluate their lifestyle and financial goals. She describes booklets, books, greeting cards, magazines, newsletters, newspapers, software, and zines as possible publishing choices. Having defined this range of choices, she prompts readers to put the specifics of their business idea on paper (and offers a sample business plan in an appendix.) Shaw offers advice on naming the business, making it legal, keeping account of costs, hiring employees, working with suppliers, and understanding the issues of taxing and zoning. Various elements of technology are discussed as a valuable option, rather than a necessity. Cash flow topics range from obtaining business credit to providing customer credit. In Day In, Day Out, readers meet some of the experts, resources and groups that will likely serve as business partners, and are given tips for staying motivated. The chapter on marketing is supplemented by an appendix which presents a sample marketing plan. Growth is a topic discussed as both a positive and a negative.

Evaluation:

Shaw begins by conveying the message that the publishing business is becoming more accessible to entrepreneurs and valuable to society. She attributes this trend to the same technology/information age that is fueling the growth of other home-based businesses. Although acknowledging that publishing can be lucrative, Shaw does not focus on the financial rewards as much as the value of controlling one's destiny. The tradeoff between security and freedom is evidenced by taking on risk to create a business. Shaw works to define realistic expectations for readers. Her own experiences provide teachings on the publishing of booklets, newsletters, books, software, and greeting cards. With each endeavor, she (similar to others featured) has found that she learned much of what she needed to know by actually going through the process. However she also stresses the importance of "doing your homework" research-wise before taking action. Another topic of importance is marketing; Shaw hits this from several angles by considering topics such as finding the time, advertising on a budget, and responding to common questions. Overall, she lays the groundwork as to what to expect, and sometimes offers specific advice such as in the technology section. But the "how to" is not often detailed.

Where To Find/Buy:

Bookstores and libraries.

Overall Rating
★★
Offers overview, but unlikely to be "Everything You Need to Know"

Design, Ease Of Use
★★
Not succinctly presented; indexed

1–4 Stars

Author:
Lisa Shaw

Lisa Shaw is a nationally renowned home publisher who owns and operates Williams Hill Publishing. She has been producing newsletters and other publications for over 14 years and recently introduced a line of greeting cards for cats and dogs.

Publisher:
Prima Publishing

Edition:
1997

Price:
$13.00

Pages/Run Time:
231

ISBN:
0671508120

Media:
Book

Principal Subject:
Setting Up & Running A Home-Based Business

V. Working From Home: The Home-Based Revolution

Setting Up & Running A Home-Based Business

STARTING A HOME-BASED BUSINESS

Description:

Readers are introduced to the general trends and conditions of the home-based business revolution, and warned of subjective obstacles such as procrastination, personal interruptions, isolation and more. Information is also provided regarding Home-Based Business Opportunities and includes a list of The 23 Best Home-Based Businesses. Planning for Success is equivalent to performing research and creating a business plan. To obtain Start-Up Financing, the editors offer suggestion to Tap Yourself First, and also cite additional sources of funds such as family and friends, banks, finance companies, and more. Issues such as legal form of operation, zoning, legislation, insurance and legal rights (i.e.: trademarks) are discussed, as is Setting Up Your Home Office. Marketing, Advertising, and Selling are addressed as components in an overall marketing strategy which is essential for the home-based business. Also pertinent to the overall marketing plan, pricing guidelines are offered. Topics related to financial planning, considered a necessity throughout the life of a business, are also included. The Personnel Question section serves those who consider hiring employees.

Evaluation:

While a lot of information is contained within the 286 pages of this book, the advice and suggestions are not necessarily worthwhile, accurate, or well presented. For example, "Be a self-starter" probably could have done without the explanation that "nobody will be there to tell you what to do or when to do it. Getting the job done is entirely up to you." Considering that many people choose to start a home-based business to provide flexibility, words of advice such as "Define Your Work Hours and Stick to Them" and "Don't Talk about Business during Family Time" come across as a bit rigid. The 23 Best Home-Based Businesses list is not particularly enlightening; for example, the editors acknowledge that the Multimedia Services business idea requires "a sophisticated computer set-up and a good dose of computer savvy." Some information from the Computerization section is a bit out of date such as the portion regarding "recently released Windows 3.1" and its "comparatively slow operating speed." In Chapter 5, Schedule C-EZ is said to require the use of a cash-accounting method to record transactions; readers are referred to Record Keeping and Taxes (Chapter 10) for more information, yet no topic heading for "cash accounting" is to be found either in chapter 10 or the index. The glossary does contain a definition for "cash basis." Cross-referencing within this text can be laborious for the reader.

Where To Find/Buy:

Bookstores and libraries.

Overall Rating

★

Although topics are relevant, information is not impressive

Design, Ease Of Use

★

Not succinct

1–4 Stars

Author:

Entrepreneur Magazine

The Entrepreneur Magazine Group also publishes Business Start-Ups and Entrepreneur in Mexico, as well as videos, audiocassettes, and software that deal with business start-up management.

Publisher:

John Wiley & Sons

Edition:

1996

Price:

$19.95

Pages/Run Time:

286

ISBN:

0471109797

Media:

Book

Principal Subject:

Setting Up & Running A Home-Based Business

Setting Up & Running A Home-Based Business

THE U.S.A. HOME BASED BUSINESS INFORMATION SUPERHIGHWAY

Non-Rated Resource

Description:
Though still in the early stages of development at the time of this review, the NAHBB's Information Superhighway has big plans that warrant a visit from home based business entrepreneurs. Currently, visitors to the site will find information about the NAHBB, links to relevant resources, and product/service advertisements for home based business needs.

Publisher:
NAHBB

Media:
Internet

Principal Subject:
Setting Up & Running A Home-Based Business

Where To Find/Buy:
On the Internet using the URL: http://www.usahomebusiness.com

HOME BUSINESS GUIDES FOR MOTHERS, WOMEN & COUPLES

The boom in home-based businesses has been echoed with a boomlet in resources available on the topic. In addition to the general audience resources profiled in the preceding chapter, there are now books, websites and other resources tailored to specific kinds of "homepreneurs." This is good news for mothers, women and couples operating a business together, three groups who can benefit enormously by having a resource designed with their unique strengths and challenges in mind.

While budding entrepreneurs need how-to information, they are also nourished by the encouragement, solidarity and humor an author provides. Stories resonate on a deeper level when we personally relate to the character or situation described. For this reason, mothers may prefer a guide written by someone who knows first hand what it's like to have a child pick up the phone and giggle into an important business call. Similarly, women may prefer to learn from an author who has "walked in her high heels." Couples who go into business together face a particular set of challenges. These families can learn from the narratives of other husband-wife teams who have learned how to make their co-preneur business *and* their marriage a success.

[For a short description of all the resources we cover that are aimed at women or parents, look in Section VII, Resources Of Interest To Specific Groups.]

Meet Me On The Net

You've heard of the "Old Boys Network," the rings of congenial relationships that provide referrals and mentors for its members. Career women have been forming their own circles of support for decades, but have been stymied in some areas because of their relatively small numbers.

The advent of the Internet, and the Web's ability to transcend distance, has served as a catalyst for bringing together like-minded people in "virtual communities." Surf the Web and you will find websites for everyone from Star Wars enthusiasts to female airline pilots. We review several websites whose raison d'être is to facilitate networking among particular groups, such as stay-at-home moms with home businesses or entrepreneurial parents.

Go online and use these groups to network, ask questions, share your knowledge or find a mentor. If you don't have access to the Internet from home, be aware that many schools, libraries and adult colleges offer free access.

For more ideas on networking websites, check out our chapter on "Resources For Networking, Support and Advice" in Section VI.

★★★★

Overall Rating
★★★★
Valuable resource for couples sharing a business

Design, Ease Of Use
★★★
Provides good game plan for entrepreneurial couples capable of frank communication

1–4 Stars

Author:
Kathy Marshack

The author is a psychologist in private practice, specializing in issues related to family-owned businesses, and a clinical social worker licensed in Washington and Oregon.

Publisher:
Davies-Black (Consulting Psychologists Press)

Edition:
1998

Price:
$26.95

Pages/Run Time:
272

ISBN:
0891061150

Media:
Book

Principal Subject:
Home Business Guides For Mothers, Women & Couples

ENTREPRENEURIAL COUPLES
Making It Work At Work And At Home

 Recommended For:
Home Business Guides For Mothers, Women & Couples

Description:
A psychologist specializing in issues related to family-owned businesses identifies the pitfalls facing entrepreneurial couples and suggests tools to achieve a healthy balance of personal, business, and family goals. Her book consists of 11 chapters; the first examines 20 different styles of entrepreneurial couples. The author goes on to examine common problems in communication, life goals, money management, "equality versus equity," parenting, and stress. In most chapters, she provides "self-assessment" exercises to help readers relate the material to their own circumstances. In the final chapter, she suggests ways in which readers can develop their own "Master Life Plan" on the basis of these exercises. Her goal is to help couples create a "holistic" plan that brings balance to their lives. The book closes with an appendix, which repeats all 15 self-assessment exercises, a bibliography, and an index.

Evaluation:
Couples working together in a family business, operating separate businesses, or considering joining forces in a new career will find this well-researched resource helpful in identifying common pitfalls and assessing their own needs and goals. The author speaks from experience, combining life stories from her practice, results from research studies, and numerous exercises to create a valuable guide to what is uncharted territory for most of us. The book is relatively free of professional and self-help jargon; the author's tone is assertive, non judgmental, and optimistic, and her presentation is logical and easy to follow. Her self-assessment exercises and numerous checklists help bring the research and anecdotal material home to the reader. However, for the author's program to work, a couple must be firmly committed to frankly examining their relationship, and personal and business goals. For maximum effect, both members of the team should read this, but if statistics bear out, women will read and attempt to inject wisdom learned into the partnership.

Where To Find/Buy:
Bookstores and libraries.

THE HOME TEAM
How Couples Can Make A Life And A Living By Working At Home

★★★

Description:

This resource offers basic tools for married couples wishing to launch a home-based business. It serves to inspire, educate, and entertain those who want to incorporate marriage, business, and home life. Addressing the rapidly growing home-business trend, this resource covers reasons to work at home together, childcare issues, the commitments necessary to make a home-business successful, and romantic potential. By using the same skills required of a good marriage, the authors assert, couples can have a successful business partnership. The authors, who are married, share their experiences along with those of numerous work-at-home couples they have interviewed. They encourage couples to gather information on the nuts-and-bolts of running a home-business from other resources and use this book as a personal supplement. Each of the 11 chapters concludes with a brief multiple-choice quiz designed to reinforce the text and prioritize goals. A four-page recommended reading list, an index, and information on the authors' businesses follow the text.

Evaluation:

This down-to-earth guide will inspire couples who want to work together or are already running a business at home. With occasional light humor, the authors explain how couples can avoid making the mistakes they did. They thoroughly cover issues couples face when opting out of the traditional work force and provide sensitive advice on how to handle criticism from outside. Especially refreshing is their progressive child-rearing attitude. While offering numerous solutions on how to juggle work, home, and family, they emphasize the benefits of child-parent contact in the first five years of a child's life. Not all couples are good candidates for a home-business, the authors explain, but there are plenty of good reasons why many couples can be successful. The easy-to-follow layout, clear writing, and quizzes keep readers focused, making this a recommended reference for work-at-home couples.

Where To Find/Buy:

Bookstores and libraries.

Overall Rating
★★★
A practical work-at-home guide for couples

Design, Ease Of Use
★★★
Well-organized and concise with helpful index and topical reading list

1–4 Stars

Author:
Scott Gregory and Shirley Siluk Gregory

The husband-and-wife authors are former newspaper reporters who run writing, publishing, and publicity businesses from their homes in suburban Chicago and northwest Florida.

Publisher:
Panda

Edition:
1997

Price:
$22.95

Pages/Run Time:
251

ISBN:
1889438324

Media:
Book

Principal Subject:
Home Business Guides For Mothers, Women & Couples

Of Interest To:
Parents

Overall Rating
★★★
Good use of individual stories to convey general teachings

Design, Ease Of Use
★★★
Good overall organization, excellent resource descriptions at back of book

1–4 Stars

Author:
Liz Folger

Liz Folger provides a successful home-based business consulting service for women and hosts two online chat rooms on the subject. She is also raising two daughters.

Publisher:
Prima Publishing

Edition:
1997

Price:
$12.00

Pages/Run Time:
290

ISBN:
0761507930

Media:
Book

Principal Subject:
Home Business Guides For Mothers, Women & Couples

Of Interest To:
Parents

Home Business Guides For Mothers, Women & Couples

THE STAY-AT-HOME MOM'S GUIDE TO MAKING MONEY
How To Choose The Business That's Right For You Using The Skills And Interests You Already Have

Description:

In Home Business Basics, Folger begins with an analogy of the decision to start a business. Before entering the process of discovery, readers are advised of some scams to avoid. That aside, Folger encourages readers to research and be open to possibilities when developing a business idea. Furthering the process, there is a worksheet that leads readers through the creation of a business plan by presenting a series of questions. Money-related topics such as financing, creating a separate business bank account, and pricing are included; and zoning, taxing and insuring are some of the technical issues that are highlighted. Part Two is a collection of twenty-nine Home Business Profiles. The following businesses are featured: craftsmaker, childcare provider, graphic artist/desktop publisher, childbirth instructor, accountant, massage therapist, alterations and sewing, tutor, upholsterer, word processor, floral designer, telecommuter, herb gardener, freelance photographer, indexer, caterer, architect, basket dealer, pet-sitter, greeting card writer, nanny-finding service, newsletter publisher, professional organizer, freelance writer and editor, soap maker, medical transcriptionist, quilter, craftsmaker, and attorney. Each profile is of an individual money-making mom and her business experiences.

Evaluation:

Folger began her family before becoming established in a profession that she could take solo. After striving to create a business that eventually failed, she did not give up. Instead she has made her dream a reality by writing this book. Folger is motivated by her compassion for mothers who are torn between work and family commitments. The can-do message found in Part One and Part Two will be especially helpful to individuals who want to start one of the businesses featured here. But moms in general will learn lessons and tricks of the (being in business for yourself) trade. Strategies for gaining the respect of friends/family for your work time are presented in Getting Down to Business. Open communication is encouraged and exemplified in How to Manage Your House, Your Family, and Your Business. Folger focuses on the well-being of the individual business owner in Staying Healthy. Lastly, she asks readers to overcome any fears that keep them from the benefits of online tools and information. In the featured business profiles, Folger describes the unique aspects of each business such as Why She Started Her Business, Skills, Equipment, Services, Rates, Marketing, Hiring Help, Mixing Kids and Business, Tips, Biggest Challenge, Rewards, Advice, and Recommended Resources. Many of the strategies revealed in these stories can be applied to other business ideas.

Where To Find/Buy:

Bookstores and libraries.

Home Business Guides For Mothers, Women & Couples

THE ENTREPRENEURIAL PARENT

★★★

Description:

Many parents are taking advantage of the SOHO revolution as a means of making money and meeting their career goals while being at home with their children. To help potential entrepreneurial parents (EPs), this site offers a variety of free and for-fee services, tools, and advice. From the home page, new users can click on Site Contents for a description of the main segments, including the 6 sections of special interest to EPs: Your Family, Your Career, Your Business, Your Profiles, Your Resources, and Your Links. Your Family focuses on parenting and lifestyle issues, while Your Career features articles from career counselors on how working at home can fit into long-term career goals. Your Business is one of the larger sections, with how-to articles, book excerpts, and tools for starting, growing, and managing your SOHO. Your Profiles, labeled "the heart and soul" of the site by its creators, is a database of EP profiles which detail the EP's business and function as advertisements. (Profiles cost $40; visitors can browse for free.) For research, there are the collections of additional resources in Your Resources and Your Links. "EP" also features a chat room, expert Q & A, a free "EP" newsletter, and for-fee Pro Help.

Evaluation:

The "EP" site is one of the rare "breakout" stars in the fast-multiplying galaxy of SOHO/entrepreneurial web resources. With its combination of lifestyle and business features, it's an idea whose time has come. Its profile has been steadily rising; its been featured on PBS and almost always turns up in working solo web guides and lists. Name recognition is hard won on the Web, and "EP's" standing is itself a good reason to visit this up-and-coming site. After all, the chief problem of most networking and "community" sites is that there aren't enough participating users to make them effective; here, the groundwork is in place for true community support. Plus, there are informative articles, start-up advice, and Q & A. You can check out the chat rooms or browse the profiles, which describe the businesses engaged in by other entrepreneurial parents—a great way to glean ideas! There is one thing to keep in mind, however: sentiment aside, this is a money-making venture for its creators. There is a $40 fee to post profiles, and Roberts and Sechrist do occasionally hock their own products and services. Also, many of the community features (most of which can be viewed for free) are membership-based. Still, for aspiring entrepreneurial parents, the potential benefits of this "community" are attractive enough to warrant a visit.

Where To Find/Buy:

On the Internet using the URL: http://www.en-parent.com

Overall Rating
★★★
Definitely worth a visit for entrepreneurial/SOHO parents

Design, Ease Of Use
★★
For-profit areas abound

1–4 Stars

Author:
Co-founders Lisa Roberts and Deborah Sechrist are both work at home moms; Ms. Sechrist is also author of *Wise Women of the Web.*

Publisher:
The Entrepreneurial Parent

Media:
Internet

Principal Subject:
Home Business Guides For Mothers, Women & Couples

Of Interest To:
Parents

V. Working From Home:
The Home-Based Revolution

★★

Overall Rating
★★
Addresses work and family issues, but not particularly original or enlightening

Design, Ease Of Use
★★★
Checklists clarify action steps, text highlights, indexed

1–4 Stars

Author:
Caroline Hull and Tanya Wallace

The two authors have eight children between them (five of whom were under the age of eight at the time this book was conceived) and over ten years of experience in combining children and business.

Publisher:
Carol Publishing Group (Citadel Press Book)

Edition:
1998

Price:
$12.00

Pages/Run Time:
242

ISBN:
0806519932

Media:
Book

Principal Subject:
Home Business Guides For Mothers, Women & Couples

Of Interest To:
Parents

MONEYMAKING MOMS
How Work At Home Can Work For You

Description:
The authors offer an overview of Getting Started, The Balancing Act, and Growing Your Business. While the title addresses Moms, the authors state that this book addresses the choices/opportunities presented to either mothers or fathers who choose to be a stay-at-home working parent. The Getting Started section primarily addresses the establishment of a business foundation which would include choosing a business, establishing a workspace, arranging childcare, researching and obtaining needed financing, establishing an accounting system, and legalizing the business. In The Balancing Act, readers are guided to clarify how the business will fit into their life. Here, there is a focus on time management skills and the development of motivational incentives/alliances. Marketing research is the theme for the last section which is about Growing Your Business. Following research, the authors talk about marketing objectives and guide readers to devise a plan to meet these objectives using marketing tools, the media, charitable activities, and a personal touch while keeping in mind that there are consequences to growing too fast. The authors believe that the guidance in this book will both get readers started and serve as a good reference/reminder once the business is underway.

Evaluation:
Like the work/family lifestyle, this book touches upon both work and family issues without ever absolutely focusing/excluding either. The authors emphasize that professionalism is a prerequisite for a successful business while acknowledging the reality of caring for young children. First readers are reminded to consider themselves as a professional, and guidance is offered regarding how to conduct their business in a professional manner. Consideration is given to the fact that when planning your business, you must also plan for some help with childcare. Suggestions are offered for office space, office equipment, business logo, and part-time childcare possibilities. A cordless telephone is described as indispensable when the commingling of personal and professional life presents a challenge. To help readers achieve a balance between the needs of work and home, the authors identify some suggestions for creating organization and efficiency. Set-up and procedures for both home and office are considered since efficiency in either one benefits both. Further, readers are advised to schedule everything, including time for the unexpected. A Personal Glimpse reveals both daily routines and unexpected experiences that real home-business owners have encountered.

Where To Find/Buy:
Bookstores and libraries.

Home Business Guides For Mothers, Women & Couples

BIZY MOMS

Non-Rated Resource

Description:
In addition to information about books and resources for work-at-home moms, Folger's site offers women an assortment of features for starting a home business. There are 180+ business ideas, "FAQs," message boards, tips from successful "bizy moms," and a list of "scams" to avoid. Folger also offers phone consultations and her own advice column.

Author:
Liz Folger

Ms. Folger is a freelance writer, author and stay at home mom. She is author of *The Stay-At-Home Mom's Guide To Making Money*.

Media:
Internet

Principal Subject:
Home Business Guides For Mothers, Women & Couples

Where To Find/Buy:
On the Internet using the URL: http:// www.bizymoms.com

IDEAS FOR HOME-BASED BUSINESSES

Computer consultant. Business plan writer. Event planner. Resume writer. Mediator. Real estate appraiser. Technical writer. Wedding consultant. These titles represent the diversity of viable home businesses in the new economy.

There are many factors to consider when selecting a home-business: income potential, barriers to entry, market potential, required skills or experience, to name just a few. But the most important factor, and one that is ignored in too many cases, is the level of personal satisfaction it delivers. A home business, like any entrepreneurial venture, will require many hours of labor before you earn your first dime. Once you open for business your work load may swell. If you enjoy what you are doing—not all aspects for sure but that which will absorb most of your time—you are more likely to succeed.

Service Businesses

Home-businesses fall into two broad categories, those offering a service and those selling a product. Service businesses are generally simpler and require less initial investment to start.

Jobs for people who provide services, whether cleaning a home or auditing medical bills, grew eight percent last year, twice the general job growth rate. People's lives are busy and they are more willing to hire someone else to do the tasks they don't have the time to accomplish themselves, such as lawn care. Others are finding that they no longer have the expertise necessary for tasks like preparing their tax return. As the population continues to gray, the need for assistance with routine chores such as pool cleaning, home repair, shopping and meal preparation will further grow the market for these services.

Another trend is the explosion in niche businesses which cater to the needs of small businesses and other self-employed professionals. For example, instead of choosing to establish a business as a generalist, a marketing consultant can specialize in one area, such as direct mail, or work with one type of client, such as shopping centers.

Product Businesses

Product-driven businesses can have steep initial start-up costs but they offer the potential of significant income as well. If you decide to manufacture the goods yourself, your learning curve will include the art and skill required in production as well as managing inventory and selling. Remember that in order to run a successful product-driven business you must sell the product. Are you skilled at making sales presentations? Do cold calls make your palms clammy? You must enjoy selling your product to potential customers, and you must be able to persevere through "nos" to be successful.

Before ramping up business, you should produce a small number of samples and send them to potential customers. Mine the data you receive from this trial run. What did they like or dislike about the product? Would they order more? Chatty customers can provide a wealth of input about everything from the color of the logo to the name of the product. Let them know you appreciate their insights and these contacts may continue to offer valuable feedback.

Traditional product businesses include handicrafts, T-shirts, jewelry and brand products sold through network marketing such as cosmetics or kitchen wares. More recent additions to the mix include gift baskets, software applications and kitchen herbs.

As you sort through the business ideas offered in the following resources, keep in mind that you are not searching for the best home business, you are looking for the best home business for you!

AVOIDING SCAMS

- The adage, "if it sounds too good to be true, it probably isn't" should be kept in mind when sorting through the business opportunity pitches that litter the landscape. Claims that you can make big money by sending away for a crafts kit or envelope stuffing business plan are notorious, but beware any promise of a quick jump to easy street.

- Surf with caution. The Internet has become the latest trolling ground for unscrupulous hucksters hoping to profit from the public's fascination with anything.com. The same rules for careful research, planning and evaluation apply to e-ventures as well.

- While it's wise to take advantage of trends and hot markets, walk away from any business opportunity that is available "for a limited time only." Ignore prodding to "act quickly." Sound business decisions take time.

Ideas For Home-Based Businesses

Overall Rating
★★★★
Well-rounded appraisal of each business, acknowledgment of choice/action paths

Design, Ease Of Use
★★★★
Introduction serves as an instruction booklet; appendix categorizes for indexing

1–4 Stars

Author:
Paul and Sarah Edwards

Paul and Sarah Edwards are the hosts of TV's *Working From Home* with Paul and Sarah Edwards and the authors of *Working From Home*. They provide advice about self-employment and home businesses on CompuServe, the Business Radio Network, and in *Home Office Computing* magazine. They work from their home in California.

Publisher:
Jeremy P. Tarcher/Putnam (Penguin Putnam Inc.)

Edition:
2nd (1994)

Price:
$14.95

Pages/Run Time:
403

ISBN:
0874777844

Media:
Book

Principal Subject:
Ideas For Home-Based Businesses

THE BEST HOME BUSINESSES FOR THE 90s
The Inside Information You Need To Know To Select A Home-Based Business That's Right For You

 Recommended For:
Ideas For Home-Based Businesses

Description:

The authors have chosen businesses based on their research conducted with the Bureau of Labor Statistics, encounters with entrepreneurs through their seminars and publications, and projections derived from sources such as *Futurist* magazine. The Best of the Best meet the following criteria: Real Businesses with a Successful At-Home Track Record, Good Income Potential (full-time employment), Reasonable Ease of Entry, Low or Modest Start-up Costs, Ability to Operate from Home, and Variety: Something for Everyone. Each of the sixty business profiles include a general description of the business, types of customers/clients, and an explanation of what makes it a good business for the '90s. Each business description also includes: Knowledge and Skills You Need to Have, Start-up Costs, Advantages and Disadvantages, Pricing, Potential Earnings, Estimate of Market Potential, Best Ways to Get Business, Related Businesses, Franchises, First Steps, and Where to Turn for Information and Help. Additional businesses that are less common, but likely to become more predominant in this decade, are listed under The Rest of the Best. Guidance for choosing the business that is right for you is offered via several questionnaires.

Evaluation:

A rather lengthy introduction explains the authors' rationale in selecting which businesses are "best" as well the method behind their calculations. For example, Potential Earnings are generally calculated based on full-time hours without employees. However only twenty billable hours are included with the rationale that the average lone entrepreneur can only bill a portion of the time spent working on their business because of other tasks entailed in operating the business. The section, Employee Trainer, further refines the Earnings calculations with the addition of training 100 days per year, a realistic assumption when a business succeeds and needs additional employees to service its clientele. Readers are advised to plan/prepare accordingly. A lesson in the transitory nature of "hot" businesses can be learned by reading the highlights of businesses that have been added or subtracted since the first publication. For example, the 900 number businesses have been eliminated from this edition due to changing regulations that have resulted in increased costs, in combination with declining public use and respect. While maintaining detailed focus on the ninety-five businesses suggestions, The Five Basic Skills Required for All Businesses is acknowledged.

Where To Find/Buy:
Bookstores and libraries.

Ideas For Home-Based Businesses

THE WORK AT HOME SOURCEBOOK

★★★★

 Recommended For:
Ideas For Home-Based Businesses

Overall Rating
★★★★
Clear, thorough, practical

Design, Ease Of Use
★★★★
Well organized, succinct

1–4 Stars

Description:

Arden's guide lists over 450 job opportunities alphabetically under topical headings. Within the more than seventy-five pages entitled "Home Business Opportunities," business titles are found that range from "Automotive Services" to "Travel." For each listing in this section, details include "Franchise, Description, Requirements, Provisions, and Profit Potential." There is another section entitled "Markets for Handcrafts" which offers details for each shop listed regarding items wanted, payment, and instructions. In "Telecommuting And Other Employee Options," companies are listed that employ significant numbers of telecommuters. Here, the author explains who is telecommuting and why. Several companies are covered in greater depth by being featured "Close Up." The section entitled "The Work-at-Home Job Bank" is another diverse listing of opportunities which includes: arts, crafts, computer-based services, office support, working with people, industrial home work, and sales. Readers are also offered a list of educational resources in "Learning at Home to Work at Home." Both an alphabetical and a location index list all of the companies described in this book.

Evaluation:

Arden's directory does an excellent job of providing people interested in working from home with ideas, leads and contacts. It also wades into subjects such as how to contact potential employers. Arden is thorough, but not excessive in conveying information on the many business opportunities presented in her lists. The author has written each individual section according to an easy to follow format, resulting in text that is both concise and substantive. The background information that accompanies each section provides the reader with an insider's view of the particular job. A good example of this occurs in the "Markets for Handcrafts" section where valuable advice on approaching shops is outlined. Another example is in the telecommuting section where background information explains the "big picture" of telecommuting from the corporation's point of view. Since negotiation and creative thinking are often required in establishing a telecommuting position, this section may provide valuable insights for readers trying to convince employers to allow the work-from-home model. This is a terrific resource for anyone who is desiring to work from home, but not necessarily interested in creating their own business.

Where To Find/Buy:

Bookstores and libraries.

Author:
Lynie Arden

Lynie Arden is the author of *Franchises You Can Run From Home* and numerous magazine articles on working from home. She has been a contributing editor for *Home Office Computing* magazine and a columnist for *Income Opportunities* magazine.

Publisher:
Live Oak Publications

Edition:
6th (1996)

Price:
$19.95

Pages/Run Time:
330

ISBN:
0911781145

Media:
Book

Principal Subject:
Ideas For Home-Based Businesses

★★

Overall Rating
★★
Serves as idea generator or resource guide; lacks detail for application

Design, Ease Of Use
★★★
Clear organization and thorough list of resources may offset lack of detail

1–4 Stars

Author:
Priscilla Y. Huff

Priscilla Y. Huff is the author of *101 Best Small Businesses for Women* and *More 101 Best Home-Based Businesses for Women.* She writes frequently for Income Opportunities, Small Business Opportunities, and Spare Time magazines.

Publisher:
Prima Publishing

Edition:
2nd (1998)

Price:
$14.95

Pages/Run Time:
389

ISBN:
0761516514

Media:
Book

Principal Subject:
Ideas For Home-Based Businesses

Of Interest To:
Women

Ideas For Home-Based Businesses

101 BEST HOME-BASED BUSINESSES FOR WOMEN

Description:
Before offering 101 Best Businesses, Huff offers some Home-Based Business Considerations where she highlights the experiences of several women and considers some practical aspects of going into business for yourself. Next, the 101 Best Businesses are introduced and detailed (if applicable) according to the following information: pricing; marketing/advertising methods and tips; essential equipment; training, experience or skills; income; type of business; best customers; helpful tips; and franchise contact. Huff also offers resource information for each job listed. The resource list may include associations, books and publications, home study, and Internet sites. Beyond the detail provided for each business, Additional Business Ideas are suggested. The 101 businesses are arranged according to the following headings: Special Event Services, Home Services, Personal Services, Health Services, Sewing Services, Pet Services, Business-to-Business Services, Entertainment Businesses, Green Businesses, Craft Businesses, Computer Businesses, Food-Related Businesses and Other Businesses which includes engraving, finding service, freelance writing, home art or music school, mail order, sign-painting, and tax preparation service.

Evaluation:
To create her collection of the 101 "best" businesses to consider, Huff researched existing businesses that are run by women. The author uses statistics and individual examples to introduce her belief that owning a home-based business can provide the flexibility that many women need in their roles as wife/mother/employee. While touching upon topics related to preparing and beginning a business, the weight of this book is in its descriptions of successful women-run businesses. The level of detail for each business is impressive. Use this guide as an idea generator, general guide, and research tool. Consider the example of "Tracy" who started out replacing zippers and sewing hems, before her business grew due to "word-of-mouth referrals and her convenient location." Additional information on her business teaches you to expect to earn "$6 to $15 per garment" and that "single men, or working women with expensive wardrobes" are your best customers. To actually create this type business for yourself, you must determine more precisely what you will charge and how you will reach your target market. The specific resources listed in conjunction with each business idea, or the more general business resources at the back of the book provide the further guidance that is necessary to establish an action plan. Although women-owned businesses are listed, the business ideas are not generally gender specific.

Where To Find/Buy:
Bookstores and libraries.

MORE 101 BEST HOME-BASED BUSINESSES FOR WOMEN

Description:

Huff begins by quoting some statistical realities and responding to several myths regarding home-based businesses. In Getting Started, she addresses guidelines for running a business from home, business plans, professional consultations, the Internet, the types of home-business opportunities, and the issue of Scams. For the 101 Home-based business ideas, Huff draws upon individual stories of real businesses. Each story is enhanced by information regarding estimated startup costs; pricing; marketing and advertising; essential equipment; recommended training, experience, or skills; income potential; best customers; success tips; and franchises, distributorships, and licenses. Additional information may include related associations, books and publications; home study courses, business startup guides, software or websites. Business ideas fall into one of the following headings: Pet and Animal, Business-to-Business, Children's, Computer and Internet, Creative, Entertainment, Environmental and Green, Food-Related, Health-Related, Home, Baby Boomer and Senior, Personal, Specialty Travel, and Word. Also included: Glossary of Business Terms, Frequently Asked Questions, Women's Business Centers, and Miscellaneous Sources of Help.

Evaluation:

Citing various statistics, Huff conveys that the work-at-home lifestyle is a growing trend; this is especially true for women who may have a great need for flexibility, such as single parents. In a discussion of certain persistent myths related to home-based businesses, Huff points out that it is vital to thoroughly research before starting your business, that the self-employed typically work longer hours, and that entrepreneurship is not for everyone. Having written this book "to suggest possibilities and give you options of entrepreneurial ideas that you may not have considered," Huff does not go into great detail in the "Getting Started" section. Instead, she dedicates the majority of this book to detailing 101 individual business ideas that she has discovered in her research. Some of the ideas are accompanied by an individual's personal success story, while other ideas are explained without mention of any individual. These business ideas may inspire readers to convert business/hobby skills into a business of their own. To implement any of these business ideas, readers would need to follow Huff's advice for extensive research. This book does not offer a detailed account of the process for choosing, preparing, establishing, and growing a business.

Where To Find/Buy:

Bookstores and libraries.

Overall Rating
★★
Limited depth; serves as an introduction to the process of creating a business

Design, Ease Of Use
★★★
Clear organization and thorough list of resources may offset lack of detail

1–4 Stars

Author:
Priscilla Y. Huff

Priscilla Y. Huff is the bestselling author of *101 Best Home-Based Businesses for Women*. She writes frequently about work-at-home issues, including articles for *Small Business Opportunities* and *Income Opportunities* magazines.

Publisher:
Prima Publishing

Edition:
1998

Price:
$14.95

Pages/Run Time:
438

ISBN:
0761512691

Media:
Book

Principal Subject:
Ideas For Home-Based Businesses

Of Interest To:
Women

Ideas For Home-Based Businesses

Overall Rating
★★
Great for business ideas but lacking in how-to advice

Design, Ease Of Use
★★
Desperately needs better search engines!

1–4 Stars

Author:
Julie and Tommy Frost, publishers of YourHomeBiz.com, began the website in 1997 to help people start and grow their own home based business. The Frosts are also representatives for I.D.E.A. Concepts, a Network Marketing Company.

Publisher:
Julie and Tommy Frost

Media:
Internet

Principal Subject:
Ideas For Home-Based Businesses

Secondary Subject:
Setting Up And Running A Home-Based Business

YOURHOMEBIZ.COM

Description:

Publishers Julie and Tommy Frost designed their website to help new entrepreneurs start and grow a home based business. Each of the site's many features are introduced on the home page: the database of hundreds of home business ideas, the archive of 65+ articles, the Business Opportunity Section, Places of Interest, the Information Marketplace. The database of business ideas is arranged alphabetically by business name; users can search by clicking on a letter of the alphabet. "A," for example, begins with Accountant, Adventure Tourism, and Advertising Copywriter. A brief description of the business follows each title, along with a link to a Recommended Reading resource. In the archive of articles, visitors will find advice and information on a wide-range of topics, including financing, marketing, networking, and success stories. Classified ads for home-based businesses are listed in the Business Opportunity Section, while Places of Interest offers annotated links to related how-to sites and websites of home-businesses currently in operation. For-sale business equipment and services are detailed in The Information Marketplace. Visitors can also subscribe to a free weekly e-mail newsletter for additional input.

Evaluation:

The key to getting the most out of this website is to visit only the worthwhile sections and religiously circumvent the rest. The Frosts are representatives of a Network Marketing Company (a variation on MLM), so visitors must be wary; the site abounds with ambiguous and suspicious solicitations. Avoid the Business Opportunity Section (unless you're interested in MLMs), avoid the Information Marketplace (which sells products), and avoid responding to the Frosts' claim that they can help you personally if you "send for information." So why go to this website at all? For one reason: the database of hundreds of home-business ideas. The database is difficult to browse (there's no search engine, so users must search alphabetically by title), but the titles listed are all first-rate options, ranging from the unusual (Air Quality Consultant) to the more traditional (Answering Service). Plus, though the description of each business is brief, there's a direct link to a Recommended Reading resource. Though some of the Recommended resources are book titles, most are online articles, so you get instant gratification. The site's 65+ articles are good to browse through too, but since you can't search them either, finding step-by-step how-to advice is near impossible. Come for the business ideas, stay for a few articles, but skip the rest.

Where To Find/Buy:

On the Internet using the URL: http://www.YourHomeBiz.com

Ideas For Home-Based Businesses

203 HOME-BASED BUSINESSES THAT WILL MAKE YOU RICH

Description:

Hicks has written this book for BWBs (Beginning Wealth Builders) who have the desire to achieve at least a six-figure income. He begins by offering BWBs guidelines that apply to topics such as product/service suppliers, financing, and publicity. An entire chapter is devoted to conveying the advice to Market Directly to Customers and Grow Rich. Also, there are several types of business that warrant their own chapter: Export Your Way to Great Wealth, Import Riches Can Be Yours, Make Big Money in High-Discount and Liquidation Sales, Find Hidden Success in "Paper" and Other Real Estate, Stake Your Claim in the Multi-Billion-Dollar Internet Market, Provide Quality Child Care and Prosper, Sell Information and Grow Enormously Rich, and Do Good Works and Get Money That Never Need be Repaid. Hicks says that most BWBs' biggest challenge is finding startup money. In the chapter devoted to this topic, he strongly encourages BWBs to use OPM (Other People's Money) and offers ideas on how to do it. The final chapter contains a table that outlines over 200 product or service providing businesses. For each business included, Hicks indicates needed sales methods, business equipment, startup time, and startup cost.

Evaluation:

Due to the strong salesmanship that Hicks employs for his own products and services throughout the entire text, readers may question the integrity of the information conveyed. Hicks begins in the introduction by encouraging readers to "come with me—your good and dependable friend—and I'll show you how to grow rich in your own business today. I'll guide you every step of the way-in person, by mail, by phone, or by fax. Call me and I'll personally answer on the first ring. Your questions will be answered quickly and clearly. You'll start to bring in a steadily rising income month after month." Doubts aside, the guidelines/tips offered throughout this text are likely to be helpful. A good example of this is in "Do Good Works . . ." which focuses on obtaining grant money that is not commonly known about, but often available. Qualifying businesses would be those that provide help to others such as weatherproofing aging homes in a low-income community, or running a recreational program for local youths. All of the chapters on business ideas are conveyed in a "how-to" format which is informative, but does necessarily consider the individual. The title of this book is a bit misleading in that there are more than 203 businesses suggested, but a much smaller number are actually covered in detail.

Where To Find/Buy:

Bookstores and libraries.

Overall Rating
★
The sales pitches throughout this book overshadow its strengths

Design, Ease Of Use
★★★
Clearly conveyed ideas and strategies including worksheets and tables; indexed

1–4 Stars

Author:
Tyler G. Hicks

Tyler G. Hicks is president of International Wealth Success Inc. and the director of a large lending organization in New York city. He is the author of many bestselling small business books, including *101 Great Home Businesses You Can Start (and Succeed in) for Under $1,000*.

Publisher:
Prima Publishing

Edition:
1998

Price:
$14.95

Pages/Run Time:
342

ISBN:
0761512594

Media:
Book

Principal Subject:
Ideas For Home-Based Businesses

V. Working From Home:
The Home-Based Revolution

Overall Rating

★

Inadequate detail not compensated by resource suggestions

Design, Ease Of Use

★

Repetitive, poorly edited

1–4 Stars

Author:

Dan Ramsey

Dan Ramsey is the author of more than 25 books on small business opportunities. He has also written articles for leading business magazines on a variety of topics. Dan is currently president of Ramsey Business Strategies, a consulting service specializing in helping small businesses grow.

Publisher:

Career Press

Edition:

1997

Price:

$14.99

Pages/Run Time:

191

ISBN:

1564142639

Media:

Book

Principal Subject:

Ideas For Home-Based Businesses

Ideas For Home-Based Businesses

101 BEST HOME BUSINESSES

Description:

Ramsey defines a "cottage company" as a home business that profits by adding value to the lives of customers. The cottage companies that he suggests are based on interviews and case histories. Each suggestion is categorized into one of the following skill areas: Best businesses using craft or physical skills, Best professional businesses, and Best service businesses. Chapter one focuses on individual skills and what types of businesses a particular skill set might imply. Then, Ramsey advises readers of the eight steps to starting a cottage company, and offers some elaboration on business financing and legalities. In chapter two, Ramsey shares 10 Steps To Success in addition to discussing the questions that "all cottage companies must answer." In Part Two, each of the 101 cottage company suggestions are detailed according to the following questions: What will I be doing? What will I need to start? Who will my customers be? How much should I charge? How much will I make? and How can I get started? In Part Three, Ramsey cites sources for free/inexpensive business counseling and tax publications. He also offers suggestions for low-budget record keeping and publicity. Sample worksheets and reports for evaluating a cottage company comprise the appendix.

Evaluation:

Similar to many books on the market that list one hundred or more business ideas, Ramsey has devoted the majority of these 191 pages to his cottage company suggestions. The introductory section conveys general information that is not particularly insightful. The 8 Steps To Starting Your Home Business are somewhat obvious: know your business, your customers, the law, and your assets as you work to add real value, keep good customers, manage money wisely and continually improve. Specific suggestions for cottage companies are often no more enlightening than the introduction. Under "Handyperson service," Ramsey points out that work requiring "a hauling truck and lots of skills and tools" will pay more than other jobs requiring less of these assets. While Ramsey declares that "the book will motivate you with examples of how others have succeeded with their home business," he does not include personal stories. Rather, the cottage company suggestions appear to be generalizations of Ramsey's research. The Contents identifies the Appendix as "Worksheets for full-time home entrepreneurs"; while the Appendix section itself is entitled "Worksheets for weekend entrepreneurs." Considering that Ramsey has presented businesses that can be "launched with as few as 20 hours a week," the implication may be that either the full-time or the weekend entrepreneur can succeed.

Where To Find/Buy:

Bookstores and libraries.

Ideas For Home-Based Businesses

HOME BASED BUSINESS OCCUPATIONAL HANDBOOK

Description:

The information contained here is derived from NAHBB membership files, letters, and telephone inquires compiled since 1984. This text was created to introduce a list of over 175 home based occupations that others have successfully managed from home. A brief overview of each listing includes: the service provided or product produced, customers and markets, skills and work/life experience required of the business owner, and an estimate of capital investment required to get started. Each listing is also assigned a Home Business Identity Classification (HBIC) number which can be used to access detailed information by either calling the NAHBB or visiting the U.S.A. Home Based Business Information Superhighway Internet site that has been created by the NAHBB. An introduction to these business listings asks readers to consider various aspects of working from the home, and to consider the choice to become an entrepreneur or "intrapreneur." Ten Reasons Why Home Managed Businesses Fail, References and Bibliography, Small Business Organizations, and a section explaining the NAHBB member and subscriber services are also included. Registration information for NAHBB is also offered.

Evaluation:

The presence of an occupation on The List of Home Based Businesses is primarily a designation of viability. Descriptions for each listing do not offer a lot of information that readers will find helpful in actually starting one of these businesses from home. The HBIC number assigned to each business, if indexed by a member of the NAHBB, is said to provide access to detailed information for the listing. But the information in this text is neither specific or thorough. For example, consider Portrait Photography which offers "Skills: Photography courses in high school, college, or private institutes necessary" and "Capital Investment: $2,500–$10,000." Several of the listings are not even presented according to the customary format which includes a brief (but individual) description of the Business Product/Service, Skills, Experience, and Capital Investment. Professional Consultant is one business that lacks any particular information beyond "See HBIC: 2510, 75612, 45100, 25000." This is not particularly helpful direction to a purchaser of this book because there is no HBIC numerical-based index available here. The value of this book is in explaining the NAHBB and describing the services it provides to its members. There are much better resources for researching potential businesses.

Where To Find/Buy:

On the Internet using the URL: http://usahomebusiness.com/book.htm

Overall Rating

★

Very brief/general occupational descriptions

Design, Ease Of Use

★

Consistent format, but inadequate depth and indexing

1–4 Stars

Author:

National Association of Home Based Businesses, Inc. (NAHBB)

NAHBB, founded in 1984, is an organization that provides support and development services to home managed businesses. This organization is establishing an Information Superhighway that will connect home-based businesses to a private database.

Publisher:

Kendall/Hunt Publishing Company

Edition:

1996

Price:

$21.95

Pages/Run Time:

111

ISBN:

0787216852

Media:

Book

Principal Subject:

Ideas For Home-Based Businesses

Ideas For Home-Based Businesses

BUSINESS OPPORTUNITIES CLASSIFIEDS ONLINE

Non-Rated Resource

Desription:
Famous for its enormous database of classified ads, "BOC Online" allows potential SOHO entrepreneurs to browse for small or home-based business opportunities or just fish for ideas. There's also a SOHO Start-Up Center, with articles on success strategies and the "basics" of starting, QuickLink web guides to related resources, and details on products and services.

Publisher:
Premier Publications

Media:
Internet

Principal Subject:
Ideas For Home-Based Businesses

Where To Find/Buy:
On the Internet using the URL: http://www.boconline.com

HOMEWORKS.COM

Non-Rated Resource

Desription:
The Edwards' site offers aspiring entrepreneurs 5 free lists of business ideas: '98 Best Home Businesses, 100 Computer Based Businesses, 1600 Self Employment Careers, Home-Based Franchises, and Business Opportunities (classifieds). Other features include a profile of the Best Home Business of the Month, links, and excerpts from the Edwards' print resources.

Author:
Paul & Sarah Edwards

The Edwards published their first book, "Working From Home," in 1985. Since then, they have been considered "self-employment experts." The Edwards are also the authors of "Secrets of Self-Employment" and "Finding Your Perfect Work."

Publisher:
Paul & Sarah Edwards

Media:
Internet

Principal Subject:
Ideas For Home-Based Businesses

Where To Find/Buy:
On the Internet using the URL: http://homeworks.com

INSIDER ADVICE

VI

SUCCESS STRATEGIES

We all learn differently. Some readers are well served by a detailed, step-by-step guide to building a business. (These are the folks that read the manual before using new software). Others enjoy learning by living vicariously through life stories. The books in this chapter are written for those who enjoy the strategy genre. These readers are apt to find their own pathway to success by learning from the "gurus" of the self-employed community. The authors are successful entrepreneurs or consultants who have distilled their real life experience into pithy tips and insider advice. If the plodding, textbook style of most how-to-build-your-business guides turns you off, you may want to pick up one of these. As a whole they are practical, street smart and quick hitting.

Although they address peripheral issues as well (How can I manage my time?), at the heart of these books is the question: What makes a successful entrepreneur? Given the high failure rate for new businesses, anyone who hopes to navigate to profitability must arm themselves with a basic set of skills. And most resources focus on the "nuts-and-bolts" of starting a business because they are the easiest part of entrepreneurial development to teach. Anyone with a desire to learn can be taught the basics. But what about the instincts needed for success as a soloist? How can one learn to develop an entrepreneurial mind set?

Experience is surely the best teacher, but another way to hone your instincts is by learning from those on top of their game. I call this section "Success Strategies" because the resources you'll find here have one central theme: entrepreneurial success. Since each writer takes a different approach to that theme, you should use the evaluations to determine which author and which approach appeals to you. Used in tandem with how-to resources, these books can be constructive tools for developing yourself as an entrepreneur.

A Success Strategy From My Mentor

I once worked with Norton Simon, a great philanthropist, and a genius. He was the owner of Hunt-Wesson Foods. I hired many of the people who became executives for the company. One thing Mr. Simon demanded was that every person I hired needed to pass an examination with a high score. And the person needed to be introduced to Mr. Simon for his final okay. By today's standards, this hiring process would probably not be legal, but it was clear to me that the company he built, made up of very smart people, gave him a competitive edge. The company grew from $120,000 in sales to $3 billion. Even the lower level persons hired were evaluated at a very high level. The lesson to cull is this: if the time comes to grow your company, surround yourself with bright, intelligent people. This philosophy has worked for me during the 30 years or so that I've been solo.

★★★★

Overall Rating
★★★★
Entertaining, insightful guide to self-styled success; a delightful read

Design, Ease Of Use
★★★★
Intertwines advice, success stories, personal anecdotes and humor; smart format

1–4 Stars

Author:
Dan S. Kennedy

Mr. Kennedy is President of Empire Communications Corporation and of LifeTech Broadcasting Corporation. His other books include *No B.S. Time Management for Entrepreneurs* and *How to Make Millions with Your Ideas*.

Publisher:
Dutton

Edition:
1997

Price:
$22.95

Pages/Run Time:
186

ISBN:
0525941983

Media:
Book

Principal Subject:
Success Strategies

Of Interest To:
Young Entrepreneurs

HOW TO SUCCEED IN BUSINESS BY BREAKING ALL THE RULES
A Plan For Entrepreneurs

Recommended For:
Success Strategies

Description:
Before the book begins, Kennedy introduces 21 "myths and lies" conventional wisdom would have you believe are the "keys" to entrepreneurial success. Among these myths are such clichés as "mind your manners," "be original," "keep your nose to the grindstone," and "think positive and life will be wonderful." These are the rules Kennedy believes should be broken. To prove his point (and to help entrepreneurs), his guide combines advice, personal anecdotes, and stories of real-life rebels who used contrarian strategies to succeed. Each of the 18 chapters illustrates one such strategy. Chapters debunk The Myth of the Born Salesman, Or Born Anything, and others demonstrate that "being rude" can be an asset, and suggest that you should Forget (Almost) Everything You've Ever Been Told About Persistence. Other contrarian success strategies include "give up forced positive thinking," use arrogance and self-promotion to advance, forget about the conventions of marketing (they no longer apply), and forget about "creativity as it is commonly perceived." Contrarian strategies for young entrepreneurs are also provided; the last chapter offers portraits of Kennedy's favorite contrarians, i.e. Ayn Rand, Walt Disney, Bill Bennett.

Evaluation:
Kennedy as an entrepreneurial advisor is, in many ways, a study in contradictions. On the one hand, he avidly denies the possibility of winning strategies or rules for success. On the other hand, he spends a considerable amount of time writing his own strategies. This book is a perfect example: it debunks conventional success strategies only to replace them with modified versions. Actually, the contrarian strategies he espouses are mostly the sort of unspoken truths we know but rarely acknowledge. For example: that arrogance (supreme self-confidence) attracts more people than it repels, that creativity isn't necessary to business success, and that "going slow" isn't better—just slower. These may not be edicts approved of by polite society but they ring true. Where Kennedy's, and the book's, contradictions vanish (or fuse) is in the philosophical heart of this work: the implicit, and often empirically demonstrated, belief that success comes from trusting your instincts (and yourself) above all else. Advice, even solid, well-researched advice, has its limits. (The irony that this insight comes from an advice giver is part of Kennedy's charm, as well as his trustworthiness.) This is a delightful, insightful, empowering guide that works on two levels: as a strategist and as a confidence-builder that enables you to leave "strategies" behind.

Where To Find/Buy:
Bookstores and libraries.

NO B.S. TIME MANAGEMENT FOR ENTREPRENEURS

 Recommended For:
Success Strategies

Description:

Time is money. It's also the key to success, according to author Kennedy, who believes that effective time management is the single greatest skill an entrepreneur can possess. He explains why he values time so much—and why you should, too—in the first chapter, which includes a formula for determining how much money your time is worth per hour. By figuring out the literal worth of your time, Kennedy hopes you'll approach the rest of the book with new vigor; after all, now you know how much money you're wasting when you waste time. Each of the following chapters focuses on one strategy for taking control of and managing your time. Chapters 2–5 help you stop time-sucking vampires (such as the "Mr. Do-You-Have-A-Minute?" and "Ms. Meeting"), field interruptions, and develop reliable self-discipline. The "Ten Time Management Techniques Worth Using" are detailed in Chapter 6. Chapters 7–9 address making the most of business trips, handling "avalanches" of information, and delegating. Tips and ideas for building productivity and achieving peak personal productivity, as well as answers to common questions about peak personal productivity, make up most of the final 5 chapters.

Evaluation:

For the most part, there aren't any revelations in this slim guide; the techniques Kennedy espouses are the same techniques you've heard before (and still haven't applied). Making appointments with yourself, ignoring phone/fax/e-mail interruptions, "laying down the law" with employees and associates who consistently "waste" your time, and clearing your mind of worries in order to focus 100% on the task at hand are "classics" in the time management repertoire. If put into practice, these strategies, and the others described, will be effective; that they're not "new" is irrelevant. What sets this book apart from other, similar themed resources is the author: his attitude, his vehemence about the topic, his personality. As is the case in all of Kennedy's works, his personality comes through loud and clear, and his genuine belief that time management is of utmost importance to success energizes his text and the reader. Don't look here for a nice career counselor feeding his audience polite rhetoric; he's a strict but noble drill sergeant who's going to whip you into shape (for your own good). It should be noted that Kennedy is very money oriented. His eye is always on the "bottom line;" much of his philosophy is based on the old adage "time is money." He can inspire anyone, but he'll inspire like-minded readers even more.

Where To Find/Buy:

Bookstores and libraries.

Overall Rating
★★★★
Practical help for mastering the crucial element of time management

Design, Ease Of Use
★★★★
Energetic tone, a quick read

1–4 Stars

Author:
Dan Kennedy

Mr. Kennedy is President of Empire Communications Corporation, a mail-order marketing firm, and of LifeTech Broadcasting Corporation, a producer of infomercials. His other books include *No B.S. Sales Success* and *How to Make Millions with Your Ideas.*

Publisher:
Self-Counsel Press

Edition:
1996

Price:
$8.95

Pages/Run Time:
108

ISBN:
1551800330

Media:
Book

Principal Subject:
Success Strategies

★★★

Overall Rating
★★★
45 smart strategies for financial success

Design, Ease Of Use
★★★★
Entertaining; combines stories and "straight talk" effectively

1–4 Stars

Author:
Dan S. Kennedy

Mr. Kennedy is President of Empire Communications Corporation, a mail-order marketing firm, and of LifeTech Broadcasting Corporation, a producer of infomercials. His other books include *No B.S. Sales Success* and *How to Make Millions with Your Ideas.*

Publisher:
Plume/Penguin

Edition:
1996

Price:
$13.95

Pages/Run Time:
264

ISBN:
0452273161

Media:
Book

Principal Subject:
Success Strategies

VI. Insider Advice

Success Strategies

HOW TO MAKE MILLIONS WITH YOUR IDEAS
An Entrepreneur's Guide

Description:
It's Kennedy's belief that success is "chaotic," rather than methodical. Entrepreneurial success, he says, comes from "grabbing this idea from here, that piece of information from there," not from following a single formula. Thus, his book contains 45 Millionaire-Maker Strategies that can be grabbed, combined, recombined, and otherwise appropriated on an individual basis by the reader. (Strategies are illustrated by stories from 50+ successful entrepreneurs.) To begin, Kennedy identifies the eight "highest probability areas of opportunity," such as direct marketing, in Chapter 1. Chapter 2 looks at ways to turn an ordinary business into "an extraordinary moneymaking machine." Chapters 3–4 address inventing, finding, reinventing and gaining control of profitable products. In Chapters 5–6, there's advice on service businesses and creating systems/franchises. The money making advantages of direct marketing (traditional and electronic) are espoused in Chapters 7–8. Chapters 9–12 cover information products, publicity and promotion, selling your business, and the "ultimate" strategy: synergy. A directory of resources, including product sources and resources on distribution channels, comprises the final chapter.

Evaluation:
In the pantheon of entrepreneurs who offer entrepreneurial advice, Kennedy is definitely one of the brightest stars. One imagines, when reading his books, the charisma he must have in person, the sheer strength of his personality, his dynamism—all of which come through in his written work. There's a wonderful mix of candid narrative, client examples, and what might best be described as "no B.S. straight talk" in this guide to business success. Kennedy admits that he can't give you a connect-the-dots strategy for success, no one can. At the same time, he believes that, if you have a vision, a million dollar idea, or the self-determination to start a business, you can succeed—but the onus is on you. The strategies explained in this book are not concrete strategies, but malleable clay; you can (and must) twist, knead and squeeze them into the shape that fits your needs. The real-life stories from entrepreneurs, which provide a couple of illustrations for each "general" strategy, demonstrate how. With 45 strategies, all of which can be mixed and matched, Kennedy's assertion that at least one will work for you is conceivable. There are no recipes for financial success, but the ingredients are all here. This is a smart book for smart people with moxie and determination.

Where To Find/Buy:
Bookstores and libraries.

Success Strategies

THE E MYTH REVISITED
Why Most Small Businesses Don't Work And What To Do About It

Description:

Why do so many small businesses fail? Answering this question and providing a solution are Gerber's goals in this guide to transforming any business into a success. Part 1 introduces the concept of the E Myth, the antecedent of entrepreneurial failure. The E Myth is America's Entrepreneurial Myth; basically, it is the mistaken belief that because you're good at your work you will be good at running a business related to that work. That a hairdresser can run a hair salon, etc. What business owners don't realize (until it's too late) is that, as an entrepreneur, you'll be doing the work you do well plus several jobs you know nothing about. You will be Entrepreneur, Manager, and Technician, and that leads to burnout, frustration, demise. While the first half of Part 1 expounds on this problem, the second half offers the first steps toward a solution. The solution takes concrete form in Parts 2 and 3, which discuss lessons learned from the Turn-Key Revolution and the Franchise Prototype (read McDonald's) and their application: The Business Development Process. The Development Process includes techniques for pinpointing your Primary Aim, Strategic Objective, Organizational Strategy, Management Strategy, and Systems Strategy.

Evaluation:

Based on the author's 20+ years of experience as a consultant for small businesses, this book (a revision of the original "The E Myth") is a 3-part strategy for overhauling both your business and your work philosophy. Its objective isn't just to help your business succeed financially, but to help you enjoy your business. Modeled primarily on the Franchise Prototype of Ray Kroc, franchiser of McDonald's, Gerber makes a compelling argument for working on your business, rather than in it. In brief, the idea is to help business owners create a system for their business that will enable the business to run itself and to create a work philosophy wherein the product is the business, not the commodity you sell. Incorporated into this mix are heavy doses of self-assessment; the Development Process is based on the owner's personal Primary Aim. Gerber communicates these concepts and his techniques clearly, alternating between straight explanatory text and an on-going dialogue with "Sarah," a burned-out business owner whose transformation to successful, happy entrepreneur epitomizes the book's goals. Believable and full of gems—like the reminder that it's not products people buy but feelings (as Revlon's founder said: we make cosmetics, they buy hope)—this is a worthwhile read that could help you start your business "the right way."

Where To Find/Buy:

Bookstores and libraries.

Overall Rating
★★★
A system for making small businesses successful; smart and believable

Design, Ease Of Use
★★★
Easy to read; Gerber alternates between plain text and Q & A-style dialogue

1–4 Stars

Author:
Michael E. Gerber
Mr. Gerber is the Chairman of Gerber Business Development Corporation, the company he founded in 1977. Since 1977, the company had helped 15,000 small and emerging business clients positively transform their businesses.

Publisher:
Harper Business

Edition:
1995

Price:
$15.00

Pages/Run Time:
268

ISBN:
0887307280

Media:
Book

Principal Subject:
Success Strategies

Overall Rating
★★
Emphasis fairly restricted to the topics of vision and business plan

Design, Ease Of Use
★★★★
Central message/philosophy thoroughly conveyed among several formats

1–4 Stars

Author:
Marc Allen

Marc Allen writes from his own experience as founder and president of a successful visionary business. Twenty years ago, he co-founded New World Library. He has guided the company from a small start-up operation with no capital to a major contributor in the independent publishing world.

Publisher:
New World Library

Edition:
1997

Price:
$12.95

Pages/Run Time:
171

ISBN:
1577310195

Media:
Book

Principal Subject:
Success Strategies

Secondary Subject:
Reflective Guides To Creating The Work And Life You Want

VI. Insider Advice

Success Strategies

VISIONARY BUSINESS
An Entrepreneur's Guide To Success

Description:
Readers will find the Keys of Visionary Business presented in the form of a quasi-novel; a Summary of business wisdom/advice accompanies each section of the fictional story. The story begins as the author is struggling to get a new business off the ground. Office space has been obtained, sparse furnishings have been pulled-together, and several informal partners and employees have worked together in the business. Only a vague description of the business has surfaced when Bernie arrives as a potential investor. Bernie asks to see a business plan, but at this point in the story no business plan has been developed. Consequently, Bernie takes the business under his wing and presents management consulting philosophies/suggestions that lead to the clarification of a business vision and a business plan. Bernie does eventually invest in the company and continues to be a mentor. As this fictional business evolves, The Keys to a Visionary Business are revealed. There is a continuation of this story in the Epilogue; here, the message is that "the ultimate purpose of visionary business is to transform the world by doing what you love to do." An Afterward lists Twenty-five Principles and Practices of Visionary Business.

Evaluation:
This is an interesting approach to conveying strategies and philosophies of business practice; this story clearly illustrates the difference between management-by-crisis and management-by-goals. Before Bernie enters the picture, the company is guided by crisis. Bernie, a fictionalized character who is both shrewd and spiritual, teaches the young start-up that a vision is the grounding force of a business. And the business plan serves as a guide to realize the vision. The challenge to research and create a business plan based on the vision are conveyed, as are the rewards of the struggle. In keeping with good business practice, Bernie continually directs a revisiting/revising of the business plan as the business and environment evolve. The business relies on this framework to overcome adversity, devise an employee handbook, establish legal safeguards, plan and evaluate sales/profits and more. Following this path, a win/win definition of success is achievable. The underlying vision is likely to range beyond making money; an epilogue continues the story/summary to consider the global implications of business choices to "transform the world." In the introduction, Allen clarifies that "this is a fictionalized account of a true story;" and he also pays tribute to Bernie Nemerov for investing $80,000 in a start-up company.

Where To Find/Buy:
Bookstores and libraries.

Success Strategies

THE STREET SMART ENTREPRENEUR
133 Tough Lessons I Learned The Hard Way

Description:

Despite the fact that Goltz grew his framing business from $70,000 in sales in 1978 to $10 million in sales in 1997, he readily admits that, in the first 15 years, he made "every mistake in the book." He learned business lessons the hard way: through experience. With this collection of 133 "tough lessons," he hopes to impart his hard-won knowledge to beginning entrepreneurs, to help them succeed. The lessons are divided into 7 parts/chapters: starting up, being the boss, management, customer service, marketing, finance, and administration (i.e. taxes). Individual lessons contain 3 sections: "What I Used To Think" (common entrepreneur myth/mistake), "Nobody Told Me . . ." (the reality, what Goltz learned), and the one-sentence lesson. For example, lesson #4 deals with competition. Goltz "used to think" that "the best competition is no competition," but "nobody told [him]" that competition is the primary indicator of demand. (Advice on conducting a competition analysis follows.) Thus, lesson #4 is: "It's easier to steal a share of the market than to create a market." Other lessons include taking advantage of remnant space for advertising, practicing controlled growth, making money by discounting bills, and keeping employees happy.

Evaluation:

To get a clear picture of the content of this guide, imagine 133 fortune cookies. Since the lessons are pithy one-liners, that's an apt analogy: these lessons are "fortunes" for entrepreneurs. Lesson #9: "Going into business with friends just because they are your friends is like betting on a horse just because you like the name." Lesson #106: "Pricing is critical. Discounting can be a critical mistake." Lesson #130: "Great companies have great computer systems." Though these lessons, and the others Goltz provides, may be "true," they're rendered practically useless when substantiated by only a couple of paragraphs of generalized advice. The lesson on computer systems, for instance, offers a quick look at the benefits of computers, i.e. maintaining customer databases, but includes no advice on choosing a computer system, software, hardware, etc. This isn't the resource for how-to tips on starting up, marketing, or finance; it simply isn't explicit enough. However, there are two sections where the lessons, while still brief, are of value: Being the Boss and Management. Here, the explanations are more specific, citing Gotlz' personal experience, and thus lend the lessons greater credence. There are also some genuine insights, especially regarding managing/hiring employees.

Where To Find/Buy:

Bookstores and libraries.

Overall Rating
★★
Bright ideas without follow-through; too pithy. Some valuable management tips.

Design, Ease Of Use
★★★
133 lessons all laid out the same way; each lesson is 1–2 pages long

1–4 Stars

Author:
Jay Goltz, with Jody Oesterreicher

Mr. Goltz founded Artists' Frame Service in 1978, the year he graduated from college. His business is now the largest retail, custom picture framing facility in the nation. Goltz is also a frequent public speaker; his "Boss School" seminars teach better business techniques.

Publisher:
Addicus

Edition:
1998

Price:
$14.95

Pages/Run Time:
235

ISBN:
188603933X

Media:
Book

Principal Subject:
Success Strategies

RESOURCES FOR NETWORKING, SUPPORT, & ADVICE

Exhilarating. Freeing. Empowering. Lucrative. These are some of the words soloists use to describe their chosen path. However, stick around long enough and you're apt to hear less positive adjectives as well. Lonely. Frustrating. Isolating. Overwhelming. The resources that follow aim to help soloists feel more of the former, and less of the latter.

The several dozen resources we've gathered can help you with the often neglected areas of support, networking and advice. Most are websites, the "cafes" of the new millennium. What can you do online? Aside from assisting in your daily business operations, the Net can provide connections to other soloists who share your interests. Perhaps you'll want to confer with other business owners like yourself, discuss ideas, find a mentor. Or perhaps you'll just want to chat with someone.

For networking (a necessity for finding clients/customers) there are networking websites, where people with similar work interests can connect online, and resources for locating business and professional associations. Networking websites are still up-and-coming. They don't yet yield the same results as traditional, person-to-person networking, but they are definitely worth a try. Business and professional associations are one of the premier avenues for networking; by joining, you can both make contacts and learn from others in your industry.

There are dozens of possibilities for support. If you need financing, you could go to SBA Online (the Small Business Administration, which details a variety of government loans and programs), or to the book "Free Help From Uncle Sam to Start Your Own Business." To contact a government agency, visit the U.S. Business Advisor site: it includes direct links to the IRS, EPA, FCC, SSA and more. If you're searching online for a specific business topic, there are several web guides you can use, like Biz Pro Web, Yahoo!, and the Smart Business Supersite. Want a list of all the publications and resources pertaining to your industry? There are guides for that, too: "The Working Solo Sourcebook" and "Women's Business Resource Guide."

If it's up-to-date advice you seek, you'll find that here as well. Advice-oriented resources include Fast Company Online, a cutting-edge "new business" magazine, the Idea Cafe, and Success Online. There's also special advice for women (i.e. WomenCONNECT.com), for parents (i.e. WAHM: Work-At-Home-Moms), and for minorities (i.e. Minority Business Entrepreneur). For expert advice, SCORE (Service Corps of Retired Executives) offers free, 24-hour e-mail counseling.

As anyone who has been self-employed for more than a week has discovered, working for yourself can be a lot of work! Whether you are a small business owner, operate a home-based business, or sell yourself as a consultant or freelancer, being CEO and COO (and perhaps everyone else in your company) can be stressful. When you are the business, keeping your business alive and healthy means taking care of YOU. Feeling connected to others in your situation can alleviate the stress of being a soloist. These resources represent a library of knowledge and thousands of real-people contacts. Take advantage of them.

Remember, even though you're going solo, you don't have to do it all alone.

★★★★

Overall Rating
★★★★
Excellent! Web guide, newsgroups, articles, networking, expert help and more!

Design, Ease Of Use
★★★★
The home page explains it all; navigating is a snap

I–4 Stars

Author:
Craig Sonnenberg

BizProWeb's creator and editor, Craig Sonnenberg, is a small business owner. Mr. Sonnenberg's goal is to create a virtual library of business resources.

Publisher:
BizProWeb

Media:
Internet

Principal Subject:
Resources For Networking, Support & Advice

Of Interest To:
Racial/Ethnic Minorities

BIZPROWEB
The Business & Professionals' Web Site

 Recommended For:
Resources For Networking, Support & Advice

Description:
Each of BizProWeb's 6 main areas are introduced on its home page: Websites, Newsgroups, Shareware, Features, and Discussion Forums. Together, these areas comprise over 700 pages of links, information, and resources for self-employed professionals and business owners. The directory of websites is organized into such categories as Entrepreneurship, Legal, Small Business, Minority Business Resources, and Women in Business. Paragraph-length descriptions of each site accompany the direct links, and superior sites are singled out with a "four star" rating. The directory of newsgroups is similarly organized into such categories as Consulting, Disabilities, Management, and Facilitators. In Shareware, users will find links to sites offering small business-oriented shareware. (Some programs can be downloaded here.) There's shareware for DOS, Macintosh, Windows 3.1, Windows 98, and Windows NT. Features provides a collection of articles and essays on an array of business issues, from market infrastructure to financial advice. Discussion Forums include 4 specialized areas: Small Business, Accounting & Finance, Sales & Marketing, and Home Office. An internal search engine is provided.

Evaluation:
While BizProWeb's web directory can't compete in scope with a giant like Yahoo! Small Business or Smart Business Supersite (see review), this one has one primary advantage: it doesn't give just a one-sentence introduction to the sites it lists, it provides paragraph-length, in depth descriptions that really give you an idea of whether or not a site is worth a click. If this site offered nothing other than the web directory, it would still be worth a visit, particularly by women and minorities, who get more attention here than at similar sites. Combined with all of the other genuinely useful features found here, this site is an absolute "must!" Newsgroup directories are relatively rare, and this one covers both the general (i.e. Management) and the specialized (i.e. Consulting). The featured articles are well-written, intriguing, and informative, and—best of all—the authors volunteer their e-mail addresses for contact/Q & A. (Information about each author and a link to their e-mail is presented at the end of each piece.) The shareware is wide-ranging and useful; take advantage! Open to networking, the discussion forums are terrific too. No matter what type of self-employment you're involved in, be it home-based business, small business, or consulting, don't miss this site.

Where To Find/Buy:
On the Internet using the URL: http://www.bizproweb.com

Resources For Networking, Support & Advice

FAST COMPANY ONLINE

 Recommended For:
Resources For Networking, Support & Advice

Description:

This is a huge site with lots of departments, including "FCToday" (daily topics, polls, an online column), "Community" (discussion forums, book clubs), the magazine's archive of articles, and a "Career Center." The home page doubles as an explicit table of contents from which visitors can navigate the site. For advice on going solo (there's a featured article on "How to Create a Killer Business Plan"), the "Career Center" is a good place to start. Of the "Center's" six sections, "Find Your Calling" (i.e. career choices, self-assessment), "Make a Choice" (i.e. career decision making), "Build Brand You" (i.e. improving skills), and "Go Free Agent," each contain advice pertinent to aspiring soloists. (There's also a "Move On" section for relocating.) Each section has links to and descriptions of pertinent "FC" articles, outside articles, and other online resources as well as book lists for additional research. In "Go Free Agent," for example, you'll find inspiration for "declaring your independence," entrepreneur profiles, articles on "free agent finance," and links to such websites as "WorkingSolo" and "The Idea Cafe." (Menu bars appear at the top and bottom of each page for ease of movement.)

Evaluation:

The print version of "FC" gains acclaim everyday with its cutting edge philosophy and style, and its online version is just as fresh, informative, and exciting! Whether you're looking for advice on career decisions, going solo, or managing your business, this is the place the go. You could spend hours and hours at this site, with pleasure; there's so much here! Aside from the magazine's articles, polls, "behind the scenes" tidbits, interviews, interactive forums, etc., the "Career Center" alone is a virtual library of valuable resources. You can find tools for determining if going solo is right for you in "Find Your Calling," read about successful leaders and entrepreneurs in "Go Free Agent," and get tips for building your skills in "Build Brand You." Plus, every section of the "Career Center" has its own mini, descriptive web guide. "FC" can be of assistance, too, after your start-up; it can help you keep up with business trends, new technology, and innovative management techniques. (It may be especially relevant to tech start-ups and consultants.) If spending "hours and hours" at "FC" sounds ominous, don't worry! This site is so well organized you can find particulars as quickly as it takes to read the succinct descriptions beneath the headings. The final verdict? Don't miss this site!

Where To Find/Buy:

On the Internet at http://www.fastcompany.com

Overall Rating
★★★★
Whatever your business needs, visit this site!

Design, Ease Of Use
★★★★
Well organized, exciting design, easy to navigate

1–4 Stars

Author:
Fast Company Online is the online product of Fast Company, Inc., the publishers of the print magazine of the same name.

Publisher:
Fast Company Inc.

Media:
Internet

Principal Subject:
Resources For Networking, Support & Advice

VI. Insider Advice

★★★★

Overall Rating
★★★★
More expansive and varied than Yahoo! Small Business—check this out!

Design, Ease Of Use
★★★★
Two easy ways to search plus an explicit Handy Reference Chart of Features

1–4 Stars

Author:
Irv Brechner is a marketing expert, author, programmer and WWW enthusiast; he is publisher and developer of SBS. Kathryn Howard created and was editor-in-chief of Florida Home & Garden Magazine before becoming SBS Editor.

Publisher:
Smart Business Supersite

Media:
Internet

Principal Subject:
Resources For Networking, Support & Advice

Secondary Subject:
Working As A Freelancer, Consultant or Contract Worker

Of Interest To:
Women

Resources For Networking, Support & Advice

SMART BUSINESS SUPERSITE

 Recommended For:
Resources For Networking, Support & Advice

Description:
The mission of SBS (Smart Business Supersite) is to be an important source of high-quality, how-to business information on the Net. In pursuit of that goal, the site serves up guides comprised of thousands of resources: articles, websites, mailing lists, checklists, reports, worksheets, book and software reviews, profiles of directories, associations, and vendors. To search the site, there's an internal search engine, or users can browse 63 categories. Categories include Consulting, Doing Business on the Net, Self-Employed, Family Business, and Women and Minority Issues, as well as general business categories such as Financing, Accounting, Legal, and Marketing. By choosing a category, the result is an annotated, direct-link list of all related resources of all types. The SBS also features daily news briefs, monthly columns, details on thousands of trade shows, message boards, and hot tips (new every weekday). There are special services, such as a free reminder service, and a "people finder" designed to help you locate experts, speakers, or consultants. To navigate the site, and to see all it has to offer, go to About SBS and click on the Handy Reference Chart of SBS Features; it functions as a site map.

Evaluation:
There's only one small problem with SBS: its "site map," the wonderfully explicit Handy Reference Chart, isn't accessible from the home page. It's only one click away though, in About SBS, and once you've found it, you're set. From there, you can navigate and familiarize yourself with the varied segments of this huge site and take full advantage of some of the terrific features it has to offer. "Stand outs" include the "people finder," for locating experts or consultants, the free reminder service, the enormous database of trade show information, and the topic-specific message boards. Of course, the primary draw to this site is the collection of thousands of how-to resources for entrepreneurs. Broader in scope than Yahoo! Small Business (SBS includes reports, profiles, articles, mailing lists and more in addition to websites), this is the premiere site for finding Net resources. It's nice, too, that you have a choice of search methods: the internal search engine or the Windows-like category box that lets you scroll through 63 categories. Plus, if you use the category search, the resulting page is equipped with internal links that let you "skip to" the type of resource you want. For instance, you can skip to Books, Products, or Net resources. Pair this site with BizProWeb (see review) and you'll have access to all the resources you need.

Where To Find/Buy:
On the Internet using the URL: http://www.smartbiz.com

Resources For Networking, Support & Advice

SCORE: SERVICE CORPS OF RETIRED EXECUTIVES
Counselor's To America's Small Business

 Recommended For:
Resources For Networking, Support & Advice

Description:

SCORE is a nonprofit organization comprised of more than 12,000 volunteer business executives. Affiliated with the SBA, SCORE is dedicated to helping entrepreneurs and small business owners. Their site (which can best be navigated via the site map) offers free e-mail counseling (to all U.S. citizens), whereby users can pose questions to the volunteer "experts." Counseling is available 24 hours a day, 7 days a week, and users choose the counselor. SCORE's other online features include archives of "success stories" and educational "workshops." The "success stories" are client profiles of successful small businesses and represent a wide array of types, i.e. ANAgraph, Inc., Better Baskets by Cindy, New York Bagel. The "workshops" are "how to" articles that cover such topics as starting and planning a business and "Technology for Small Business." In "Technology," users will find information on creating a company website, setting up a network, and e-commerce. For additional research, SCORE provides a "Business Resource Index," with links for specific issues, i.e. domain naming, and an annotated web guide titled "Business Hotlinks."

Evaluation:

There is absolutely no reason not to take advantage of the free counseling offered by SCORE's army of volunteer business executives. Not only is it free "expert" advice, it couldn't be more convenient or user-friendly. The service is available all the time, it's confidential, you initiate contact, and you pick the counselor from a wide range of choices. (You must be a U.S. citizen to be eligible.) (Keep in mind, too, that the site provides information on locating local SCORE chapters, so it may be possible to meet person-to-person.) You could visit every entrepreneur site on the Net and you won't find a better offer than that! Of course, though the counseling is the best reason to drop by this site, there are other good reasons to visit. The "success stories" are inspirational and the web guide is absolutely a "must" for browsing or bookmarking. The "workshops" are educational and useful, too, particularly the articles in "Technology for Small Business," which function nicely as introductions to the business benefits of e-commerce and the Web. The site is well-organized, so it's easy to find particulars. There's a constant side-bar "menu," but familiarize yourself with the contents, via the site map, first. The site map is explicit and includes everything, i.e. all the archived workshops, etc. The home page is a bit ambiguous.

Where To Find/Buy:

On the Internet at http://www.score.org

Overall Rating
★★★★
Free e-mail counseling, informative workshops, a great web guide, plus lots more!

Design, Ease Of Use
★★★
User friendly and well organized; use the site map for initial navigating

1–4 Stars

Author:
The SCORE association (Service Corps of Retired Executives) is a resource partner with the U.S. Small Business Administration. It is a nonprofit organization dedicated to the formation, growth, and success of small businesses nationwide.

Publisher:
SCORE Association

Media:
Internet

Principal Subject:
Resources For Networking, Support & Advice

VI. Insider Advice

Overall Rating
★★★★
Informative, yet concise; contacts should be current due to recent revision

Design, Ease Of Use
★★★
Considering the vast applications, could be enhanced by a more detailed index

1–4 Stars

Author:
William Alarid

William Alarid is an entrepreneur who has used government aid to start several small businesses. He's the author of two business books. Alarid is an engineer, a member of Mensa and is listed in Who's Who In California. He resides in Santa Maria, California with his wife and children.

Publisher:
Puma Publishing Company

Edition:
4th (1997)

Price:
$15.95

Pages/Run Time:
312

ISBN:
0940673665

Media:
Book

Principal Subject:
Resources For Networking, Support & Advice

Of Interest To:
Racial/Ethnic Minorities

VI. Insider Advice

Resources For Networking, Support & Advice

FREE HELP FROM UNCLE SAM TO START YOUR OWN BUSINESS
Or Expand The One You Have

Description:
Success Stories About Some of Uncle Sam's Citizens carry titles such as Zero-Cost Consultant Spots Problem, Takes Community by Storm After Tornado, and more. StartUps on a Shoestring lists some big success stories, such as Nike, who began very small. Assistance and Information lists where to go if you currently are not in business, would like to learn how to avoid common pitfalls, and want to learn from the experiences of others. The New Products heading contains the following sections: License a Government Invention, How to File for a Patent, Registering a Trademark, Obtaining a Copyright, Where to Get Information on Foreign Research, Help to Stimulate the Innovative Process, Stuff Made Out of Wood, Factory of the Future, Shop of the '90s. Selling To The Feds is self-explanatory. Everything You Ever Wanted To Know, But Were Ashamed To Ask lists sources for research information, statistical analysis training, automating expertise, and more. Financial Help lists 37 sources that may serve particular individuals, loss situations, or business types. The International Trade section leads off with Trade Information Center. Women, Minorities, and Disadvantaged refer to special assistance for these groups.

Evaluation:
This compilation of information indirectly offers readers an overview of our government's organization, while focusing on how government supports businesses in the private sector. The first two chapters tell stories that exemplify the wide range of businesses that stand to gain from government assistance/interaction. Chapters three and four tend to focus on the possible alliances between the private sector and government that facilitate delivery of products and services to the marketplace; an example of this is private licensing of government-created inventions. Selling to the Feds conveys that various segments/departments of government satisfy internal demand for products/services through a procurement network; readers are directed to sources that will get them in the loop to supply government needs. Chapter six explains that government shares statistical data with private industry; this research might be valuable to either a startup or an existing private business. Loans, grants and guarantees are listed in Financial Help; similar to previous reference sections, sources are clearly defined as to what is offered and who is served. Alarid says that more emphasis has been placed on international trade and minority enterprises in this latest edition because these are entrepreneurial areas that are growing. Appendixes are basically a quick reference for contact information.

Where To Find/Buy:
Bookstores and libraries.

Resources For Networking, Support & Advice

IDEA CAFE
The Small Business Channel

Description:

Created by business owner Francie Marks Ward to help users "solve problems and have fun," The Idea Cafe serves up a variety of dishes for both current and potential entrepreneurs. The home page provides access to the site's main areas, such as the "Coffee Talk with Experts," "Q & A" forum, the "Biz Comm Zone's" articles, and the "Financing Your Business" "menu." The "Financing" menu includes articles on "women getting money," "minorities getting money," "cleaning up your credit," and sources of money, i.e. borrowing money, getting investors, and "creative financing." There are also "self-exams" for determining the "right financing for you" and "getting ready emotionally," and an "All-In-One Budget Calculator" for finding out how much money you need. For "cyberschmoozing" with other small business owners, there are two chat rooms: one on financing and one on starting, running and managing your business. Reviews of hardware and software are also provided, and the site has a variety of "fun" features, too, i.e. horoscopes, "Dilbert" comics, contests, etc. Links to other online resources are organized into the Cafe's web guide, the "Business Directory."

Evaluation:

The Idea Cafe is one of the more famous sites on the Net for current and budding entrepreneurs. Since it's a relatively high-traffic site, it's definitely worth checking out the "cyberschmooz" chat rooms for informational networking. There are lots of other terrific features, too. The section on "Financing Your Business" is particularly well done, with an extensive "menu" of options for figuring out your personal financial needs and getting the money. Of special note is the "creative financing" segment, which explores such possibilities as "strategic partners," "convertible debt," and borrowing from friends and family. Take advantage, too, of the online "Business Directory;" it's well-organized and offers links to resources on such subjects as "Starting & Running a Business," "Protecting Intellectual Property," and "Accounting, Taxes & Business Law." The site is basically well-formatted, though there isn't a site map and the constant metaphorical language (the food/Cafe allusions are used throughout, i.e. the "Idea Cafe Fridge") can make navigating slightly difficult. (The "Idea Cafe Fridge" seems to be a mini-map of the "Biz Comm Zone's" contents.) Still, whether you want coffee chat or a hearty advice stew, the Cafe is certainly worth a visit!

Where To Find/Buy:

On the Internet at http://www.ideacafe.com

Overall Rating
★★★★
A fun "hangout" for entrepreneurs; a great place for financial advice and networking

Design, Ease Of Use
★★★
Engaging design, but navigating can be a slight problem

1–4 Stars

Author:
Francie Marks Ward
Ms. Ward is a veteran business owner who has started and run a variety of small businesses.

Publisher:
Idea Cafe

Media:
Internet

Principal Subject:
Resources For Networking, Support & Advice

VI. Insider Advice

★★★

Overall Rating
★★★
Useful and unusual articles, plus other nice features

Design, Ease Of Use
★★★
Use the site map for navigating

1–4 Stars

Author:
The Small Business Advisor was developed and is maintained by Information International. Information International is dedicated to assisting individuals who are starting a business; they also help companies do business with the U.S. Government.

Publisher:
Information International

Media:
Internet

Principal Subject:
Resources For Networking, Support & Advice

Resources For Networking, Support & Advice

THE SMALL BUSINESS ADVISOR

Description:
The best starting point for new visitors is the site map, accessible from the home page. From the map, users can navigate the site's main sections. There's The Advisor, a collection of 100+ articles from author Robert Sullivan that covers such topics as Start-Up, Operations, Marketing, Selling, Legal, and Internet. (Sullivan is the author of "The Small Business Start-Up Guide" and other books available for purchase in the site's Books for Sale section.) Articles address a wide range of issues: steps to increase profits, guidelines for choosing a bank, 800-telephone numbers, networking tips, writing sales letters. The site also offers daily marketing tips, daily news items, and weekly tax tips. A glossary of small business terms, advice on doing business with the U.S. government, and book reviews comprise other sections. Other features include checklists (i.e. Entrepreneurial Aptitude, Choosing a Partner), links to websites and related newsgroups, mailing lists, and information about website design services. State-specific data, e.g. the phone numbers of state agencies and services, is available, too. An internal search engine is provided.

Evaluation:
There are some attractive features at this site for small and home-based business owners. Sullivan's articles are one such feature, well worth the time it takes to browse the titles/short descriptions. They're perceptive, informative, and they tackle pertinent yet seldom-seen topics. For example, one article presents a detailed guide to evaluating a merchant card provider while another explores alternative, start-up financing sources. The Marketing articles are the best, however, with lots of writing tips for creating everything from business cards to classified ads. The number of articles that focus on networking (in Operations, in Marketing) is noteworthy, too, since so many entrepreneurial advice sites seem to forget the importance of "contacts." Still, as good as the articles are, they don't add up to a complete how-to-start-up picture; you'll have to go elsewhere for that. (The links will help you.) The state-specific data, such as the phone number for your state's SBA district office and incorporation information, is a nice inclusion, but skip the checklists, they're simplistic. If you're interested in doing business with the government, this is a good place to start; it's the site's specialty. Overall, this is a reliable, useful resource. Just be sure to head straight for the site map to navigate or you may find yourself clicking in circles.

Where To Find/Buy:
On the Internet using the URL: http:// www.isquare.com

Resources For Networking, Support & Advice

★★★

WAHM: WORK AT HOME MOMS

Description:

Despite styling itself as an "online magazine" (a flavor that carries throughout its many pages), WAHM is more accurately described as an online networking "hub" for work at home moms and potential work at home moms. Ms. Demas contributes a weekly editorial column whose subject matter focuses on the particular needs, joys and concerns of her fellow home-based moms. The site also contains "advice and FAQs" on general home-business issues. Other sections feature an online bookstore, classifieds, and links to related resources. However, the primary focus is on networking. There are three ways to network with other WAHMs (work at home moms): you can search for a "WAHM Near You" by state, you can search by "WAHM Businesses" type, i.e. "Home Decorating," "Writer," etc., or you can browse in "Business Opportunities." In any case, the results of your search will either be a personal or business home page or an e-mail address for the work at home mom you chose. Since all of the work at home moms accessible through WAHM are willing to discuss their businesses, you can write to them for advice, query, ideas, information, etc.

Evaluation:

The last couple of years have seen the emergence of a new breed of website: those dedicated to women's business networks. WAHM is a perfect example of these female-oriented networking "hubs." If a home-based business is your bread-and-butter, or your dream, this site is a must visit! Valuable advice can be gleaned from those who have "been there, done that," and such mentoring is the paramount attraction at WAHM: it's a virtual network of work at home experts! The contacts available via WAHM have a wide range of careers; they are freelance writers, children's clothiers, desktop publishers, etc. Perhaps you'll find a work at home mom in your area to confer with and exchange ideas. Or perhaps this is a site where you can offer advice or encouragement. The down sides: the original content is skimpy and there isn't much practical "how-to" advice. (A word of caution: be aware that folks use this and similar sites to troll for recruits for their multi-level marketing businesses.) Bookmark this page and keep tabs on its growth and development. It is poised to take off as its audience of work at home moms reaches critical mass. Given the phenomenal growth in full- and part-time mother-run home businesses, this site is one to watch.

Where To Find/Buy:

On the Internet at http://www.wahm.com

Overall Rating
★★★
The content is skimpy, but the networking possibilities are endless!

Design, Ease Of Use
★★★
Simple format and search mechanisms; easy to navigate

1–4 Stars

Author:
Cheryl Demas

Ms. Demas is a work at home mother with two daughters. She began WAHM when she started working from home in 1994.

Publisher:
Miracle Communications

Media:
Internet

Principal Subject:
Resources For Networking, Support & Advice

Of Interest To:
Women

VI. Insider Advice

★★★

Overall Rating
★★★
1,200 resources for going solo; a good "one stop" reference book

Design, Ease Of Use
★★★
Well organized; uses icons for ease of reference

1–4 Stars

Author:
Terri Lonier

Ms. Lonier is president of Working Solo, Inc. She advises such clients as Microsoft, Hewlett-Packard, and Claris on how best to access and communicate with the small business and SOHO (Small Office Home Office) market.

Publisher:
John Wiley & Sons

Edition:
2nd (1998)

Price:
$14.95

Pages/Run Time:
315

ISBN:
0471247146

Media:
Book

Principal Subject:
Resources For Networking, Support & Advice

VI. Insider Advice

WORKING SOLO SOURCEBOOK

Description:
Where do you go to find the information you need for starting and/or managing your own business? How do you make contacts or take advantage of Internet resources? Ms. Lonier's "sourcebook" for going solo provides over 1,200 listings for all types of entrepreneurial-related help: magazines, books, websites, professional associations, support groups, government agencies, etc. The listings are arranged in chapters by category. Categories/chapters include "Business Planning," "Choosing a Business," "Computers and Technology," "Consulting," "Legal Information," "Taxes," and "Women-Owned Businesses." Each chapter has an introductory paragraph followed by the listings. Listings detail pertinent information (i.e. book titles are followed by price, ISBN number, etc., organizations contain contact addresses, etc.) and are accompanied by brief descriptions. (Descriptions are usually only one or two sentences long.) Easy-reference icons appear beside each listing; for example, a spider-web icon appears beside a website listing, a book icon beside a book, etc. An alphabetized index of resources can be found in the back.

Evaluation:
If you feel overwhelmed by the plethora of resources available to entrepreneurs, Ms. Lonier's "sourcebook" may be for you. It's a concise, straightforward, well-organized grouping of the most popular, well-respected, and generally well thought of resources "out there." And it covers them all, from print to Internet sites to professional associations. By dividing the listings into categories, such as "Starting a Business," the author makes it easy to browse or to search the text for specifics. (Familiarize yourself with the table of contents first, though, to make sure you're in the right category.) The icons are helpful, too; you can see what you're getting without having to read the whole description. The only shortcoming here is that Lonier makes no subjective comments about the resources; that is, she doesn't tell you which ones she finds most valuable. There are no "ratings" or other mechanisms for comparing resources on similar subjects; choosing a book or website may come down to a case of "eeny-meeny-miney-mo." Still, if you want a "yellow pages" for going solo, this is the one to choose. (Keep in mind that similar material can be found online at Lonier's "Working Solo" website. It has an even better search engine, of course, plus it's free.) (See review.)

Where To Find/Buy:
Bookstores and libraries.

Resources For Networking, Support & Advice

WOMANOWNED.COM

Description:

When Christina Blenk created her website, it was to elicit support via networking for her own business venture, At First Site. With her Web Studio now up and running, Blenk has developed her site into a networking hub for all entrepreneurial women. There are 3 ways to network: the Networking Center, Message Boards, and the WomanOwned Database. The Networking Center allows users to ask for assistance and/or provide help and sales to fellow business owners; the Message Boards are communal Q & A boards. The Database is a volunteer, no-fee directory of women owned businesses from around the country. (A business must be at least 51% "woman owned" to be listed.) The businesses here are both advertising their services/products and offering their expertise; users can contact them for advice. In addition to networking, this site provides a selection of women-authored informational guides, which focus on such subjects as Budgeting for Start-Up and financing. There's also a step-by-step tutorial for creating/revising your business plan. Other features include a Government section with details on winning contracts and a Working the Web section with tips on e-commerce and marketing.

Evaluation:

Networking is a fantastic way to help build a business. Plus, for women, it's a way to support and encourage other women entrepreneurs while helping yourself at the same time. The most effective networking, however, is still the old-fashioned grass roots kind: person to person, not online. Eventually, the Web will be the networking vehicle of choice, but not yet. Use simply isn't wide spread enough (though more and more users log on every day). That said, this site is still worth a visit; its a great example of the networking venues the Web can offer today. It provides 3 different ways of networking, which is more than most sites, and the directory has great potential. Blenk hopes that women will use the Database to form networking groups in their area, which is certainly a possibility. (Don't expect lots of listings for every geographic area; the directory is still growing.) You can contact the businesses listed for personal assistance, too, which is always a plus. In that way, this site is similar to WAHM (see review), and may work well in tandem with that online resource: you could (feasibly) double your list of women business owners/contacts. (Keep in mind, too, that you can use the Database to browse for business ideas.) The rest of the site features only a handful of articles, but the Business Plan section is valuable. Try it out!

Where To Find/Buy:

On the Internet using the URL: http://www.womanowned.com

Overall Rating
★★
Lots of networking possibilities, plus a few good tips

Design, Ease Of Use
★★★
Features a Welcome page that tells you how to "get the most" from the site

1–4 Stars

Author:
Christina Blenk developed WomanOwned.com in 1997 in order to build her business, At First Site, Inc., Web Studio, through networking. Today, she hopes the site will help other women who are starting their own businesses.

Publisher:
At First Site, Inc.

Media:
Internet

Principal Subject:
Resources For Networking, Support & Advice

Of Interest To:
Women

VI. Insider Advice

★★

Overall Rating
★★
A mix of articles, links, and chat; best for the links

Design, Ease Of Use
★★
Smart navigation tools; straightforward

1–4 Stars

Author:
Ed Martin

Mr. Martin has started 3 businesses, holds an MA in International Management, and served as a counselor at a Small Business Development Center.

Publisher:
MiningCo.com

Media:
Internet

Principal Subject:
Resources For Networking, Support & Advice

Of Interest To:
Women

MININGCO.COM: SMALL BUSINESS INFORMATION

Description:

Martin's MiningCo. Guide to small businesses shares the same format and features found in all of the MiningCo. GuideSites: NetLinks, articles (both original and off-site), chat rooms, message boards, and a marketplace of subject-related books, videos, and services. All of the main areas of the site are accessible from the home page, as is a "guide bio" describing Martin's background in entrepreneurship and qualifications. (Martin is "always available" to answer e-mail questions, and he regularly visits the chat room.) Articles run the gamut from advice on "Putting the SBA to Work" to "Hiring a Lawyer." Weekly-updated business tips are spotlighted, and there are links to sites where free business and legal forms can be downloaded. There's also a free e-mail newsletter, Small Business HotLine, and a calendar of events. Netlinks, the Guide's annotated web guide, organizes links into such categories as Accounting, E-Commerce, Financing Your Biz, SOHO, and Women and Minority-owned Businesses. There are also links to MiningCo.'s related GuideSites, such as Entrepreneurs, Management, and Marketing. A search interface allows users to search either "this site" or all of MiningCo.

Evaluation:

Since every MiningCo. GuideSite has its own author, quality varies from site to site. As captain of this site, Martin does an adequate job; his articles are informative, but there aren't many to choose from. (One article that is definitely worth reading is the one on using the SBA; Martin does a terrific job of explaining how to navigate and get the most from that immense resource.) He is on hand for Q & A—via e-mail—which is a plus; it's always advantageous to have your questions answered by an actual person. However, the real boon here is the web guide. NetLinks covers a wide variety of subjects, from Accounting to Y2K preparedness, with seldom-seen inclusions such as Women and Minority-owned Business, Kids in Business, and Ergonomics. For the links alone, this is a site to check out. The search interface, which can search either just this site or all of the MiningCo. sites, is a valuable feature too; it enables the site to act as a doorway to all of the MiningCo. Guides that may have relevant information. For a web guide with extras (a few good articles, chat, etc.), this a reliable choice, but it pales in comparison to BizProNet or the Smart Business Supersite, two websites with similar concepts and a lot more information. (See reviews.)

Where To Find/Buy:

On the Internet using the URL: http://sbinformation.miningco.com

Resources For Networking, Support & Advice

THE WOMEN'S BUSINESS RESOURCE GUIDE
A National Directory Of More Than 800 Programs, Resources, And Organizations To Help Women Start Or Expand A Business

Description:

Believing that women face special challenges that "often mean working overtime just to get to square one," Littman has designed this book in an attempt to level the playing field. She aims to inspire readers by introducing role models who used resources to start and expand their business in Business Women Talk. Littman then supplies a variety of resources available through the federal, state and private sectors. Information Sources lists offices, agencies, books, magazines, and government publications. Training, Technical Assistance, and Counseling describes sources of counseling, mentoring, training and consulting. Business Financing provides general information on types of financing available and describes specific financing programs. Selling to the Government lists publications, databases and assistance centers with programs specifically for women. Membership Organizations is a directory of women's business and professional associations; this includes a description of professional development opportunities and other benefits available to members. Resource, Program, and Agency Listings provide contact information for more than eight hundred organizations, offices, programs, and agencies that are referred to throughout the guide.

Evaluation:

There is a vast multitude of free and priced information available to address all facets of establishing and growing a business. Cost conscious readers may be disappointed to find that the price of information is not consistently placed for quick reference, and may be altogether absent. On the contrary, each resource that is Exclusively for Women is clearly indicated by the notation of EW at the section heading. Resources are adequately described so that readers know what type information will be delivered by a particular resource. How to Proceed is included with each resource suggestion and may designate telephone, fax, online and/ or physical addresses detail. The Quick-Find Guide is a comprehensive list of all contact information that does not duplicate the descriptive detail present in earlier chapters. When detail of services/information is supplied separately from the contact information, the two components of a particular resource are always clearly linked. Even the Business Women Talk section provides cross-references to resource information that is highlighted by each interview. This Q & A format illustrates personal perspectives of the challenges that these small and large business owners confronted, and how resources were used to help create solutions.

Where To Find/Buy:

Bookstores and libraries.

Overall Rating
★★
Directs to resources, but does not eliminate the guesswork completely

Design, Ease Of Use
★★
Thoroughly cross-referenced and indexed, but text is a bit dry

1–4 Stars

Author:
Barbara Littman

Barbara Littman, whose background is in applied design and education, has been self-employed most of her adult life. She owns Information Design Northwest, a communications consulting firm located in Eugene, Oregon.

Publisher:
Contemporary Books (NTC/ Contemporary Publishing Co.)

Edition:
2nd (1996)

Price:
$18.95

Pages/Run Time:
302

ISBN:
0809231662

Media:
Book

Principal Subject:
Resources For Networking, Support & Advice

Of Interest To:
Women

VI. Insider Advice

Overall Rating

★

Focuses more on financial news and investing than entrepreneurial how-to

Design, Ease Of Use

★★★

Search engines and side-bar menu lend ease to navigation

1–4 Stars

Author:

Black Enterprise.com is the website for the print publication of the same name.

Publisher:

Earl G. Graves, Ltd.

Media:

Internet

Principal Subject:

Resources For Networking, Support & Advice

Of Interest To:

Racial/Ethnic Minorities

VI. Insider Advice

Resources For Networking, Support & Advice

BLACK ENTERPRISE.COM
The Virtual Desktop For African Americans

Description:

To navigate this online version of Black Enterprise magazine, visitors can use the side bar menu (which functions as a "site map") or use the internal search engine. The site's major sections include Features (featured articles), Departments, *B.E.* Unlimited, Archives, News, Market Data, and Personal Finance. Entrepreneurs may want to start in Departments, which organizes articles into such categories as Enterprise, Techwatch, and Motivation. In Enterprise, articles address such issues as customer satisfaction, boosting profits through referrals, and getting media mentions. Techwatch offers articles on using technology in business; Motivation provides strategies for enhancing personal effectiveness. In *B.E.* Unlimited, there's information on conferences, "kidpreneurs," and newsletters. Archives house back issues, News covers current events, and Market Data contains updates on U.S. Index Movers. The site also provides tax tips, a web guide to related links, bulletin boards, and tools such as a "lease or buy calculator." Entrepreneurs can browse the Small Business Directory, too; it's a list of business offers divided into categories: Consulting, Franchising, Information Technology, Start-Up, etc.

Evaluation:

While there are lots of general audience entrepreneurial magazines on the Web, Black Enterprise.Com is one of the few to address the African American entrepreneur specifically. For that reason alone, this is a site worth visiting. The articles in Departments, which are directed primarily toward business owners, are relevant and educational; they cover technology, personal motivation, financial planning, and customer relations quite well. The articles also focus on issues of special interest to African Americans, such as loan funds made available through diversity initiatives. However, since B.E.com's audience includes both self-employed persons and traditionally employed persons, the rest of the site is a mix of general financial advice and at-work advice, with little left over for business owners. As a general interest website, B.E.com delivers; however, for entrepreneurs, it simply doesn't offer enough how-to guidance, especially not for starting a business. For the nuts-and-bolts of starting up, you'll have to go elsewhere; try the links. Also, beware of the Small Business Directory; it's full of MLM schemes and some very dubious offers. (It may give you a few ideas though; one listing is for Scholarship Consultant, another for African Style Clothing.)

Where To Find/Buy:

On the Internet using the URL: http://www.blackenterprise.com

Resources For Networking, Support & Advice

SUCCESS ONLINE

Description:

This online version of "Success Magazine" details its contents on the home page. A side menu offers access to the magazine's various Departments (collections of articles) and Resources, and there are teasers for this month's featured articles. (The articles frequently profile successful entrepreneurs/enterprises.) Departments include Direct Selling, E-commerce, Franchising, Going Public, Raising Capital, and Tech Edge. By clicking on a Department, you'll find a list of articles to choose from. In Tech Edge, for instance, articles highlight new office equipment, computer hardware, and business-applicable technological breakthroughs. Resources encompass such features as an online archive, classifieds, an interactive forum, information about business schools and about the site itself, product and subscription information, and The Source, an annotated web guide for entrepreneurial resources. The Source contains direct links to online resources for such subjects as Academia, Electronic Commerce, Entrepreneurship, Finance and Venture Capital, Government Agencies, and Industry Information. There are also links for Law and Taxes, Management, Marketing and Market Research, and Technology.

Evaluation:

While some of the articles available at this site are intriguing and educational, there aren't enough of them to make this a viable how-to site. What little learn-by-example direction you can glean from these few articles can't compare with the depth and variety offered at sites like EntrepreneurMag.com or Entrepreneur Online. (See reviews.) Also, while most online magazine sites provide full content (or close to full content) access to their periodicals, this one doesn't. Back issues have to be bought, and the scant number of free articles suggests that the producers of "Success" are using this site primarily to advertise their print product, rather than to provide help to aspiring entrepreneurs. You'll find, too, as you navigate via the ambiguous headings on the home page (there is no site map), frustrating advertisements popping up where you expected free information and, in some cases, no information at all. At the time of this review, there were no articles posted "this month" in the Raising Capital Department, nor were there any "past articles currently available." So why bother with this site at all? For The Source, the direct-link web guide. Bookmark The Source's page, because it offers lots of fantastic links to a wide variety of online, entrepreneurial resources. Final verdict: visit for the web guide and skip the rest.

Where To Find/Buy:

On the Internet using the URL: http://www.successmagazine.com

Overall Rating
★
A fabulous web guide—bookmark it!—But not much else

Design, Ease Of Use
★
Ambiguous headings disguise missing information and advertising

1–4 Stars

Author:
Success Online is the website for *Success Magazine*, a print magazine which targets entrepreneurs.

Publisher:
Success Magazine

Media:
Internet

Principal Subject:
Resources For Networking, Support & Advice

VI. Insider Advice

Resources For Networking, Support & Advice

AFRICAN AMERICAN WOMEN ENTREPRENEURS AT HOME

Non-Rated Resource

Description:
Similar to Bizy Moms.com, AAWEH functions primarily as a networking hub for African American women who work at home. The site also features current events, a place to post and respond to contracting opportunities, and a resource "library." The library includes links to Business Resources and phone numbers for African American women's organizations.

Author:
Marie Parham
Ms. Parham is an entrepreneur who works out of her home.

Media:
Internet

Principal Subject:
Resources For Networking, Support & Advice

Where To Find/Buy:
On the Internet using the URL: http://www.wix.com:80/vss/aaweh_m.htm

AMERICAN INDIVIDUAL MAGAZINE AND COFFEEHOUSE

Non-Rated Resource

Description:
In addition to message boards, chat "houses," and a "library" of print resources, this site offers a descriptive web guide for entrepreneurs. From the home page, under "Places to Go," visitors can find links for such topics as "Starting A Business," "Working From Home," and "Career Information." Just click on a topic for an alphabetical list of relevant websites.

Publisher:
Kasia Communications

Media:
Internet

Principal Subject:
Resources For Networking, Support & Advice

Where To Find/Buy:
On the Internet at http://www.aimc.com/aimc

CAREER RESOURCE CENTER

Non-Rated Resource

Description:
The Career Resource Center is an index of career-related web sites; it contains thousands of links for a variety of job searching needs. There are links to sites for small businesses and home offices, career service professionals, and research-related sites. CRC 's "Regional Pages" organizes sites by location (e.g. U.S. state or Canadian province).

Author:
Marc D. Snyder
Mr. Snyder is both the director of Career Resource Center and its webmaster. He is co-author of *How To Get A Job In Seattle And Western Washington (4th Editon) 1998* (Surrey Books).

Media:
Internet

Principal Subject:
Resources For Networking, Support & Advice

Where To Find/Buy:
On the Internet at http://www.careers.org/index.html

Resources For Networking, Support & Advice

CYBERGRRL

Non-Rated Resource

Description:
For women in technology, the Cybergrrl site offers networking forums, Tech Tips (which include articles on creating a website and choosing an ISP), and expert Q&A. The She's So Savvy feature offers profiles of successful women business owners. There's also access to Webgrrls, a technology-and-women-related networking site and nationwide organization.

Publisher:
Cybergrrl, Inc.

Media:
Internet

Principal Subject:
Resources For Networking, Support & Advice

Where To Find/Buy:
On the Internet using the URL: http://www.Cybergrrl.com

ENTREWORLD.ORG

Non-Rated Resource

Description:
To help entrepreneurs find "the best of the Web," this site provides annotated links to articles and websites on all aspects of self-employment, from Starting Your Business to Growing Your Business. Categories of links include Legal & Taxes, Finances, and Special Interest Groups. Other features include Perspectives, Discussions, and a Glossary of terms.

Publisher:
Kauffman Center for Entrepreneurial Leadership

EntreWorld is a collaborative project created and maintained by entrepreneurs and coordinated by the Kauffman Center for Entrepreneurial Leadership at the Ewing Marion Kauffman Foundation, a non-profit organization.

Media:
Internet

Principal Subject:
Resources For Networking, Support & Advice

Where To Find/Buy:
On the Internet using the URL: http://www.entreworld.org

EVERYTHING BLACK.COM: BUSINESS RESOURCES

Non-Rated Resource

Description:
As its name suggests, this Yahoo!-style web guide provides annotated links to African American-related websites; its Business Resources page contains links to a variety of entrepreneurial resources. Links include online magazines, organizations, news agencies, networking forums, and sites that list (for free) African American Internet businesses.

Publisher:
The Freedom Group

Media:
Internet

Principal Subject:
Resources For Networking, Support & Advice

Where To Find/Buy:
On the Internet using the URL: http://www.everythingblack.com/Resources/2a.html

Resources For Networking, Support & Advice

THE FEMINIST MAJORITY FOUNDATION ONLINE

Non-Rated Resource

Description:
To help women locate and contact relevant professional associations, this site offers lists of women's business, legal, and medical organizations. Entries include "American Association of Black Women Entrepreneurs" and "American Society of Women Entrepreneurs." Each entry contains contact information and a link to the association's website (where possible).

Publisher:
Feminist Majority Foundation

The Feminist Majority and The Feminist Majority Foundation are nonprofit organizations commited "to empowering women."

Media:
Internet

Principal Subject:
Resources For Networking, Support & Advice

Where To Find/Buy:
On the Internet at http://www.feminist.org/gateway/womenorg.html

HISPANSTAR: THE HISPANIC INFORMATION NETWORK

Non-Rated Resource

Description:
In addition to cover stories from last month's "Hispanic Business" magazine, visitors to this site will find chat rooms and bulletin boards, a calendar of events, and a list of related "bizlinks." There's also HispanTelligence, a private data archive of marketing information on the U.S. Hispanic market, other U.S. minority markets, and international economics.

Publisher:
Hispanic Business Inc.

Hispanstar is the official website for *Hispanic Business* magazine and HsipanData National Diver Recruitment Services.

Media:
Internet

Principal Subject:
Resources For Networking, Support & Advice

Where To Find/Buy:
On the Internet using the URL: http://www.hispanstar.com

MINORITY BUSINESS DEVELOPMENT AGENCY

Non-Rated Resource

Description:
To help minority entrepreneurs, the MBDA's site provides information on its activities and services, local MBDA centers, and such MBDA partners as Minority Business Development Centers and Minority Business Opportunity Committees. Other features include a resource locator and an annotated list of links. A Spanish-text version is also available.

Publisher:
Minority Business Development Agency

The Minority Business Development Agency is part of the U.S. Department of Commerce; it was created to encourage creation, growth, and expansion of minority-owned businesses in the U.S. The MBDA provides a variety of business programs and services to minorities.

Media:
Internet

Principal Subject:
Resources For Networking, Support & Advice

Where To Find/Buy:
On the Internet using the URL: http://www.mbda.gov

Resources For Networking, Support & Advice

MINORITY BUSINESS ENTREPRENEUR

Non-Rated Resource

Description:
MBEMAG is the online version of *Minority Business Entrepreneur (MBE)* magazine, a publication for minority and women business owners. The site features articles from current and back issues of MBE, as well as a business resource directory, related links, and access to the Women's Business Executive site, a newsletter for women business owners.

Author:
Ginger Conrad

Ms. Conrad started MBE magazine in 1984; today, the Los Angeles-based bimonthly reaches over 60,000 minority and women readers. Ms. Conrad is also co-founder and Publications Director of "Women's Business Exclusive," a bimonthly newsletter for women entrepreneurs

Publisher:
Minority Business Entrepreneur

Media:
Internet

Principal Subject:
Resources For Networking, Support & Advice

Where To Find/Buy:
On the Internet using the URL: http://www.mbemag.com

NATIONAL ASSOCIATION OF WOMEN BUSINESS OWNERS

Non-Rated Resource

Description:
At this site, women entrepreneurs can learn about and/or join NAWBO, the National Association of Women Business Owners. Emerging business owners can become members for a $50 annual fee; membership benefits include partner/vendor discounts, networking locally and nationally, public policy representation, and international affiliations.

Publisher:
National Association of Women Business Owners

The NAWBO is the only dues-based national organization representing the interests of women entrepreneurs in all types of businesses. It has over 60 chapters and is affiliated with the World Association of Women Entrepreneurs in 33 countries.

Media:
Internet

Principal Subject:
Resources For Networking, Support & Advice

Where To Find/Buy:
On the Internet using the URL: http://www.nawbo.org

THE NATIONAL CENTER FOR AMERICAN INDIAN ENTERPRISE DEVELOPMENT

Non-Rated Resource

Description:
The NCAIED is a full-service center offering economic development services to Native Americans. Their site provides contact information for the organization's 3 regional offices, an introduction to NCAIED services, such as the Native American Business Consultant, and a hyperlinked list of Native American-owned businesses.

Publisher:
NCAIED

The NCAIED begain its 27-year history as UIDA, organized by 6 Native American businessmen. Today, through management contracts with the MBDA, NCAIED services Native American entrepreneurs through regional offices in LA, Seattle, and Phoenix.

Media:
Internet

Principal Subject:
Resources For Networking, Support & Advice

Where To Find/Buy:
On the Internet using the URL: http://www.ncaied.org

VI. Insider Advice

Resources For Networking, Support & Advice

NETWORKING MOMS

Non-Rated Resource

Description:
Another networking site for work-at-home moms, this one revolves around the Mom-to-Mom Solutions Club, a chat room for sharing information, advice, and ideas. Other features include Pulse Polls (weekly "hot topic" Q&A), current news items, and Working Mom Gateway, an annotated web guide to work-at-home mom resources.

Author:
Melanie Berry

Ms. Berry is creator of "Executive Baby," a newsletter for working mothers, as well as the NetWorking Moms Directory and Networking Moms website. Berry's goal is to create a community of working moms who can help one another.

Publisher:
NetWorking Moms

Media:
Internet

Principal Subject:
Resources For Networking, Support & Advice

Where To Find/Buy:
On the Internet using the URL: http://www.networkingmoms.com

U.S. BUSINESS ADVISOR

Non-Rated Resource

Description:
This government site offers entrepreneurs direct-link access to business-related information from such government agencies as the U.S. Postal Service, IRS, SBA, EPA, FCC, SSA, and OSHA (Occupational Safety and Health Assistance for Small Businesses). Answers to "FAQs" are provided, as is a search interface and a categorical topic list for browsing.

Publisher:
National Technical Information Service

The U.S. Business Advisor provides businesses with access to federal government information, services, and transactions.

Media:
Internet

Principal Subject:
Resources For Networking, Support & Advice

Where To Find/Buy:
On the Internet using the URL: http://www.business.gov

WOMEN CONNECT.COM

Non-Rated Resource

Description:
An online resource for women in all types of business, this site features chat rooms, business and career workshops, and money and health segments, as well as news items and current events. A keyword search using "entrepreneur" will result in a number of articles and profiles on entrepreneurism, including minority entrepreneur issues.

Publisher:
Women CONNECT.com

WomenCONNECT.com is a women-owned company committed to building and strengthening the community of women in business. Site content contributors include *Working Woman Magazine*, *Working Mother Magazine*, and *National Journal Inc.*

Media:
Internet

Principal Subject:
Resources For Networking, Support & Advice

Where To Find/Buy:
On the Internet using the URL: http://womenconnect.com

Resources For Networking, Support & Advice

WORKING SOLO ONLINE

Non-Rated Resource

Description:
Entrepreneurs, consultants, free agents, e-lancers, and other self-employed persons will find over 1,000 listings for publications, professional associations, tech help, and online resources at this advice site from entrepreneur and author Terri Lonier. The site is searchable by keyword and also includes small business "FAQs," news and events, and a free newsletter.

Author:
Terri Lonier

Ms. Lonier is an author and president of Working Solo, Inc. She advises such clients as Microsoft, Hewlett-Packard, and Claris on how best to access and communicate with the small business and SOHO (Small Office Home Office) market.

Publisher:
Working Solo, Inc.

Media:
Internet

Principal Subject:
Resources For Networking, Support & Advice

Where To Find/Buy:
On the Internet at http://www.workingsolo.com

YAHOO! SMALL BUSINESS

Non-Rated Resource

Description:
A relatively new addition to Yahoo!, this annotated web guide to self-employment resources offers direct links for such topics as Starting a Business, Finance, E-commerce, Technology, and Office Supplies. Like other Yahoo! pages, this one also includes articles, chat rooms, business tools, news features, and related services.

Publisher:
Yahoo! Inc

The two developers of Yahoo!, David Filo and Jerry Yang, started their guide in April 1994 to keep track of their personal interests on the Internet. Today, Yahoo! contains information on tens of thousands of computers linked to the Web.

Media:
Internet

Principal Subject:
Resources For Networking, Support & Advice

Where To Find/Buy:
On the Internet using the URL: http://smallbusiness.yahoo.com

RESOURCES OF INTEREST TO SPECIFIC GROUPS

VII

WOMEN

Having enjoyed rapid growth over the past two decades, women-owned enterprises are a significant contributor to our nation's economy. In 1997, the nation's 8.5 million women-owned businesses represented over one-third of all businesses in the U.S. They generated $3.1 trillion in revenue, an astounding increase of 209% in ten years!

These women-run enterprises employ more than 23.8 million workers, an increase of 262% since 1987. By 2000, it is projected that half of all businesses will be women-owned. As a whole, women-owned businesses outpace all other small business sectors in growth and, significantly, they fail less often.

What's behind this phenomenal growth? Entrepreneurism's siren call to women can be summed up in one word: control. Controlling one's career was once considered a man's prerogative. Today, women are finding, or creating, business arrangements that suit their need for flexibility and their desire for interesting, rewarding work in a family-friendly environment.

For many women, the journey to self-employment includes a time of working in the traditional work world. Though gains have been made, women still earn 72 cents to a man's dollar for the same work. Having faced real or perceived limits imposed on them because of their gender, these women have decided to surmount the "glass ceiling" by building their own home, with their own blueprint.

Frustration with gender discrimination is only one factor in the move toward self-employment. Many mothers yearn to spend more time with their children, and find that being their own boss allows them to cut back or tailor their hours around their family's schedule. But it's not only mothers who are looking for balance. While the 80s idolized financial success and tolerated, if not celebrated, workaholism, the 90s witnessed a reordering of values. As the millennium approaches, the concept of success is broadening, into a holistic notion encompassing work, family, and personal fulfillment.

Going solo has allowed many women to be The Boss for the first time in their career. As a self-employed woman, you are CEO and founder: you control the product, you take the credit (or the hits), you choose which hours to work, how long to work, and where to work. You can implement your knowledge and expertise; you can test your limits. You can employ and mentor other women. You can work in your home while your kids are at school and stop when they come in the door. You can start a dream business after you've retired.

You can bring in income, fulfill ambitions, and strive for greatness, all on your own terms. And best of all, you may never have to wear panty hose again!

The resources we highlight in this chapter are written by women, for women, or contain significant sections of interest to women. (Be sure to read the full reviews to get all of the details.) There are how-to guides for starting a business, websites for networking with working moms and entrepreneurial women, and resources for locating women's business associations. You'll also find web guides, ideas for home businesses, and information on government loans and assistance programs. (Note: Moms, check out the Parents section for other resources of interest).

Women

Title:	**BizProWeb**
Subtitle:	The Business & Professionals' Web Site
Author:	Craig Sonnenberg
Overall Rating:	★★★★
Media Type:	Internet
Short Description:	Visitors to BizProWeb will find over 700 pages of business links, information, and resources in this combination Net guide and networking hub for entrepreneurs and self-employed professionals. Divided into 6 main areas, the site includes directories of websites, newsgroups, and shareware sites, a collection of featured articles, and 4 discussion forums.

■ **Read The Full Review Of This Resource On Page 148.**

Title:	**Consulting On The Side**
Subtitle:	How To Start A Part-Time Consulting Business While Still Working At Your Full-Time Job
Author:	Mary F. Cook
Overall Rating:	★★★★
Media Type:	Book
Short Description:	According to Cook, it can take as long as 12–18 months for a consulting business to bring in enough income to sustain its creator. So why not start a consultancy while still employed? In this guide, Cook explores both the practical and ethical questions of on-the-side consulting, as well as the logistics and how-to basics of starting-up.

■ **Read The Full Review Of This Resource On Page 83.**

Title:	**Free Help From Uncle Sam To Start Your Own Business**
Subtitle	Or Expand The One You Have
Author:	William Alarid
Overall Rating:	★★★★
Media Type:	Book
Short Description:	Alarid advises that although government assistance may entail some "red tape," in many cases it is well worth the effort. He also offers a contact in case assistance is needed to overcome this obstacle. In its eleventh printing, this source provides detail/contacts regarding grants, loans, information, education, and more.

■ **Read The Full Review Of This Resource On Page 152.**

Title:	**HERS**
Subtitle	The Wise Woman's Guide To Starting A Business On $2,000 Or Less
Author:	Carol Milano
Overall Rating:	★★★★
Media Type:	Book
Short Description:	In regards to starting a business, Milano writes "a key question is, should you?" While acknowledging that business ownership is not everyone's choice, Milano believes that it is possible to create a successful business on $2000 or less. She offers examples and advice in an effort to help readers make informed choices.

■ **Read The Full Review Of This Resource On Page 35.**

Women

Title:	**Minding Her Own Business**
Subtitle:	The Self-Employed Woman's Guide To Taxes And Record Keeping
Author:	Jan Zobel, EA
Overall Rating:	★★★★
Media Type:	Book
Short Description:	Zobel looks at the self-owned business with a focus on tax considerations. She considers taxes from the reference of the employer and the employee. Attention is given to deductions and the calculations of taxes. Intending to support both business needs and IRS requirements, Zobel offers a variety of suggestions for records keeping.

■ **Read The Full Review Of This Resource On Page 36.**

Title:	**The Online Women's Business Center**
Overall Rating:	★★★★
Media Type:	Internet
Short Description:	Described by its creators as an interactive business skills training site, the "OWBC" offers hundreds of how-to articles and tutorials on every aspect of entrepreneurism. The contents include sections on Starting Your Business, Growing, and Expanding, as well as a Finance Center, Management Institute, and Marketing Mall. Chat and Q&A features are provided.

■ **Read The Full Review Of This Resource On Page 32.**

Title:	**SBA Online**
Overall Rating:	★★★★
Media Type:	Internet
Short Description:	The SBA site offers a variety of informational and educational resources for small business owners, including sections on "Starting Your Business," "Financing," and SBA offices and services. There are "FAQs," links to related online resources, counseling and research help, advice, and a "Startup Kit," with tools and "tutorials" for every aspect of starting.

■ **Read The Full Review Of This Resource On Page 33.**

Title:	**Smart Business Supersite**
Overall Rating:	★★★★
Media Type:	Internet
Short Description:	The SBS site is more than a Net guide, though it does contain links to thousands of articles, websites, mailing lists, and profiles. It also features news columns, information on thousands of trade shows, interactive forums, hot tips, a "people finder," and a free reminder service. Users can browse 63 categories or use the internal search engine to find specifics.

■ **Read The Full Review Of This Resource On Page 150.**

Title:	**The Home Team**
Subtitle:	How Couples Can Make A Life And A Living By Working At Home
Author:	Scott Gregory and Shirley Siluk Gregory
Overall Rating:	★★★
Media Type:	Book
Short Description:	Written as a guide for couples interested in launching a home-business, this resource offers advice and insights based on the authors' experiences and those of couples they have interviewed. Family issues, prerequisites for successful at-home businesses, and work styles are highlighted.

■ **Read The Full Review Of This Resource On Page 121.**

Women

Title:	**WAHM: Work At Home Moms**
Author:	Cheryl Demas
Overall Rating:	★★★
Media Type:	Internet
Short Description:	Created by a work-at-home mom, WAHM offers a variety of networking and support resources for women who currently work or wish to work in the home. In addition to the advice, book selections, and links to related websites, users can find/contact "WAHMs Near You" and/or learn about "WAHM businesses" from their female founders.
■ **Read The Full Review Of This Resource On Page 155.**	

Title:	**Your Small Business.com**
Subtitle:	Helping Your Small Business Become Successful
Overall Rating:	★★★
Media Type:	Internet
Short Description:	Whether you're a work-at-home parent, SOHO, small business or Internet business entrepreneur, this online "resource center" is designed for you. There are sections for Starting a Biz, Women in Biz, Home Biz, Website Owners, Marketing Ideas, and Money Issues. The site also boasts 250+ how-to and informational articles, as well links to related sites.
■ **Read The Full Review Of This Resource On Page 111.**	

Title:	**101 Best Home-Based Businesses For Women**
Author:	Priscilla Y. Huff
Overall Rating:	★★
Media Type:	Book
Short Description:	Huff considers some general aspects of home-based business ownership, and lists 101 individual business ideas. The businesses featured offer examples of how to convert work/hobby skills into a home-based business. Although the businesses featured are all owned by women, the ideas could apply to anyone.
■ **Read The Full Review Of This Resource On Page 130.**	

Title:	**MiningCo.com: Small Business Information**
Author:	Ed Martin
Overall Rating:	★★
Media Type:	Internet
Short Description:	Like other MiningCo. Guides, the one to small businesses combines original articles, NetLinks, message boards, chat rooms, Q&A, and a marketplace of selected books, videos, and related services. Articles address such topics as "Putting the SBA to Work" and business and technology; links include sites where you can download free business and legal forms.
■ **Read The Full Review Of This Resource On Page 158.**	

Title:	**More 101 Best Home-Based Businesses For Women**
Author:	Priscilla Y. Huff
Overall Rating:	★★
Media Type:	Book
Short Description:	Huff begins with an overview of common topics related to researching and establishing a business. Current topics such as "The Internet" and "Home-Based and Work-at-Home Business Scams" are included. The remainder of the book details 101 business ideas.
■ **Read The Full Review Of This Resource On Page 131.**	

Title:	**The NAFE Guide To Starting Your Own Business**
Subtitle:	A Handbook For Entrepreneurial Women
Author:	Marilyn Manning & Patricia Haddock
Overall Rating:	★★
Media Type:	Book
Short Description:	The National Association for Female Executives asks women to "Dare to Dream Big." The blueprint for your business is established by defining your vision, values and ethical standards. Personal development strategies are based on the profiles of successful women business owners. Exercises, information and additional resources are included.

■ **Read The Full Review Of This Resource On Page 17.**

Title:	**The Women's Business Resource Guide**
Subtitle:	A National Directory Of More Than 800 Programs, Resources, And Organizations To Help Women Start Or Expand A Business
Author:	Barbara Littman
Overall Rating:	★★
Media Type:	Book
Short Description:	Littman begins with interviews of four women business owners who have used one or more of the resources contained in this book to establish and grow a business. Over 800 resources are described according to who is served, what is offered, what it costs, and how to get connected to the resource. Many of the resources are especially for women.

■ **Read The Full Review Of This Resource On Page 159.**

Title:	**WomanOwned.com**
Overall Rating:	★★
Media Type:	Internet
Short Description:	Providing networking opportunities and business information is the goal at this site for entrepreneurial women. There's an assortment of guides and articles authored by women, and there are 3 networking vehicles: a Networking Center, Message Boards, and a database of women-owned businesses. A step-by-step tutorial for business plans is also included.

■ **Read The Full Review Of This Resource On Page 157.**

Title:	**The Enterprising Woman**
Subtitle:	An Inspirational And Informational Guide For Every Woman Starting, Running, Or Redefining Her Business
Author:	Mari Florence
Overall Rating:	★
Media Type:	Book
Short Description:	According to the SBA, women are starting small businesses at twice the rate of men. Yet, women still face entrepreneurial challenges particular to their gender. In this combination inspirational and informational guide, Florence explores 10 different industries, shares the stories of successful women, and provides tips and advice for starting/managing a business.

■ **Read The Full Review Of This Resource On Page 51.**

Women

Title:	**African American Women Entrepreneurs At Home**
Author:	Marie Parham
Overall Rating:	N/R
Media Type:	Internet
Short Description:	Similar to Bizy Moms.com, AAWEH functions primarily as a networking hub for African American women who work at home. The site also features current events, a place to post and respond to contracting opportunities, and a resource "library." The library includes links to Business Resources and phone numbers for African American women's organizations.

■ **Read The Full Review Of This Resource On Page 162.**

Title:	**Bizy Moms**
Author:	Liz Folger
Overall Rating:	N/R
Media Type:	Internet
Short Description:	In addition to information about books and resources for work-at-home moms, Folger's site offers women an assortment of features for starting a home business. There are 180+ business ideas, "FAQs," message boards, tips from successful "bizy moms," and a list of "scams" to avoid. Folger also offers phone consultations and her own advice column.

■ **Read The Full Review Of This Resource On Page 125.**

Title:	**Cybergrrl**
Overall Rating:	N/R
Media Type:	Internet
Short Description:	For women in technology, the Cybergrrl site offers networking forums, Tech Tips (which include articles on creating a website and choosing an ISP), and expert Q & A. The She's So Savvy feature offers profiles of successful women business owners. There's also access to Webgrrls, a technology-and-women-related networking site and nationwide organization.

■ **Read The Full Review Of This Resource On Page 163.**

Title:	**The Feminist Majority Foundation Online**
Subtitle:	Directory Of Women's Organizations
Overall Rating:	N/R
Media Type:	Internet
Short Description:	To help women locate and contact relevant professional associations, this site offers lists of women's business, legal, and medical organizations. Entries include "American Association of Black Women Entrepreneurs" and "American Society of Women Entrepreneurs." Each entry contains contact information and a link to the association's website (where possible).

■ **Read The Full Review Of This Resource On Page 164.**

Title:	**Minority Business Entrepreneur**
Author:	Ginger Conrad
Overall Rating:	N/R
Media Type:	Internet
Short Description:	MBEMAG is the online version of *Minority Business Entrepreneur* (MBE) magazine, a publication for minority and women business owners. The site features articles from current and back issues of MBE, as well as a business resource directory, related links, and access to the "Women's Business Executive" site, a newsletter for women business owners.

■ **Read The Full Review Of This Resource On Page 165.**

Women

Title:	**National Association Of Women Business Owners**
Overall Rating:	N/R
Media Type:	Internet
Short Description:	At this site, women entrepreneurs can learn about and/or join NAWBO, the National Association of Women Business Owners. Emerging business owners can become members for a $50 annual fee; membership benefits include partner/vendor discounts, networking locally and nationally, public policy representation, and international affiliations.
■ **Read The Full Review Of This Resource On Page 165.**	

Title:	**NetWorking Moms**
Author:	Melanie Berry
Overall Rating:	N/R
Media Type:	Internet
Short Description:	Another networking site for work-at-home moms, this one revolves around the Mom-to-Mom Solutions Club, a chat room for sharing information, advice, and ideas. Other features include Pulse Polls (weekly "hot topic" Q & A), current news items, and Working Mom Gateway, an annotated web guide to work-at-home mom resources.
■ **Read The Full Review Of This Resource On Page 166.**	

Title:	**WomenCONNECT.com**
Subtitle:	The Source For Women In Business
Overall Rating:	N/R
Media Type:	Internet
Short Description:	An online resource for women in all types of business, this site features chat rooms, business and career workshops, and money and health segments, as well as news items and current events. A keyword search using "entrepreneur" will result in a number of articles and profiles on entrepreneurism, including minority entrepreneur issues.
■ **Read The Full Review Of This Resource On Page 166.**	

RACIAL/ETHNIC MINORITIES

Minority-owned businesses are a vital part of the U.S. economy, and their ranks and influence are rapidly growing. Between 1987 and 1997, minority-owned businesses grew 168% to total more than 3.25 million enterprises. These businesses now generate $425 billion in revenue, an astonishing increase of 343% in the last decade. Employing nearly 4 million workers, minority-owned businesses are more likely to recruit, train and promote racial and ethnic minorities. (The U.S. Small Business Administration's Office of Advocacy produced these impressive numbers; in this context, "minority-owned" includes African-American, Hispanic, and Asian-owned ventures. Our use of the term "racial/ethnic minorities" is similarly inclusive.)

The history of entrepreneurism among minority communities reflects the history of the United States as a whole. Immigrants to America often bring an entrepreneurial culture with them, and many earn a livelihood by starting their own business. Hispanic, Asian and Jamaican newcomers are particularly likely to be self-employed.

In the "land of opportunity," many members of minority groups have found that their best opportunities can be found in the arena of self-employment. Having experienced real or perceived discrimination in the traditional work force, many African-Americans have opted for the risks and rewards of striking out on their own. Many of the estimated 880,000 African-American-owned enterprises were started by men and women who saw a need for products or services in their community that mainstream businesses missed or ignored. Because racial advocacy groups have placed a renewed emphasis on keeping "Black dollars in Black communities," many African-American owned and operated businesses enjoy strong customer support and loyalty.

In this section, we highlight books and websites directed to specific racial and ethnic communities. There are websites for networking with peers and finding support organizations, information on government loans and programs, and advice on minority-related issues. One site offers data on Hispanic and other minority markets; another provides a networking hub for African-American work-at-home moms. (Be sure to read the complete review for a full description.)

Going solo is no easy task. It takes a great deal of planning, research, hard work, and motivation. With technological advances and a trend toward small business, however, now is a better time than ever to put your dreams into action.

Minorities

Title:	**BizProWeb**
Subtitle:	The Business & Professionals' Web Site
Author:	Craig Sonnenberg
Overall Rating:	★★★★
Media Type:	Internet
Short Description:	Visitors to BizProWeb will find over 700 pages of business links, information, and resources in this combination Net guide and networking hub for entrepreneurs and self-employed professionals. Divided into 6 main areas, the site includes directories of websites, newsgroups, and shareware sites, a collection of featured articles, and 4 discussion forums.

■ **Read The Full Review Of This Resource On Page 148.**

Title:	**Free Help From Uncle Sam To Start Your Own Business**
Subtitle:	Or Expand The One You Have
Author:	William Alarid
Overall Rating:	★★★★
Media Type:	Book
Short Description:	Alarid advises that although government assistance may entail some "red tape," in many cases it is well worth the effort. He also offers a contact in case assistance is needed to overcome this obstacle. In its eleventh printing, this source provides detail/contacts regarding grants, loans, information, education, and more.

■ **Read The Full Review Of This Resource On Page 152.**

Title:	**SBA Online**
Overall Rating:	★★★★
Media Type:	Internet
Short Description:	The SBA site offers a variety of informational and educational resources for small business owners, including sections on "Starting Your Business," "Financing," and SBA offices and services. There are "FAQs," links to related online resources, counseling and research help, advice, and a "Startup Kit," with tools and "tutorials" for every aspect of starting.

■ **Read The Full Review Of This Resource On Page 33.**

Title:	**Smart Business Supersite**
Overall Rating:	★★★★
Media Type:	Internet
Short Description:	The SBS site is more than a Net guide, though it does contain links to thousands of articles, websites, mailing lists, and profiles. It also features news columns, information on thousands of trade shows, interactive forums, hot tips, a "people finder," and a free reminder service. Users can browse 63 categories or use the internal search engine to find specifics.

■ **Read The Full Review Of This Resource On Page 150.**

Minorities

Title:	**The NAFE Guide To Starting Your Own Business**
Subtitle:	A Handbook For Entrepreneurial Women
Author:	Marilyn Manning & Patricia Haddock
Overall Rating:	★★
Media Type:	Book
Short Description:	The National Association for Female Executives asks women to "Dare to Dream Big." The blueprint for your business is established by defining your vision, values and ethical standards. Personal development strategies are based on the profiles of successful women business owners. Exercises, information and additional resources are included.

■ **Read The Full Review Of This Resource On Page 17.**

Title:	**Black Enterprise.com**
Subtitle:	The Virtual Desktop For African Americans
Overall Rating:	★
Media Type:	Internet
Short Description:	To assist African American entrepreneurs and professionals, this online version of *B.E.* offers articles, links, financial news, and market data. Users can search the last 12 print issues by topic, browse featured selections, or look through the small business directory. Advice on using technology, investment strategies, and personal motivation techniques is included.

■ **Read The Full Review Of This Resource On Page 160.**

Title:	**African American Women Entrepreneurs At Home**
Author:	Marie Parham
Overall Rating:	N/R
Media Type:	Internet
Short Description:	Similar to Bizy Moms.com, AAWEH functions primarily as a networking hub for African American women who work at home. The site also features current events, a place to post and respond to contracting opportunities, and a resource "library." The library includes links to Business Resources and phone numbers for African American women's organizations.

■ **Read The Full Review Of This Resource On Page 162.**

Title:	**Everything Black.com: Business Resources**
Overall Rating:	N/R
Media Type:	Internet
Short Description:	As its name suggests, this Yahoo!-style web guide provides annotated links to African American-related websites; its Business Resources page contains links to a variety of entrepreneurial resources. Links include online magazines, organizations, news agencies, networking forums, and sites that list (for free) African American Internet businesses.

■ **Read The Full Review Of This Resource On Page 163.**

Title:	**Hispanstar: The Hispanic Information Network**
Overall Rating:	N/R
Media Type:	Internet
Short Description:	In addition to cover stories from last month's *Hispanic Business* magazine, visitors to this site will find chat rooms and bulletin boards, a calendar of events, and a list of related "bizlinks." There's also HispanTelligence, a private data archive of marketing information on the U.S. Hispanic market, other U.S. minority markets, and international economics.

■ **Read The Full Review Of This Resource On Page 164.**

Minorities

Title:	**Minority Business Development Agency**
Overall Rating:	N/R
Media Type:	Internet
Short Description:	To help minority entrepreneurs, the MBDA's site provides information on its activities and services, local MBDA centers, and such MBDA partners as Minority Business Development Centers and Minority Business Opportunity Committees. Other features include a resource locator and an annotated list of links. A Spanish-text version is also available.

■ **Read The Full Review Of This Resource On Page 164.**

Title:	**Minority Business Entrepreneur**
Author:	Ginger Conrad
Overall Rating:	N/R
Media Type:	Internet
Short Description:	MBEMAG is the online version of *Minority Business Entrepreneur (MBE)* magazine, a publication for minority and women business owners. The site features articles from current and back issues of MBE, as well as a business resource directory, related links, and access to the "Women's Business Executive" site, a newsletter for women business owners.

■ **Read The Full Review Of This Resource On Page 165.**

Title:	**The National Center For American Indian Enterprise Development**
Overall Rating:	N/R
Media Type:	Internet
Short Description:	The NCAIED is a full-service center offering economic development services to Native Americans. Their site provides contact information for the organization's 3 regional offices, an introduction to NCAIED services, such as the Native American Business Consultant, and a hyperlinked list of Native American-owned businesses.

■ **Read The Full Review Of This Resource On Page 165.**

YOUNG ENTREPRENEURS

There was a time, not so long ago, when the term "young entrepreneur" conjured up two standard images: the gee-whiz kid with brilliant ideas and scruffy hair, and the kids who mowed lawns, set up lemonade stands, or babysat. Today, "young entrepreneur" is a catch phrase used to describe a new generation of independent business types under 30. Though the media is filled with stories of young, tech-savvy entrepreneurs making waves—and big bucks—not all of today's success stories involve high technology.

Certainly the advent of the Internet and the widespread use of technology (which young people tend to have both greater interest and experience in than their older counterparts) has contributed significantly to the rise of under-30 entrepreneurship; but it is not the sole factor. Generations "X" and "Y" grew up amid downsizing and recessions; many of them were personally affected by a family member suffering a lay-off or firing. Young people today understand that "job security," as their grandparents knew it, is an endangered (if not extinct) species. So, how do you "feel secure in an insecure world?" You take control. You start your own business.

A 1996 Gallup Poll found that nearly 7 out of 10 high school students wanted to start their own business; primarily, they said, because they wanted to be their own boss. That same year, *U.S. News & World Report* stated that 62% of people under 30 wanted to be self-employed. Those statistics haven't translated into an equal number of start-ups, but they do reflect a growing trend. Young entrepreneurship is on the rise in every industry. People under 30 are finding success in Internet, import/export, sales-rep and home-based businesses. They are producing new fashions, new beverages, new software. Once, people would have told you that it was rash to start a business in your twenties. Today, people are not only eager to hear your business ideas, they're more eager to invest, too.

Whatever your business goals, as an entrepreneur under 30, you will probably face challenges and concerns unique to your peer group. The younger you are the more specific guidance you will need. The resources collected in this section were created to assist you in your travails—providing how-to knowledge, advice or an opportunity to network with like-minded peers. In these books and websites, you'll find information on gaining the trust (and money) of lenders and investors, instruction for combating age discrimination, and tips on how to present yourself, your business plan, and your business. You'll also find stories from other young entrepreneurs and profiles of a wide range of businesses. In "No Experience Necessary," the author even tells you how to conduct meetings in bars or restaurants if you're under 21. (Don't forget to read the complete review for a full description of this and other resources.)

Use these resources as supplements, but be sure to visit other chapters of this guide for help with your particular business type. Preparation is a vital element of start-up success, and the more you know before you begin your venture, the greater your chances of staying afloat. With preparation and commitment, you can make your solo dreams come true. Good luck!

Young Entrepreneurs

Title:	**How To Succeed In Business By Breaking All The Rules**
Subtitle:	A Plan For Entrepreneurs
Author:	Dan S. Kennedy
Overall Rating:	★★★★
Media Type:	Book
Short Description:	Just as the title states, Kennedy's purpose is to show you how to break the rules and succeed in business. Forget such aphorisms as "it takes money to make money," "you can't get rich quick," and "think positive!" In this guide, Kennedy uses his own experiences and other real-life success stories to prove that contrarian, rule-breaking strategies work best.
■ **Read The Full Review Of This Resource On Page 140.**	

Title:	**Inc. Online**
Subtitle:	The Web Site For Growing Companies
Overall Rating:	★★★
Media Type:	Internet
Short Description:	While Inc. Online does offer the full contents of the 14 annual issues of "Inc." and 4 annual issues of "Inc. Technology" online (as well as archived issues), it goes beyond the print publications with site-only features and interactive networking opportunities. Sections include Online Entrepreneur for online businesses, and Zinc, for young entrepreneurs.
■ **Read The Full Review Of This Resource On Page 44.**	

Title:	**Upstart Start-Ups**
Author:	Ron Lieber
Overall Rating:	★★★
Media Type:	Book
Short Description:	You're under 30 and you have a fantastic business idea—maybe even a revolutionary one—but the "suits" won't take you seriously. How do you turn your "youth and inexperience" into an asset? Lieber tells you how in his guide, which also offers success stories and advice on such issues as business plans, obtaining financial backing, and establishing credibility.
■ **Read The Full Review Of This Resource On Page 41.**	

Title:	**MiningCo.com: Small Business Information**
Author:	Ed Martin
Overall Rating:	★★
Media Type:	Internet
Short Description:	Like other MiningCo. Guides, the one to small businesses combines original articles, NetLinks, message boards, chat rooms, Q&A, and a marketplace of selected books, videos, and related services. Articles address such topics as "Putting the SBA to Work" and business and technology; links include sites where you can download free business and legal forms.
■ **Read The Full Review Of This Resource On Page 158.**	

Young Entrepreneurs

Title:	**No Experience Necessary**
Author:	Jennifer Kushell
Overall Rating:	★★
Media Type:	Book
Short Description:	Young entrepreneurs ("YEPs") face their own set of problems when it comes to starting a business. Kushell understands that; she founded her company at the age of 24. In her guide, she covers the need-to-know basics, such as developing "the idea," writing a business plan, and raising money, and offers advice tailored to "YEPs," i.e. commanding respect.

■ Read The Full Review Of This Resource On Page 47.

Title:	**Black Enterprise.com**
Subtitle:	The Virtual Desktop For African Americans
Overall Rating:	★
Media Type:	Internet
Short Description:	To assist African American entrepreneurs and professionals, this online version of *B.E.* offers articles, links, financial news, and market data. Users can search the last 12 print issues by topic, browse featured selections, or look through the small business directory. Advice on using technology, investment strategies, and personal motivation techniques is included.

■ Read The Full Review Of This Resource On Page 160.

Title:	**Generation E**
Subtitle:	The Do-It-Yourself Guide For Twentysomethings & Other Non-Corporate Types
Author:	Joel and Lee Naftali
Overall Rating:	★
Media Type:	Book
Short Description:	If you're a twenty-something or "non corporate type" with no money and no business experience, this guide to self-employment was written just for you. The first half helps you find your passion and presents 300+ businesses you can start or customize. The second half offers advice on starting up, turning a profit, accounting, and taxes.

■ Read The Full Review Of This Resource On Page 50.

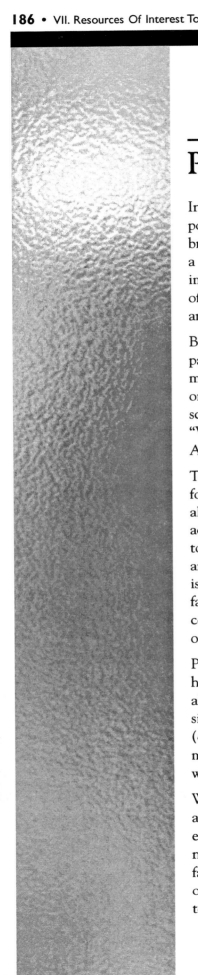

PARENTS

In the 80s, the image of the Working Woman in a shoulder-padded power suit, balancing a baby on her hip while preparing her family's breakfast, fed the belief that women could have it all—a career and a family—if only they worked hard enough. Women believed that image, and worked themselves to weariness following the rigid rules of corporate America by day, pouring themselves into their children and house management tasks evenings and weekends.

Because long hours, willingness to relocate and uninterrupted career paths are often requirements for promotion in the corporate world, many mothers felt they were sacrificing the needs of their children in order to be successful in their career. Kay James, a Dean at a graduate school in Virginia, speaks for many mothers when she concludes: "Women *can* have it all: they just can't have it all at the same time." At least not if you play by somebody else's rules.

Today, millions of parents are playing by their own rules. They have found that creating their own business, or becoming a consultant, allows them to live life, and balance their career and family, according to their priorities. Parents, like other soloists, are drawn to the independence of doing work that they love, on their terms, and in their way. But the benefit most often cited by moms and dads is the ability to tailor their work schedule around the needs of their family. Although women are still the primary caregivers, surveys consistently show that both moms and dads place a high priority on spending more time with their children.

Parents are the driving force behind the decade's explosion in home-based businesses. Home-based businesses aren't new. After all, mothers have run income-producing ventures out of their homes since the beginning of civilization. However advances in technology (cell phones, email, and computers under $1,000) and changes in the marketplace have made it easier for parents to use professional skills while maintaining time for family.

When websites and how-to resources for self-employed moms and dads began to appear regularly in the mainstream media, entrepreneurial parents knew their time had come. There are networking websites to visit, books on businesses for mothers (or fathers), and advice on everything from setting up a home office to on-the-job parenting. For a full description of each resource, be sure to read the complete review.

In the movie "Baby Boom", Diane Keaton plays a harried corporate executive who gives up her lucrative job to raise her daughter. She winds up rediscovering herself, creating her own home-based baby food company, and making millions. In today's entrepreneur-friendly market, her happy ending is being lived out by millions of parents.

Parents

Title:	**The Entrepreneurial Parent**
Overall Rating:	★★★
Media Type:	Internet
Short Description:	Designed to be both a community and a career resource, the "EP" site offers parents who want to work at home services, tools, lifestyle and entrepreneurial advice. The 6 main sections include information on Your Family (i.e. parenting), Your Career (i.e. long term goals), and Your Business (i.e. tips on starting and growing your SOHO business).
■ **Read The Full Review Of This Resource On Page 123.**	

Title:	**The Home Team**
Subtitle:	How Couples Can Make A Life And A Living By Working At Home
Author:	Scott Gregory and Shirley Siluk Gregory
Overall Rating:	★★★
Media Type:	Book
Short Description:	Written as a guide for couples interested in launching a home-business, this resource offers advice and insights based on the authors' experiences and those of couples they have interviewed. Family issues, prerequisites for successful at-home businesses, and work styles are highlighted.
■ **Read The Full Review Of This Resource On Page 121.**	

Title:	**The Stay-At-Home Mom's Guide To Making Money**
Subtitle:	How To Choose The Business That's Right For You Using The Skills And Interests You Already Have
Author:	Liz Folger
Overall Rating:	★★★
Media Type:	Book
Short Description:	Folger believes that preparing with research and taking action are the two key steps mothers need to take to become a home-based entrepreneur. She features twenty-nine individuals who've achieved work and family goals by creating a business that is uniquely their own. Also included: overview of the business process and resource suggestions.
■ **Read The Full Review Of This Resource On Page 122.**	

Title:	**Moneymaking Moms**
Subtitle:	How Work At Home Can Work For You
Author:	Caroline Hull and Tanya Wallace
Overall Rating:	★★
Media Type:	Book
Short Description:	Here is guidance for Moms and Dads who wish to work from home in order to share more of life with their children. Discussion of business-related topics is qualified by the special need to achieve and maintain a comfortable balance between work and family. Work/family issues are covered in-depth.
■ **Read The Full Review Of This Resource On Page 124.**	

Parents

Title:	**NetWorking Moms**
Author:	Melanie Berry
Overall Rating:	N/R
Media Type:	Internet
Short Description:	Another networking site for work-at-home moms, this one revolves around the Mom-to-Mom Solutions Club, a chat room for sharing information, advice, and ideas. Other features include Pulse Polls (weekly "hot topic" Q & A), current news items, and Working Mom Gateway, an annotated web guide to work-at-home mom resources.

■ **Read The Full Review Of This Resource On Page 166.**

INDICES

TITLE INDEX

AUTHOR INDEX

PUBLISHER INDEX

MEDIA INDEX:

Note: This media index is created using the media **reviewed**. In a number of cases, resources are also available in other media formats (audiotape, videotape, etc.); the availability of these other formats is noted in the "Where To Find/Buy" section found in the full-page reviews of such resources.

Book

Internet

Book + Software

Videotape

SUBJECT INDEX
1–4 Stars (4 = Best)

Setting Up & Running A Home-Based Business

Home Business Guides For Mothers, Women & Couples

Ideas For Home-Based Businesses

Success Strategies

Resources For Networking, Support & Advice

ABOUT THE EDITOR

Stanley I. Mason, Jr. is the founder (1973) and CEO of Simco, Inc. a product development enterprise. A successful entrepreneur for over three decades, he has created and patented many well-known products including the first shaped disposable diaper and the first granola bars. He was *Inc.* Magazine/Ernst & Young 1989 Entrepreneur of the Year, and holds 55 U.S. patents and 8 foreign patents in a diversity of fields. Mason was the University of Connecticut's Director of Entrepreneurial Development, and an adjunct professor, for seven years. He currently teaches Entrepreneurship at Sacred Heart University in Fairfield, Connecticut in the MBA program and serves on their Board of Regents. He is a member of the Board of Trustees of the National Council for Industrial Innovation (NCII), a member of the Institute of American Entrepreneurs, and a member of the Board of Directors of the National Congress of Inventor Organizations. In addition to Simco, Mason has created several other businesses, including Masonware, Inc., Crisis Communications, Inc., Family Security Co. and Appropriate Village Technology, Inc. He is the author of *Inventing Small Products*.

GUIDEBOOKS FOR
LIFE'S BIG DECISIONS

For every important issue we face, there are resources that offer suggestions and help. Unfortunately, we don't always know much about the issue we've enountered and we don't know:

- Where to find these sources of information

- Much about their quality, value, or relevance

Resource Pathways guidebooks help those facing an important decision or challenging life-event by directing them to the information they need to understand the issues they face and make decisions with confidence. In every Resource Pathways guidebook:

- We **describe and evaluate virtually all quality resources** available in any media (books, the Internet, CD-ROMs, videotape, audiotape, and more).

- We **explain the issues** that are typically encountered in dealing with each subject, and **classify each resource** reviewed according to its primary focus.

- We **make a reasoned judgment** about the quality of each resource, give it a **rating**, and decide whether it should be **recommended**. We select only the best as "Recommended" (roughly 1 in 4).

- We **provide information on where to buy or how to access** each resource, including ISBN numbers for books and URL "addresses" for Internet websites.

- We **publish a new edition of each guidebook frequently**, with updated reviews and recommendations.

Those who turn to Resource Pathways guidebooks will be able to locate the resource they need, saving time, money, and frustration as they begin their research and learning process.

LIFECYCLES SERIES

■ *"... a calm and hope-filled guide ..."*

Anxiety & Depression: The Best Resources To Help You Cope

Editor: Rich Wemhoff, PhD
ISBN: 1-892148-09-9 (2nd Ed); 292 Pages

■ *"... an invaluable tool for couples and therapists ..."*

Marriage: The Best Resources To Help Yours Thrive

Editor: Rich Wemhoff, PhD
ISBN: 1-892148-05-6; 244 Pages

■ *"... positive, user-friendly guidebook ..."*

Divorce: The Best Resources To Help You Survive

Editor: Rich Wemhoff, PhD
ISBN: 1-892148-00-5 (2nd Ed); 324 Pages

■ Eldercare: The Best Resources To Help You Help Your Aging Relatives

Editor: Marty Richards, MSW, ACSW
ISBN: 1-892148-07-2; 256 Pages
Available: November 1999

PARENTING SERIES

■ *"... well-organized, easy-to-read, and to-the-point."*

Having Children: The Best Resources To Help You Prepare

Editor: Anne Montgomery, MD, IBCLC, FAAFP
ISBN: 1-892148-06-4 (2nd Ed); 312 Pages

■ *"... a practical guide through the often dense forest of parenting information ..."*

Infants & Toddlers: The Best Resources To Help You Parent

Editor: Julie Soto, MS
ISBN: 1-892148-10-2 (2nd Ed); 372 Pages

■ *"... an incredible resource guide ..."*

Raising Teenagers: The Best Resources To Help Yours Succeed

Editor: John Ganz, MC, EdD
ISBN: 1-892148-04-8; 262 Pages

■ Stepparenting: The Best Resources To Help Blend Your Family

Editor: Marty Richards, MSW, ACSW
ISBN: 1-892148-13-7; 256 Pages
Available: March 2000

HIGHER EDUCATION & CAREERS SERIES

■ *"... quintessential guide to the guides..."*

College Choice & Admissions: The Best Resources To Help You Get In

Editor: Dodge Johnson, PhD
ISBN: 0-9653424-9-2 (3rd Ed); 336 Pages

■ *"... comprehensive ... a real time and money saver..."*

College Financial Aid: The Best Resources To Help You Find The Money

Editor: David Hoy
ISBN: 1-892148-01-3 (3rd Ed); 222 Pages

■ *"... thorough, honest, and complete..."*

Graduate School: The Best Resources To Help You Choose, Get In, & Pay

Editor: Jane Finkle, MS
ISBN: 1-892148-11-0 (2nd Ed); 278 Pages
Available: February 2000

■ *"... a clear and concise roadmap..."*

Starting Your Career: The Best Resources To Help You Find The Right Job

Editor: Laura Praglin, PhD
ISBN: 1-892148-03-X; 248 Pages

■ *"Great resources gathered with an eye for the practical..."*

Career Transitions: The Best Resources To Help You Advance

Editor: David Goodenough, MS, CMHS
ISBN: 1-892148-08-0; 268 Pages

■ Going Solo: The Best Resources For Entrepreneurs & Freelancers

Editor: Stanley I. Mason, Jr.
ISBN: 1-892148-12-9; 268 Pages
Available: October 1999

Your favorite bookstore or library may order any of these guidebooks for you, or you can order direct, using the pre-paid postcards on the following pages.

ORDERING INFORMATION

Order by phone: 888-702-8882 (Toll-free 24/7)
Order by fax: 425-557-4366
Order by mail: Resource Pathways, Inc.
                        22525 SE 64th Place, Suite 253
                        Issaquah, WA 98027-5387

ORDER FORM

Order by phone: 888-702-8882 (Toll-free 24/7)
Order by fax: 425-557-4366

Order by mail: Resource Pathways, Inc.
22525 SE 64th Place, Suite 253
Issaquah, WA 98027-5387

☐ *Anxiety & Depression:* The Best Resources To Help You Cope
☐ *Marriage:* The Best Resources To Help Yours Thrive
☐ *Divorce:* The Best Resources To Help You Survive
☐ *Eldercare:* The Best Resources To Help You Help Your Aging Relatives

☐ *Having Children:* The Best Resources To Help You Prepare
☐ *Infants & Toddlers:* The Best Resources To Help You Parent
☐ *Raising Teenagers:* The Best Resources To Help Yours Succeed
☐ *Stepparenting:* The Best Resources To Help Blend Your Family

☐ *College Choice & Admissions:* The Best Resources To Help You Get In
☐ *College Financial Aid:* The Best Resources To Help You Find The Money
☐ *Graduate School:* The Best Resources To Help You Choose, Get In, & Pay
☐ *Starting Your Career:* The Best Resources To Help You Find The Right Job
☐ *Career Transitions:* The Best Resources To Help You Advance
☐ *Going Solo:* The Best Resources For Entrepreneurs & Freelancers

_____ copies at $24.95 = _____

Shipping (USPS Priority Mail): $3.95 for first copy; $2.00/copy for additional copies
We will include an invoice with your shipment

+ Shipping & Handling = _____
Total = _____

Name (please print) _____
Organization _____ Title _____
Address _____
City _____ State _____ Zip _____
Phone _____ Email _____

ORDER FORM

Order by phone: 888-702-8882 (Toll-free 24/7)
Order by fax: 425-557-4366

Order by mail: Resource Pathways, Inc.
22525 SE 64th Place, Suite 253
Issaquah, WA 98027-5387

☐ *Anxiety & Depression:* The Best Resources To Help You Cope
☐ *Marriage:* The Best Resources To Help Yours Thrive
☐ *Divorce:* The Best Resources To Help You Survive
☐ *Eldercare:* The Best Resources To Help You Help Your Aging Relatives

☐ *Having Children:* The Best Resources To Help You Prepare
☐ *Infants & Toddlers:* The Best Resources To Help You Parent
☐ *Raising Teenagers:* The Best Resources To Help Yours Succeed
☐ *Stepparenting:* The Best Resources To Help Blend Your Family

☐ *College Choice & Admissions:* The Best Resources To Help You Get In
☐ *College Financial Aid:* The Best Resources To Help You Find The Money
☐ *Graduate School:* The Best Resources To Help You Choose, Get In, & Pay
☐ *Starting Your Career:* The Best Resources To Help You Find The Right Job
☐ *Career Transitions:* The Best Resources To Help You Advance
☐ *Going Solo:* The Best Resources For Entrepreneurs & Freelancers

_____ copies at $24.95 = _____

Shipping (USPS Priority Mail): $3.95 for first copy; $2.00/copy for additional copies
We will include an invoice with your shipment

+ Shipping & Handling = _____
Total = _____

Name (please print) _____
Organization _____ Title _____
Address _____
City _____ State _____ Zip _____
Phone _____ Email _____

BUSINESS REPLY MAIL
FIRST-CLASS MAIL   PERMIT NO. 176   ISSAQUAH, WA

POSTAGE WILL BE PAID BY ADDRESSEE

RESOURCE PATHWAYS INC.
22525 SE 64TH PL STE 253
ISSAQUAH WA 98027-9939

BUSINESS REPLY MAIL
FIRST-CLASS MAIL   PERMIT NO. 176   ISSAQUAH, WA

POSTAGE WILL BE PAID BY ADDRESSEE

RESOURCE PATHWAYS INC.
22525 SE 64TH PL STE 253
ISSAQUAH WA 98027-9939